Tofu, Tempeh, & other Soy Delights

Enjoying traditional Oriental
soyfoods in American-style cuisine

Camille Cusumano

 Rodale Press, Emmaus, Pennsylvania

Printed in the United States of America on recycled paper, containing a high percentage of de-inked fiber.

Production Coordination: Carol M. Kosik
                           Editing, Design & Production, Inc.
Cover Design: Linda Jacopetti
Cover Illustrations: Jean Gardner
Interior Illustrations: Diane Ness Shaw
Recipe Development: Debra Deis
                      Marie G. Harrington
                      Camille Cusumano
                      Susan Hercek
                      Susan Jaffer
                      Betty Stechmeyer

Recipe Development Manager: Linda C. Gilbert

Recipe Testing: Nancy J. Ayers, Susan Leggett Pearson, Kimberly A.
                  Kuder, Karen Haas, Pat Singley, JoAnn Coponi,
                  Adrienne Redd

Photography: Michael Kanouff, Mitch Mandel, Pat Seip, Christie C. Tito

Library of Congress Cataloging in Publication Data

Cusumano, Camille.
  Tofu, tempeh, & other soy delights.

  Includes index.
  1. Cookery (Bean curd) 2. Cookery (Soybeans)
3. Cookery (Soy sauce) I. Title. II. Title: Tofu, tempeh, and other soy
delights.
TX814.5.B4C87 1983   641.6′3   83-26891
ISBN 0-87857-489-1   paperback

2 4 6 8 10 9 7 5 3 1   paperback

Contents

Acknowledgments

This book represents efforts and contributions beyond my own.

I express my appreciation to the people who answered my many questions and who shared with me their years of experience with soyfoods. William Shurtleff and Akiko Aoyagi are two of the most dedicated workers in soyfoods whom I have met. Their enthusiasm for the subject is infectious. I came away from our meeting with a great respect for their never-ending quest to awaken Westerners to the attributes of soy. I wish them the best of luck with *The History of Soyfoods,* a book they are now writing.

Betty Stechmeyer and Gordon McBride were further inspiration. As dedicated microbiologists, they focused their efforts on the study of tempeh and other types of molds. They generously responded to my many questions on tempeh-making. Betty provided some delectable tempeh recipes.

Richard Leviton, author of the Japanese Soyfoods section, is another soyfoods dynamo. Because of his long involvement with Soycrafters Association and the *Soyfoods Magazine,* he was able to provide me with a true picture of the soyfoods culture in America. I thank him also for supplying me with the many contacts in the soyfoods business that resulted in the colorful profiles in this book.

I thank both Jon Lee and Michael Cohen for the tours of Tomsun Foods tofu manufacturing plant and the Tempeh Works, respectively.

ix

Both tours were fascinating, instructive, and indispensable to my total understanding of soyfoods.

Any cookbook is only as good as its recipes. In addition to my own, this book includes the recipes of Susan Jaffer, Betty Stechmeyer, Debra Deis, and Marie Harrington. Debra and Marie, who work in the Product Development division of Rodale's Test Kitchen, deserve special recognition for their persistence and eagerness in perfecting each recipe. They are directly responsible for the success of many recipes in this cookbook.

Last and perhaps most important, I would like to acknowledge the contributions of Charles Gerras, senior editor at Rodale Press, whose editorial style I strive to emulate. He taught me more about putting together a book than anyone else, and I will always value his guidance.

The Coming of Age of Soyfoods Cuisine

My experience with soyfoods goes back to a time long before I realized that the tofu, tamari soy sauce, and soybeans I loved all came from the same source. This cookbook is the result of my discoveries (and of those who shared recipe development), and it is designed to make you feel comfortable with soyfoods. We want to share the many inspired ways to use soyfoods that we discovered through years of trial-and-error recipe testing.

Although I don't remember the first time I tasted soyfoods, I do know it was in California during the seventies. I had just moved to San Francisco and was discovering all kinds of new and exciting foods. The neighborhood food co-op had a wide variety of fresh produce as well as a great stock of interesting dried foods.

Among the barrels brimming with flours, whole grains, and dried beans were containers of soybeans. Customers could tap the spigots of large plastic containers filled with oils and various other liquids, including deep dark tamari soy sauce. Metal tins were stuffed with nut and seed butters and peanut buttery miso. There were also sealed plastic tubs of tofu.

Like everyone else I would bring my own bags and containers and fill them with a sampling of everything. I must confess my natural curiosity for these foods did not include a natural instinct for cooking them. I had my share of failures before I realized I needed guidance. My experience with Soy-Stuffed Cabbage convinced me of that. The stuffing was a spiced herbed puree of soybeans, and the mixture tasted delicious. But when I added the neatly stuffed rolls to the cooking tomato sauce, the soy mixture mysteriously vanished. I ended up with a pot of empty cabbage leaves and grainy tomato sauce. Lesson number one: Soybeans are high-protein but low-starch; you must add some starchy carbohydrates to make a cohesive mixture.

Then a friend gave me a recipe using soybeans in combination with cooked oats, millet, wheat germ, minced vegetables, herbs, and spices. I used the same mixture for years, varying it as I pleased: as sautéed vegetable patties for sandwiches, eggplant parmesan casseroles, and a stuffing for vegetables, including cabbage rolls.

My experience with other soyfoods was not quite as episodic. Tofu, for example, seemed to turn out quite well no matter what I did to it. But I must admit that for a long time I used it in very conventional ways. I enjoyed tofu as Asians often do, simply steamed or fried and seasoned lightly with soy sauce.

Soon I realized that tofu, like many other soyfoods, is the perfect substitute for eggs, cheese, and other dairy products in many American-style recipes. But, it was the pleasant taste and texture tofu added to quiche, lasagna, cheesecakes, spreads, salads, and other favorite recipes that excited me more than anything. At the same time, I unwittingly gained a deeper reward in becoming acquainted with these culinary delights: the nutritional bonus of soyfoods. Replacing eggs, meat, cheese, and fat-rich dairy foods with tofu in these dishes, I learned, cut down on my intake of cholesterol and saturated fats as well as calories. To see for yourself how favorably soyfoods compare with standard American foods, check the table on Nutrient Content of Various Soyfoods and Other Foods on page 3.

Tempeh, one of my more recent soyfood discoveries, works some of the same nutritional magic as tofu when used in place of meat. One of the first dishes I ever made with tempeh, the pungent Indonesian fermented soyfood, was a Tempeh Parmigiana. I served the dish at a buffet-style meal for my brothers and sisters—all raised on traditional Italian foods as I was. The dish was devoured so fast that I never had a chance to taste it! Only a few of the diners even noticed there was anything different about this family favorite. So with the confidence that comes from generally good results, I proceeded to use tofu and tempeh in more and more of my regular recipes.

Of the whole soyfood family, tofu and tempeh are the most versatile and familiar to American cooks. This is probably because these

Nutrient Content of Various Soyfoods and Other Foods
(100 grams)

Food	Water (%)	Calories	Protein (g)	Fat (g)	Total Carbohydrates (g)	Fiber (g)	Calcium (mg)	Phosphorus (mg)	Iron (mg)	Sodium (mg)	Potassium (mg)	Vitamin A (IU)	Thiamine (mg)	Riboflavin (mg)	Niacin (mg)	Vitamin C (mg)
Tofu	84.8	72	7.8	4.2	2.4	0.1	128	126	1.9	7	42	—	0.06	0.03	0.1	—
Tempeh, Soy	60.4	157	19.5	7.5	9.9	1.4	142	240	5.0	—	—	—	0.28	0.65	2.52	—
Soymilk	92.4	33	3.4	1.5	2.2	—	21	48	.8	—	—	40	0.08	0.03	0.2	—
Hamburger, Cooked	54.2	286	24.2	20.3	—	—	11	194	3.2	47	450	40	0.09	0.21	5.4	—
Ham, Roasted	45.5	374	23.0	30.6	—	—	10	236	3.0	—	—	—	0.51	0.23	4.6	—
Chicken Drumstick, Fried	55.0	235	32.6	10.2	1.0	—	15	236	2.3	—	—	140	0.07	0.40	7.1	—
Cow's Milk	87.4	65	3.5	3.5	4.9	—	118	93	Tr.	50	144	140	0.03	0.17	0.1	1
American Cheese	39	398	25.0	32.2	2.1	—	750	478	1.0	700	82	1,310	0.03	0.46	0.1	—
Potatoes, Baked in Skin	75.1	93	2.6	0.1	12.1	0.6	9	65	0.7	4	503	Tr.	0.10	0.04	1.7	20
Rice, White Enriched, Cooked	72.6	109	2.0	0.1	24.2	0.1	10	28	0.9	374	28	—	0.11	—	1.0	—
Spaghetti, White Enriched, Cooked	72.0	111	3.4	0.4	23.0	0.1	8	50	0.9	1	61	—	0.14	0.08	1.1	—
Cottage Cheese 4.2% Fat	78	106	13.6	4.2	2.9	—	94	?	0.3	229	85	170	0.03	0.25	0.1	—
Eggs 11.5% Fat	74	163	13	11.5	0.9	—	54	?	2.3	122	129	1,180	0.11	0.30	0.1	—
Yogurt 3.4% Fat	88	62	3	3.4	4.9	—	111	?	—	47	132	140	0.03	0.16	—	0.1

Tofu, tempeh, and soymilk, the high-protein soyfoods, are much lower in fat and calories when compared to our typical American high-protein foods.

two soyfoods blend easily into everyday sandwiches and casseroles as well as more elegant dishes, such as stroganoff and teriyaki. In addition, tofu and other soyfoods can be transformed into wonderfully rich-tasting desserts for those with a sweet tooth.

But now a word about the other soy delights—creamy soymilk, fresh green soybeans, soy flour, soy oil, soy grits, soy sprouts, soy nuts, and miso. This group of soyfoods—so unlike each other in flavor, appearance, and cooking properties—increases the ways protein-rich soyfoods can be used in American cooking. So rather than featuring a collection of soyfood recipes based on Eastern cuisine, we have incorporated soyfoods into innovative American-style dishes. Each of these recipes has the same simplicity, versatility, and creativity found in today's new-style American cuisine.

In this cookbook, you'll find classic American favorites and new creations as well—all featuring protein-rich soyfoods. Some of these unique recipes are: Jerusalem Artichokes and Tofu Au Gratin, Maple Walnut Pie, Armenian Stretched Bread, Cherry Custard, Barbecued Tempeh Cheeseburgers, Bean and Sausage Enchiladas, Indonesian Sprout Fritters, Salade Nicoise, Shoo-fly Pie, Lamb and Apricots with Soy Grits, Soy-Marinated Mushrooms, and Miso-Sesame Eggplant.

Don't limit your use of soyfoods to these recipes, but be on the lookout to discover ways to use them in your favorite recipes, too. Here are some easy ideas for adding soyfoods to everyday fare:

- Add fresh cubes of tofu and soy sprouts to your soups, salads, or omelets.
- Use soymilk in any soup, sauce, or dessert in place of milk or cream.
- Sprinkle soy nuts into breakfast cereal, snack mixes, or any baked goods batter or dough.
- Substitute soy oil for other saturated oils or butter in breads, pancakes, or salad dressings.
- Stir tamari soy sauce into soups, sauces, and other dishes instead of salt for a low-sodium condiment with a rich beefy flavor.

When you have sampled some of these recipes, another pleasurable surprise awaits you—the treat of home-produced tofu, tempeh, and soymilk. Of course, if you're as busy as I am, you will not be producing these on a regular basis because it does take extra time. But once in a while you will make the time because you want the marvelous taste of fresh tofu, tempeh, and soymilk.

Whether you make your own soyfoods or buy them, you will be pleased with the wonders they can work for your budget, your health, and most of all, your dining pleasure.

Menu Suggestions

Tofu, tempeh, and the other soyfoods can be worked into your everyday menus. A glance through these suggested menus shows that soyfood meals can be light and simple or rich and elegant. Menus for quick-cooking meals and vegetarian meals are also given. Use these menus as starting points and make your own adjustments depending on the tastes of your family and friends.

BREAKFAST MENUS

Buckwheat Almond Pancakes, page 67
Peanut Sauce, page 129, or maple syrup
Honeyed Soymilk, page 139

scrambled eggs
Pumpkin Tempeh Bread, page 113
fresh fruit

Soy-Granola Cereal, page 215
fresh fruit
Maple Soymilk, page 140

Brunch Tempeh, page 96
fried eggs
Fruit Soy Shake, page 140

plain yogurt
Okara Pudding with Raisins and Cinnamon, page 81
Strawberry-Banana Drink, page 140

vegetable omelet
Orange-Apricot Muffins, page 214
butter and fruit preserves

BRUNCH MENUS

Walnut Sticky Buns, page 209
Pineapple, Sprout, and Rice Salad, page 189
Eggplant Muhtar, page 33

TOFU, TEMPEH, &
OTHER SOY DELIGHTS

Quick Blender Tofu Souffle, page 38
Fruit and Nut Roll, page 132
sliced apples, oranges, and grapefruit

Curried Tropical Salad, page 54
Soy Crepes, page 207, filled with stewed fruit or Tofu and Pineapple
   Pastry Filling, page 71

Salad Niçoise, page 180
Russian Caraway Bread, page 205
Almond-Banana Pudding, page 66

Tofu-Zucchini Quiche, page 48
green salad
Basil Walnut Dressing, page 166
Morningstar Muffins, page 70

LUNCHEON MENUS

Monastery Bean Soup, page 178
Tempeh Burgers, page 104
Sunrise Salad, page 57

Corn and Tempeh Fritters, page 112
Cheese Souffle, page 122
Soy-Banana Nut Bread, page 207

Vegetable Terrine, page 218
Shrimp Egg Roll, page 190
Spicy Peanut Butter Spread, page 234
celery sticks

Italian Meat Loaf, page 213
Tamari-Marinated Mushrooms, page 230
Kiwi Custard Pie, page 136

Korean Hot Beef Soup, page 53
Broiled Tofu Burgers, page 32
Cherry Custard, page 135

DINNER MENUS

Hawaiian Tofu with Chinese Cabbage, page 34
Indonesian Sprout Fritters, page 188

6

green salad
Sesame Seed Salad Dressing, page 227
Vanilla Ice Cream, page 138

Linguine a la Tofu, page 36
Italian-Style Green Soybeans, page 178
Ice Box Cake, page 69

Tempeh Stroganoff, page 105
Sweet-Pungent Stir-Fried Beans, page 181
steamed brown rice
Carob-Tofu Pudding, page 67

Chinese Chicken and Sprouts in Hot Pepper Oil, page 187
India-Spiced Rice Casserole, page 97
vegetable salad
Sunflower Brownie Drops, page 71

Bean and Sausage-Filled Enchiladas, page 158
Tofu, Peas, and Yogurt, page 58
Orange Ice Milk, page 137

QUICK MEALS

Broiled Tofu Burgers, page 32
whole grain buns
tomato slices
Pina-Colada Shake, page 140

Quick and Creamy Curry, page 38
whole wheat toast points
dates stuffed with walnuts

Macaroni, Beans, and Cheese, page 160
spinach salad
Bread Pudding, page 135

Tuna Pasta Salad, page 166
Miso Soup, page 233
fruit and yogurt

Teriyaki Beef, page 230
steamed brown rice
Soy Shake, page 139

ELEGANT DINNER MENUS

Tofu Moussaka, page 52
Bread and Butter Bean Medley, page 174
Stuffed Grape Leaves, page 217
Raspberry Chiffon Pie, page 137

Miso Soup, page 233
Hot and Spicy Pork-stuffed Tofu, page 34
steamed brown rice
Rich Eggnog Mousse, page 70

Fancy Seafood, page 121
Pasta with Nut Sauce, page 189
fresh fruit

baked salmon
Tahini Sauce, page 62
Fettuccine with Green Soybeans, page 175
whole grain rolls
Grasshopper Pie, page 68

VEGETARIAN MENUS

Tofu Strips and Snow Peas, page 46
Okara Patties, page 80
steamed brown rice
Giant Old-Fashioned Cookies, page 194

Top-of-the-Stove Casserole, page 49
Calico Vegetable Salad, page 162
green salad with light dressing
fresh pineapple slices

Tempeh-Stuffed Peppers, page 107
Sauteed Apples, Cabbage, and Sprouts with Noodles, page 190
Deep and Dark Carob Pie, page 68

Tempeh Parmesan, page 105
cooked pasta or rice
mixed green salad
Dill Dressing, page 130
Almond-Banana Pudding, page 66

Pennsylvania Dutch-Style Beans and Corn Custard, page 179
Broadway Salad, page 54
Linzer Cookies, page 204

Rosemary, Bean, and Pasta Soup, page 163
Chicken-Fried Tofu Cutlets, page 50
Walnut Torte, page 219

Soyfoods Glossary

age (AH-gay) Japanese name for deep-fried tofu pouches.

bean curd   See *tofu*.

bittern   The bitter by-product of salt-making that is used as a coagulant in making tofu.

coagulant   The substance, usually a natural chemical, used to curdle soymilk in making tofu.

defatted   Refers to soybeans that have had most of their oil pressed from them.

doufu or *dowfoo*   (DOH-foo) Chinese name for tofu.

dried-frozen tofu   Tofu that has been frozen, then slowly dried in an oven.

forming box   The mold used to form curds in tofu-making into a specific solid and cohesive shape.

forming box cloth   The cloth—usually cotton or cheesecloth—used to line the forming box for making tofu.

fresh green soybeans   Soybeans picked from the vine before drying has occurred.

full-fat   Refers to soybeans that have not been pressed of their oil.

ganmo   (GAHN-moh) Japanese word for a deep-fried tofu burger.

go   (GOH) Japanese word for the cooked soy puree.

hatcho miso   (HACH-oh MEE-soh) A rich-flavored, dark-colored miso made by inoculating soybeans and allowing them to ferment for a period of two to three years.

kinugoshi   (kee-nu-GOH-shee) Japanese word for silken or soft tofu.

koji   (KOH-jee) Japanese word for the fermented grain starter used to make miso.

miso   (MEE-soh) Japanese name for nutrient-rich paste-like soy sauce made by grinding and fermenting a mixture of steamed rice, cooked soybeans, and salt.

natto   (NAT-oh) A cake of sticky soybeans with a mustard-like flavor used most often as a seasoning; natto is made by inoculating cooked soybeans with a bacterium.

nigari (nih-GAH-ree) Japanese name for bittern, a popular tofu coagulant derived from sea water.

okara (oh-KAR-uh) Japanese name for the high-fiber puree that remains when soymilk is strained from pureed soybeans.

Rhizopus oligosporus (RY-zoh-puss ah-lee-goh-SPOH-russ) Bacteria mold used to inoculate soybeans in making tempeh.

shoyu Japanese name for soy sauce; in this country it refers to natural soy sauce.

soybean curd See **tofu.**

soy flakes Soybeans that are treated briefly with radiant heat then rolled mechanically yielding flat flake-shaped beans that cook in about one hour.

soy flour Raw or toasted soybeans ground to a fine powder.

soyfoods A group of nutritious foods all derived from the soybean, using low-technology methods; these foods are generally high-protein, low-fat, and cholesterol-free.

soy granules A product similar to soy grits but quicker cooking.

soy grits Defatted or full-fat soybeans mechanically ground into smaller pieces making them quicker cooking and eliminating the need to soak them.

soy mash See *okara.*

soymilk The high-protein creamy beverage made by cooking, pureeing, and straining soybeans.

soy nuts Nut-like snack soyfood made from roasted soaked soybeans.

soy oil The lecithin-rich oil pressed from soybeans; also called soybean oil.

soy powder A commercial product that can be used to make soymilk and tofu or used as a nutritious food supplement.

soy pulp See *okara.*

soy puree Soybeans that have been soaked and/or cooked then ground to a puree.

soysage A savory meatless loaf seasoned very much like sausage, first developed by the Farm Commune in Tennessee.

soy sauce Any of several soy condiments including shoyu, tamari, and miso, all made by various processes of fermenting soybeans.

soy sprouts The tender edible shoots that grow when whole dry soy beans (seeds actually) are soaked in water and cultivated for several days; also called soybean sprouts.

tamari (tah-MAR-ee) A soy sauce made by fermenting soybeans with salt, but no wheat as is used in making shoyu.

tempeh (tem-PAY) A high-protein, high-fiber fermented soyfood that is made by injecting soybeans with a beneficial mold.

textured vegetable protein (TVP) A commercially produced soyfood made through a refining process and the use of chemicals; TVP is used to make artificial meat products and to extend meats.

tofu (TOE-foo) The high-protein, low-fat cheese-like soyfood made from soymilk; also called **bean curd** and **soybean curd.**

trypsin (TRIP-sin) A substance in soybeans that interferes with the body's assimilation of protein unless the trypsin is deactivated through cooking.

whey The yellowish liquid that is separated from the curds in soymilk in order to make tofu.

whole dry soybeans An annual legume (*Glycine max*) grown for its oil-rich and high-protein content and for its soil-improving qualities; see also **fresh green soybeans.**

yuba (YOU-bah) A nutritious and rich soyfood made by drying out the skin that forms when cooking soymilk.

Tofu

Tofu, bean curd, soybean curd, or soy cheese—this beige-white cake has many identities, and none of them even suggests its soybean source in either taste or appearance. Its custard-like consistency is reminiscent of creamy cottage cheese, yet it is not a dairy product and not really a cheese. Of all the marvelous foods the Eastern world has created from soybeans, this soy cheese has the most appeal because of its mild flavor. Tofu blends easily into many different cuisines: herby Mediterranean flavors, spicy exotic Mid-Eastern dishes, and the fiery piquancy of South American classics. Tofu can also be substituted for the cottage or ricotta cheese in any dessert recipe, and it has fewer calories, too. While Western cooks like myself are still learning to meld tofu's adaptable nature to our own cuisine, the Eastern world enjoys this staple in many traditional ways.

Known most widely as tofu in this country, it has many names in Eastern countries reflecting subtle differences in the many ways it can be made. *Doufu* or *dowfoo* are popular names for the firm Chinese type. Tofu (pronounced TOE-foo) is actually a Japanese name for just one kind of soy cheese, and it is the name that has caught on in this country. Deep-fried, grilled, wine-fermented, and silken-smooth represent other popular commercial forms of tofu in the East (see Japanese Soyfoods, page 144).

Even if you have not cooked with tofu, you have probably seen it—in the fresh produce or dairy section of supermarkets or in Chinese restaurants where it is often billed as bean curd. It is also very likely to appear in creative dishes in natural food or vegetarian restaurants. In the soyfood delicatessens and restaurants that are becoming very popular, you can find freshly made tofu as well as numerous take-out dishes created with tofu. It appears in savory main dishes and sweet desserts alike.

Tofu is the refined essence of the soybean's goodness. It is much more digestible than soybeans, because the process of making it removes the crude fiber and the water-soluble carbohydrates that can cause intestinal gas. Yet like soybeans, tofu is a high-protein food, containing all the essential amino acids. The usable protein of tofu is equal to that of chicken. Combine tofu with whole grains, seeds, nuts, or small amounts of dairy products, and you increase its usable protein content significantly. Like soybeans, it has no cholesterol and is low in saturated fats. Tofu is even lower in calories than soybeans. In fact, it has one of the lowest ratios of calories to protein of all foods. One gram of usable protein is equal to only 12 calories. Equal weights of eggs and beef contain about three and five times as many calories as tofu. Tofu is low in sodium, but its healthy supply of calcium makes it ideal for people who must follow dairy-free diets. Tofu is by tradition a naturally pure food that may be prepared as simply today as it was thousands of years ago. Soybeans, water, and a coagulant, or curding agent, are the only ingredients.

TOFU-CHEESE BLENDS

If you like the flavor of certain rich dairy cheeses, here's a way to continue to enjoy them but with a vast reduction in their calories, fat, and cholesterol (see Nutritional Content in Cheese and Cheese-Tofu Blends, page 14). Combine firm or soft tofu with equal amounts of cream cheese, grated Parmesan, shredded cheddar cheese, or any of your favorite hard or soft cheeses. Just mash the tofu into the cheese in a bowl, and store it in the refrigerator. Use the tofu-cheese blend as you would normally use cheese.

Buying Tofu

Many supermarkets carry good quality tofu in their refrigerated dairy section. Unfortunately, some supermarkets store tofu in the produce section. Since tofu must be refrigerated at 38°F or colder, tofu stored at warmer temperatures quickly sours. In general, I prefer to buy tofu from soy dairies where tofu is made fresh every day or two.

Nutritional Content in Cheese and Cheese-Tofu Blends (100 grams)

	Moisture (%)	Calories	Protein (g)	Carbohydrates (g)	Fats (g)	Unsaturated Fat (g)	Cholesterol (mg)	Sodium (mg)	Potassium (mg)	Vitamin A (IU)	Thiamine (mg)	Riboflavin (mg)	Niacin (mg)	Calcium (mg)	Iron (mg)	Phosphorus (mg)
Cream Cheese	22	374	8	2.1	37.7		120	250	74	1539	0.02	0.24	0.09	62	0.22	95
Cream Cheese with 50% Tofu	68.19	220.34	7.92	2.27	20.66	8.21	54.66	126.44	57.73	756.99	0.04	0.13	0.10	95.76	1.08	110.59
Grated Parmesan Cheese	17	467	42.7	3.5	30.8			870	177	1260	0.02	0.87	0.2	1352	0.5	926
Grated Parmesan with 50% Tofu	64.61	190	18.21	2.61	12.21	5.36	35.00	274.84	81.42	390.53	0.05	0.29	0.14	501.05	1.37	367.11
Shredded Cheddar Cheese	32.8	398	25	2	32.2			700	82	1310	0.03	0.46	0.09	750.5	.97	478
Shredded Cheddar Cheese with 50% Tofu	69.5	176.20	13.34	2.32	13.14	5.77	31.73	228.84	54.82	419.26	0.05	0.17	0.10	327.48	1.61	238.53

You can usually buy fresh tofu in one of three ways: water-packed in a plastic tub, vacuum-packed in plastic wrapping, or in cakes from a soy deli. Pre-packed tofu usually comes in cakes weighing anywhere from 8 to 22 ounces. Packaged tofu should have its ingredients listed. Often a date is stamped on packaged tofu indicating the date by which it should be used. Usually, but not necessarily, the date is 7 to 10 days from when it was made, though no law requires tofu manufacturers to date their products. Without a standardized dating procedure, you can't tell how fresh the tofu really is. However, if you find out when the tofu is delivered, you will have a better clue to its freshness.

The ingredients are always the same for plain tofu: soybeans, water, and a coagulant (see page 22 for the different safe coagulants that may be used). Herbs and spices may be added to commercial tofu, but it's best to buy plain tofu and add your own flavorings. Never buy tofu that has added preservatives—they are just not necessary. Some tofu is pasteurized. If it is, it will remain fresh a few days longer than tofu that is not.

Tofu's mild, delicately sweet flavor is most pronounced when it is first made and still warm and fresh. This initial freshness fades rather quickly, though the tofu remains receptive to seasonings that can readily perk it up. Avid tofu lovers often begin to make their own tofu just because they want to experience this peak freshness.

If you buy tofu, search for the freshest product possible. Check the appearance. Prime tofu should be an even eggshell white and have a smooth surface. If it is stored in water, the water should be clear. If the tofu appears to have a slimy surface, it is a sign of age. When buying loose tofu ask to have a sniff. The tofu should have a very mild fresh water aroma. If the tofu smells faintly like soured milk products, it is sour.

Although its flavor and freshness will diminish the longer it is stored, tofu is not nearly so perishable as eggs, cream, and milk. Even if it is a bit old, tofu can still be safely used in recipes where it will be blended with other ingredients and cooked or baked. I often add small amounts of leftover tofu to breads. It hardly alters the recipe; but, if necessary, I adjust the liquid. Tofu can also be refreshened by parboiling.

Storing Tofu

Tofu that you make or that you buy as loose cakes or in plastic tubs should be immersed in water in a tightly sealed container and refrigerated. It should be used within a week to 10 days from when it was made. Though the tofu may still be usable after 10 days, its flavor will be greatly diminished, and the tofu may be somewhat sour. Like soured milk it can still be used in baked goods or in recipes where its flavor will not be apparent. Or you can completely transform the tofu by freezing it (see below).

To insure maximum freshness change the water of stored tofu every day, if possible, and at least every other day. Although the tofu you buy in plastic tubs is already in water, you should remove it from the container when you get home, and store it in fresh water in a sealed container. Vacuum-packed tofu need not be opened and stored in water. It will keep for about a month if unopened. Once opened, though, it should be stored the same as loose tofu and used within a week to 10 days.

Firm and Soft Tofu

In Eastern countries the various types of tofu reflect preferences for different tastes, textures, and appearances. In this country, most tofu is simply designated as soft or firm. Chinese or firm tofu is the most commonly found here. Perhaps that is because it is the easiest to work with. Japanese tofu is usually a softer one. *Kinugoshi* or silken tofu is a kind of Japanese tofu especially prized by gourmet cooks for its smooth custardy texture. It is very fragile and its exquisite consistency is a nice complement to the crunchy texture of stir-fried dishes.

The consistency of tofu usually determines how it can best be used in recipes. Some recipes call for a certain firmness of tofu, but in most cases you will find that firm or soft tofu can be used interchangeably. As you become familiar with tofu and its physical properties, you can easily determine which consistency is best for a particular purpose. A general rule of thumb is: Firm tofu for dishes where the tofu must retain its shape and soft tofu for recipes where it will be blended, creamed, or mashed, such as in salads, dressings, sauces, spreads, or baked goods. You can easily firm up soft tofu by lessening its water content (see pressing, page 18), since it is the water content that determines firmness. Because the firmer tofu is simply a denser cake of soymilk curds it is also higher in protein than the soft tofu.

FREEZING TOFU

Freezing tofu puts an almost completely new product at your disposal. The freezing process changes the soft cheesy texture to a chewy meatlike one that I find very pleasant and versatile. In fact, many cooks prefer frozen tofu in recipes where a meat flavor and texture is desired. The color of tofu also changes slightly as it freezes. It turns to a golden amber when frozen. As it thaws the amber will fade to a creamy beige, and the water content will lessen so the tofu will be higher in protein. You will be able to squeeze more water from it just as you squeeze water from a sponge. The tofu will not crumble as easily as it did before being frozen.

I often freeze tofu that is slightly old in order to prolong its usefulness. When thawed its new porous texture will soak up the flavors even more readily than unfrozen tofu.

To freeze tofu simply remove it from the water in which it is stored, and wrap it tightly in plastic. You may freeze a whole block of tofu but to accelerate freezing and defrosting, I cut it into slices and wrap them separately. For best results freeze tofu for at least 10 hours. You can keep it frozen for up to 6 months. I find its chewy texture may seem tough and dry if you keep it much longer than this.

Frozen tofu will thaw fairly quickly at room temperature. You can leave it wrapped or unwrapped in a colander so the water can drain from it. Speed up the thawing by placing the unwrapped frozen tofu in a pot and covering it with boiling water. Allow whole blocks of tofu to remain immersed for about 20 minutes, or about 10 minutes for smaller pieces.

Preparing Tofu

Cooking with tofu is simple. But if tofu is new to you, here are a few basic techniques for working with it:

- Drain tofu from the water it is stored in before using it. Use a colander or let it stand about 15 minutes on absorbent paper. Gently pat it dry with paper towels to remove excess moisture.
- Rinse tofu before using it if it feels slippery to the touch. You may also rinse it when changing the water it is stored in to keep it as fresh as possible.
- Squeeze tofu with your hands to remove water, but only do so when it is not necessary for the tofu to retain its shape, as it will crumble easily. Frozen tofu can be easily squeezed without losing its shape. You can facilitate squeezing water from fresh or frozen tofu by wrapping it securely in a dish towel and twisting the gathered ends tightly.

17

• Press tofu when you wish to remove water but retain its shape. This will make a firmer tofu. Press tofu in a whole block or in smaller uniformly cut pieces. Place the block or pieces on absorbent paper, then cover them with more paper and a flat platter or a cutting board. Place a three- to five-pound weight —a big jar or a pot of water —on the board or platter and allow to stand for 30 to 60 minutes, depending on how firm you want the tofu to be.

• Crumble or mash the tofu with your hands or with a fork in a bowl. This is usually done before blending with other ingredients for salads, spreads, patties, loaves, breads, or baked goods. You can even beat tofu with an electric beater for a finer consistency.

• Purée or cream tofu in a blender or a food processor for dips, spreads, sauces, dressings, puddings, and pie fillings. Purée tofu in small amounts—about one-half cup at a time. If the tofu is too firm to blend, add small amounts of water, soymilk, stock, or any liquid called for in the recipe. You can puree a batch of tofu to keep on hand for different recipes. Refrigerate it in a tightly sealed container. You need not cover it with water. You can also freeze puréed tofu in a sealed container. Of course, its texture will change.

TOFU EQUIVALENT MEASUREMENTS

(1 pound firm tofu)

Form	Amount
1-inch cubes	2⅔ cups
Crumbled or mashed	2 cups
Pressed or squeezed and crumbled	1¼ cups
Beaten with electric beater	1¾ cups
Puréed	1½ cups

19

- Par-boil slightly aged tofu to refreshen it, firm it up a bit, and make it more absorbent of flavorings. Gently slide a whole block or uniformly cut pieces of tofu into a pot of boiling water—using enough water to cover the tofu. Remove the pot from the heat, and let stand five minutes. Remove tofu from water and drain.

Dried Frozen Tofu

Textured Vegetable Protein (TVP) is a popular commercial product made by an extraction from soy flour. Various chemical solvents are used in the process, and it is a highly refined product—a junk soyfood, if you can believe it. It is used to simulate meat, fish, poultry, and cured meats and to make various meat analogues such as bacon and sausage. These products are usually artificially colored and flavored and have many additives.

You can make something that is much better than TVP and has many of the same uses. Dried frozen tofu is fresher and meatier, and it is pure. It also has the advantage over fresh or frozen tofu of being storable at room temperature for many months. Keep it in a plastic bag in the cupboard.

To make it first freeze tofu (see page 16). Thaw and squeeze as much water from it as possible, using a towel to get it really dry. The more water you get out, the faster it will dry in the oven. You can dry it in any form depending how you would like to use it later—in slices or cubes, or mashed and crumbled to any coarseness. (Mashed and seasoned, it can extend or double for the ground beef in many meat dishes). Its new absorbent nature will drink up seasonings such as soy sauce and garlic or onion powder, beef or chicken bouillon, clam juice, or any vegetable or meat marinade. It can also be used in snack mixes (see recipe, page 167).

To dry frozen tofu: Spread the thawed, very well-drained and squeezed slices or crumbled mixture on a lightly oiled cookie sheet. Place in 175°F oven, and allow to dry for 6 hours, or until all moisture is gone.

Check occasionally to make sure it is not burning. It should turn a golden tan, but not brown at all. Toss or turn pieces if necessary to promote even drying. Allow to cool thoroughly before storing in a plastic bag at room temperature. Be sure all moisture is gone before you store it, or it will quickly give way to mold growth.

Reconstituting dried-frozen tofu: Mix dried-frozen tofu, cup for cup, with hot tap water, stock, or whey. Stir and let stand about 15 minutes, or until the previous spongy consistency returns. Drain off any liquid that has not been absorbed. You can also rehydrate it in a marinade—full strength or diluted with water—depending on how strong you want it to be. You can add dried frozen tofu directly to dishes that have enough moisture in them to rehydrate the tofu, such as soups, meat loaves or moist vegetable patty mixtures, and casseroles.

Making Tofu

After tasting my first fresh tofu from a soy dairy, I quickly abandoned the stale product I'd been buying from unconscientious stores. But when I tasted my first batch of my own homemade tofu, I wished I'd had the time to make it every week. There is no comparison, and now I understand why buying freshly made cakes of tofu in Japan is as much a daily ritual as buying a fresh loaf of bread is in other countries. Most Americans, because many of us are still learning the properties of this curious and exotic food, settle for a slightly less than fresh product unless we are lucky enough to live near a soy dairy, or to make our own. Just as bread bakers praise the superior taste of freshly baked bread, tofu lovers gloat over the special treat of homemade tofu.

If you find that tofu is a regular part of your menu, it may be worthwhile to start making your own. I have always appreciated bread baking's sensual qualities, and I find that making tofu offers a similar satisfaction. It is certainly no more time-consuming than making a yeast bread, and no more mysterious. Even if you do not intend to make tofu regularly, it is worth trying once. Most likely you have all the needed equipment in your kitchen already, and you will certainly enjoy the pleasure of fresh tofu.

THE INGREDIENTS

With so few ingredients needed it is very easy to insure that only the best ones go into making tofu. You can find good quality soybeans in many supermarkets, co-ops, and natural foods and ethnic stores. The light yellow ones they usually carry are the best.

Good water that is chemical-free is very important since water plays an important role in making tofu. If your tap water has a lot of chlorine or other chemicals in it, use bottled spring water. The difference it will make in the final product is well worth the slight extra expense.

COAGULANTS

To make tofu, you must first make soymilk. This creamy rich-tasting beverage may be used in many of the same ways you might use the dairy milk it resembles. (See Soymilk, page 115). To the soymilk, you add a coagulant.

All the coagulants discussed here are perfectly natural ingredients. They are used to curdle soymilk into tofu as rennet is used to curdle dairy milk in cheese-making. Most of the coagulant does not actually remain in the curds that are compressed into tofu, but is drained off.

There are several types of coagulants you can use, and each one contributes its own quality so that subtle variations in taste are possible. Japanese tofu is usually made with natural *nigari* (bittern), or a *nigari*-type solidifier, such as calcium chloride or magnesium chloride. *Nigari* is available in many natural foods stores or in Oriental grocery shops. *Nigari* and *nigari*-type solidifiers are the most expensive but they give tofu a very delicate subtle sweetness.

The choice of coagulants also includes calcium sulfate (gypsum) and magnesium sulfate (epsom salts) both carried by pharmacists and both inexpensive. They also make a delicate tofu, creamier but a little blander than the tofu made with *nigari* coagulants. Calcium sulfate also enriches the tofu with about 40 percent more calcium than tofu made with other coagulants. It is the coagulant used by most commercial tofu manufacturers.

Fresh lemon juice or vinegar may also be used to coagulate soymilk. These will flavor the tofu with their distinct tartness and produce a coarser textured tofu.

You may mix solidifiers when making tofu, if you like, for different results in the end product.

GETTING STARTED

The following recipe yields about 1 pound of tofu. You may double or triple the recipe, but then you will need to increase the capacity, thus the size, of your equipment accordingly. This recipe is especially good for first-time tofu makers who do not want to invest in equipment other than what is usually found in most kitchens.

Equipment needed
    3-quart bowl
    colander
    electric blender
    measuring cups and spoons

2 6-quart pots

forming box cloth (about 30 square inches of fine mesh, gauze, loosely woven dish towel, or tightly woven cheesecloth. Its shape should conform to that of the container you will be using to mold the tofu.)

wooden spoon

forming box* with lid that fits inside (see Homemade Forming Boxes for Making Tofu, page 25)

large pan to catch the whey

2- to 3-pound weight (a jar filled with water will do)

Ingredients

1 cup dry soybeans

14 cups water, approximately

1½ teaspoons of coagulating salts (see Coagulants, page 22), or 3 tablespoons of vinegar or lemon juice

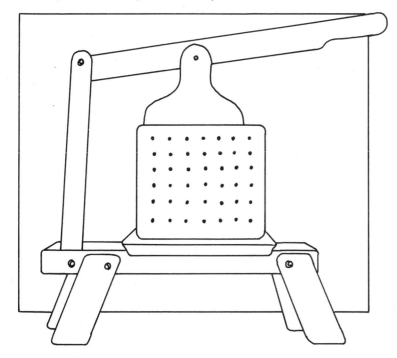

A Home Soyfoods Equipment tofu-press (see Mail Order Sources, page 247).

*NOTE that you can also purchase at reasonable prices tofu kits that supply a forming box and cloth. Ask at a natural foods store or see Soyfoods Mail Order Sources, page 247.

*Hand-thrown tofu mold, available from CIS
(see Mail Order Sources, page 247).*

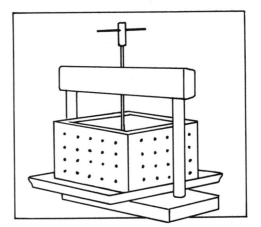

Large home-built press for regular tofu-making.

PROCEDURE

1. Rinse the beans. Place them in the bowl and cover them with enough cold water to allow for expansion. Soak 8 hours or overnight. Drain the beans and rinse again before using.
2. Grind beans in an electric blender, using 1½ cups water to 1 cup of soaked beans. Add blended beans to one large pot. Rinse the blender with 1 cup water, and add to pot.

HOMEMADE FORMING BOXES FOR MAKING TOFU

Just about any type of forming box or mold can be used to make tofu as long as it meets two specifications:

1. It must allow you to apply a lid that fits inside of it in order to apply pressure at the top.
2. It must allow liquid to run off.

Examples of forming boxes that may be used are a colander or a large can (a coffee can or a large cooking-oil can with its top removed—save the top) with holes punched in the sides and bottom. You can also punch holes in a large plastic container and use it as a mold.

The shape of the mold does not matter, but be sure you can find something to use as a lid that is flat and will fit inside the mold with a clearance of about ¼ to ½ inch all around the circumference or perimeter. A plate or a piece of plywood, or the top of a metal can, if you use one, can all be used as lids for the mold.

EASY FORMING BOX FOR UP TO 1½ POUNDS OF TOFU

You will need two round one-quart plastic or sturdy waxed cardboard containers with one lid. Large yogurt and ricotta cheese containers are the right size. Poke lots of holes in the bottom and lower half of the sides of one container. If the container is a very rigid plastic, you may have to use a drill with a small bit. Buy or make a jelly bag of fine nylon mesh shaped to fit inside the container. Place this bag inside the container with the holes.

To mold tofu, set the container with holes inside a colander. Proceed with instructions for making tofu. Fill the matching container (with no holes) with water, and put on its lid. Use this one as the weight. When the tofu is almost set, gently remove it from the mold, flip it over, and replace it upside-down into the mold again. Replace the weight and let it set until firm.

For a square-sided block of tofu, follow the same procedure using one-quart plastic freezer containers.

3. Cook the fresh soy puree over medium heat, loosely covered. Bring to a rolling boil, reduce heat, and simmer for 15 to 20 minutes. This cooking period is very important to deactivate an enzyme in soybeans called trypsin. Unless properly cooked, the trypsin will interfere with the body's assimilation of the protein in the beans.

4. Dampen the forming box cloth and arrange it in the colander, then place the colander over the second large pot.

5. Pour the cooked soy puree into the forming box cloth to separate the solids from the soymilk. Rinse the empty pot with 1 cup of water, and pour the residue into the cloth. Transfer the strained soymilk to the large cooking pot, and place on the range again.

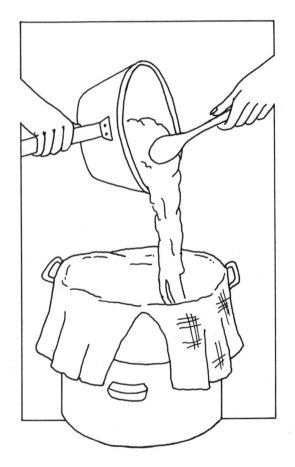

PRESEASONING TOFU

Tofu seasoned with herbs and spices is becoming more widely available commercially. However, if you make your own tofu you can easily preseason it yourself using the flavors you prefer. Most seasonings are added before the curds are molded. We offer here some winning combinations that Debra Deis worked out at the test kitchen. Feel free to experiment with any standard herb and spice blends or with different combinations that you like. When adding herbs, chop them very finely for best results. The resulting tofu will be attractively flecked with green.

Fines Herbes: Add 2 tablespoons finely chopped parsley, 1 tablespoon fresh chopped basil, 1 tablespoon finely chopped fresh chives, and 1 teaspoon chopped fresh thyme leaves to coagulated soymilk right before ladling into mold.

Italian Sausage Tofu: Add ½ teaspoon hot pepper flakes and 1 tablespoon fennel seed, slightly crushed, before bringing soymilk to a boil. After curds have formed add 2 teaspoons dried oregano, 2 teaspoons garlic powder, 1 tablespoon Parmesan cheese, and ½ teaspoon coarsely ground black pepper.

Onion and Herb Tofu: Add 2 tablespoons finely chopped mild onion and 2 cloves garlic, minced, to soymilk before bringing to a boil. After curds have formed, add 2 teaspoons chopped fresh dillweed and 2 teaspoons finely chopped fresh parsley.

Curry Powder: Add 1 tablespoon curry powder to soymilk before bringing to a boil.

Use 5 cups of cold water to cool the mixture so that it can be handled. To do this: Pour the cold water through the soy puree, and allow it to drain into the second pot. After the last of the water is added, you can begin to press and squeeze as much moisture as possible from the pulp. Add this soymilk to that already on the range. Heat again to boiling.

At this point you will have made about 1½ cups of soymilk. You can stop here if you wish, or you can reserve a small amount of soymilk, and use the rest to make tofu. (To make soymilk intended for use as a beverage, see Making Soymilk, page 118.)

You will also have at this point in the forming cloth about 2½ cups of the okara or soy mash. Reserve this very nutritious residue in a container in the refrigerator. It has many uses also (see Cooking with Okara, next page).

At this point if you intend to make pre-seasoned tofu, you may add the seasonings (see Pre-seasoning Tofu, page 27).

6. Prepare the coagulant. If using coagulating salts, dissolve in 1 cup of water. If using vinegar or lemon juice, do not dilute.

When the soymilk returns to a boil, remove it from the heat to add the coagulant. Sprinkle about one-third of the coagulant over the soymilk and stir very gently to distribute it evenly throughout the soymilk. When the milk becomes still, sprinkle another third of the coagulant over the top of the soymilk, stir gently, and cover the pot.

After 5 minutes, examine again. If the soymilk has properly curdled, the whey will appear clear and yellowish. You will not need to add the remaining coagulant. If it is still milky, add the remaining coagulant slowly until the curds definitely separate from the whey.

7. Rinse the forming box cloth well and line the tofu mold with it. Place the mold over the large pan set in the sink. Ladle as much of the clear whey as possible from the pan, and pour it

COOKING WITH OKARA

Okara (also called soy mash) is the pulp resembling mashed potatoes that remains when soymilk is pressed from soybeans. It has many uses in cooking and should not be discarded. Containing some of the soybean's protein, it has virtually all the fiber of the soybean.

One of the most attractive uses of okara is as a meat extender. Mixed with ground meat, it adds a good dose of fiber, some texture, and it reduces cholesterol. Combined with the ingredients for baked goods it adds all these, plus protein. Okara holds moisture in baked goods, too, so they stay fresh longer.

Okara's flavor is very bland, so it is ideal for mixing with highly flavored ingredients where it will add its goodness unintrusively. It can even be the base for a spicy vegetarian loaf that has a meaty texture. Try adding okara to any of your recipes for crackers, breads, pie crusts, puddings, loaves, stuffings, and croquettes. Mixed with pimientos, herbs, and spices, it makes a savory spread for sandwiches or appetizers.

You can store okara in tightly sealed containers in the refrigerator for up to two weeks or in the freezer for about six months.

DRIED OKARA

If you make your own tofu and you have a lot of okara, you can dry it for easier and longer storage. You can also purchase okara very cheaply from soy dairies, and preserve it this way. Removing the moisture reduces its volume and its perishability.

You can dry okara in an electric dehydrator or in your oven. To dry it in the dehydrator, spread the okara in a thin even layer on the trays, and dry it at a medium heat until crisp and thoroughly dry, about 8 to 12 hours. To dry okara in the oven, spread it on cookie sheets, and place them in the oven. Turn the oven to the coolest possible setting, stirring occasionally. When all moisture is gone, about 6 to 8 hours, remove the okara and allow it to cool before storing. Store the dried okara in tightly sealed glass jars.

Because okara dries into small clumps, you may have to pound it or grind it to a finer consistency in a blender or food processor to facilitate its storage and use.

Use dried okara in breading mixes and in much the same way you would use bran or wheat germ in baked goods.

You can rehydrate the dried okara quickly by pouring 2 cups boiling water or other hot liquid over 1 cup of tightly packed okara. The dried okara doubles in volume when rehydrated.

WHEY

Whey is the liquid that remains when the protein in soymilk is coagulated into tofu. Like okara, it has several uses in cooking and shouldn't be discarded.

Whey contains some of the soybean's protein, and also the water-soluble B vitamins as well as some simple sugars.

Whey is an excellent substitute for the water in soups, stews, sauces, and gravies. Vegetables cooked in whey instead of water have a slightly sweeter flavor. Even yeast breads benefit from whey. The whey's sugar content hastens the yeast activity, making for a nicely risen bread.

You can store whey in the refrigerator for about a week. If you cannot use it before then, water your plants or outdoor garden with it.

through the cloth to strain it. Ladle the curds gently into the forming box cloth. When all the curds are in the mold, fold the forming box cloth over the curds, place the lid on top of the draining curds, and place the weight on the lid. Press the tofu for 30 to 50 minutes, or until the whey has stopped dripping from the mold.

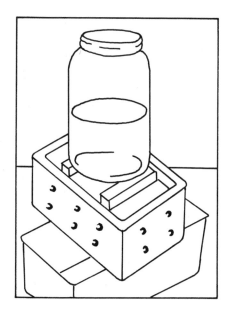

The tofu may be either removed under cold water, or left in the mold until cool. Store tofu in water in the refrigerator.

Main and Side Dishes

Broiled Tofu Burgers

2 cups mashed tofu
  (1 pound)
½ pound ground beef
2 tablespoons soy sauce
2 teaspoons cider vinegar
2 cloves garlic, minced
¼ teaspoon black pepper
¼ cup tomato paste

Serve these as you would any hamburger—as an entrée, with a sauce or on a bun. Looks just like a hamburger—the fat in the beef is necessary for broiling. If you use lean ground beef there may not be enough fat for broiling, so add a little extra meat.

Combine the tofu, beef, soy sauce, vinegar, garlic, pepper, and tomato paste; mix together well, using a large spoon or your hands. Set aside for about 30 minutes. Form into 8 (3–inch) patties and broil for 5 to 7 minutes on each side, or until browned.

4 servings

Chili Con Tofu

2 tablespoons olive oil
1 large onion, chopped
1 green pepper, chopped
2 cloves garlic, pressed or
  minced
2 teaspoons chili powder
¼ teaspoon ground cumin
1½ cups mashed tofu
2 teaspoons soy sauce
2 cups tomatoes, canned or
  fresh
1 cup corn, fresh or frozen
½ teaspoon dried oregano
2 cups drained cooked
  pinto beans

A delicious high-protein vegetarian tofu chili.

Heat the oil in a large Dutch oven and sauté the onion, green pepper, and garlic until the vegetables are just tender. Stir in the chili powder, cumin, and mashed tofu. Sprinkle mixture with soy sauce and add tomatoes, corn, and oregano. Simmer gently, uncovered, for 30 minutes, stirring occasionally.

Add the pinto beans and cook 10 minutes more. Taste for seasonings.

4 to 6 servings

Eggplant Muhtar

This versatile dish makes an attractive hors d'oeuvre as well as a different main or side dish.

Steam eggplants skin-side up until tender (about 20 to 25 minutes). Carefully remove the insides of the steamed eggplants. Reserve the shells, even though they will be droopy. Puree the eggplant pulp in a blender.

Preheat oven to 350°F. In a bowl, thoroughly combine the eggplant pulp, tofu, bread crumbs, and basil. Sauté the onion and garlic in the butter until soft and add to the eggplant mixture, along with 1 cup of the cheese. Divide the stuffing between the eggplant shells—reforming the shells around the stuffing.

Lightly butter a baking dish and place the stuffed eggplants inside. Sprinkle with the remaining cheese, sunflower seeds, and paprika. Bake for 40 minutes or until hot.

4 servings

2 medium-size eggplants, cut in half lengthwise
1 cup mashed tofu (½ pound)
1½ cups fresh whole grain bread crumbs
1 teaspoon dried basil
1 medium-size onion, finely chopped
2 cloves garlic, minced
1 tablespoon butter
1½ cups shredded mild cheddar cheese
raw sunflower seeds
paprika, to taste

Golden Eggplant and Tofu

Serve this hot or cold, as a filling for pita bread, or as an entrée accompanied by bread and salad.

In a large skillet with a cover, heat 2 tablespoons of the olive oil and sauté the onion over medium-low heat for several minutes, until wilted. Remove onion from pan.

Heat the remaining 3 tablespoons of oil and add the eggplant. Toss to coat the eggplant with oil, and sauté for 5 minutes. Stir in the onion, garlic, turmeric, curry powder, and water. Bring to a boil, cover, and simmer over low heat until the eggplant is very tender, about 15 minutes. Add the tofu, mashing it down and sprinkling with the soy sauce. Cover and cook 5 minutes more.

5 to 8 servings

5 tablespoons olive oil
1 large onion, sliced
1 large eggplant, peeled and cut into ¾-inch cubes
1 clove garlic, minced
1 teaspoon turmeric
1 teaspoon curry powder, or to taste
1 cup water
1 pound tofu, diced
1 tablespoon soy sauce

1½ cups unsweetened
    pineapple juice
2 tablespoons soy sauce
2 tablespoons cider vinegar
⅔ cup catsup
2 tablespoons vegetable oil
2 pounds tofu, cut into
    3×1-inch strips (6 to 7
    cups)
1 small head Chinese
    cabbage, thinly sliced
3 to 4 tablespoons
    cornstarch
¼ cup water
8 cups hot cooked brown
    rice

STUFFING

⅔ cup finely chopped
    cold roast pork or
    sauteed ground pork
    (¼ pound raw)
2 scallions, finely chopped
    (reserve the green part
    to use as garnish)
2 cloves garlic, minced
½ to 1 teaspoon hot
    pepper paste* or to taste
    or dash of hot pepper
    sauce
1 tablespoon plus 2
    teaspoons soy sauce
1 teaspoon honey
2 tablespoons plus 2
    teaspoons cornstarch

*Available in Oriental food
stores.

34

Hawaiian Tofu with Chinese Cabbage

This stir-fry dish is an ideal quick meal for a small crowd.

In a bowl combine the pineapple juice, soy sauce, cider vinegar, and catsup. Reserve.

Heat the oil in a wok or large skillet and add the tofu. Stir-fry for a few minutes over medium-high heat until thoroughly heated. Add the Chinese cabbage and stir until slightly wilted.

Stir the sauce ingredients once again, lower heat to simmer, and add sauce to the skillet. Stir cornstarch and water together. When sauce begins to bubble, stir in ⅔ of the cornstarch mixture. Cook just until the sauce is thickened. Add remaining cornstarch mixture if necessary. Serve immediately over brown rice.
8 servings

Hot and Spicy Pork Stuffed Tofu

This is best made with the small pillow-shaped tofu blocks from Oriental food stores. However, instructions are also given for the more common block tofu. Although pork is especially appropriate, any leftover meat or combination of meats may be used to make the stuffing. Serve as an appetizer or main course.

To make the stuffing: In a small bowl combine the pork, white part of scallions, ½ teaspoon garlic, hot pepper paste, 2 teaspoons soy sauce, and honey. Sprinkle with 2 teaspoons cornstarch. Mix in only enough of the egg as is needed to hold the mixture together.

If using pillow-shaped tofu, cut each piece in half diagonally. Using a sharp knife, carefully hollow a deep pocket into the cut side of each piece.

If using block tofu, cut the tofu into 8⅝×2½-inch blocks. Cut each block in half diagonally. You will have smaller pieces than when using the above method. Using a small sharp paring knife, carve a pocket into the long side of the triangle.

Pack as much stuffing as possible into each pocket and smooth the stuffed edge. Reserve any leftover stuffing to put in the sauce.

Heat a thin layer of oil in a medium skillet. Over medium heat, sauté the stuffed side of the tofu triangles first to seal the edge. Then, using kitchen tongs and a small spatula to turn the tofu, sauté the large sides of the tofu, 1 minute on each side, just to form a light skin.

To make the sauce: Mix tomato paste, onion, ginger, chili, vinegar, szechwan peppercorns, remaining garlic, and soy sauce, into the stock and pour over tofu. Simmer for 10 minutes shaking pan occasionally. Transfer tofu pieces with a slotted spoon to a warm shallow casserole dish. Keep hot.

Mix remaining cornstarch and water to form a smooth paste and add to the stock in the skillet. You may also add leftover stuffing. Stir until the sauce is thickened and a few bubbles appear. Pour sauce over tofu and serve, garnished with the scallion tops.

4 to 8 servings

1 egg, lightly beaten
4 pieces molded, pillow-
   shaped firm tofu or 1 to
   1¼ pound block of tofu
vegetable oil, for frying

SAUCE

2 tablespoons tomato paste
1½ cups Chicken Stock
   (page 243) or Beef Stock
   (page 243)
1 small onion, finely
   chopped
1 teaspoon minced, peeled
   ginger root
1 small dried chili pepper,
   with seeds removed, or
   another dash of hot
   pepper sauce
1 tablespoon red wine
   vinegar
6 Szechwan peppercorns,*
   lightly crushed
2 tablespoons water

*Available in Oriental food
stores

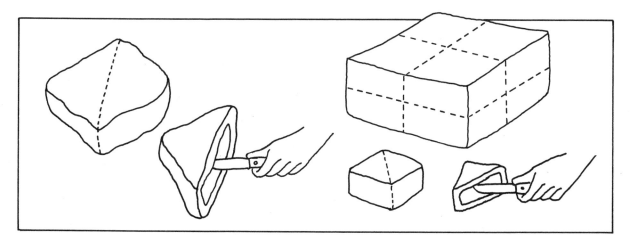

Jerusalem Artichokes and Tofu au Gratin

This dish offers one of my favorite combinations of textures and flavors.

4 medium-size Jerusalem
  artichokes
½ pound firm tofu, cut
  into 1-inch cubes (1½
  cups)
3 tablespoons butter
3 tablespoons whole wheat
  flour
⅔ cup rich Chicken Stock
  (page 243), Beef Stock
  (page 243), or Vegetable
  Stock (page 244)
⅔ cup soy milk or dairy
  milk
4 ounces sharp cheddar or
  Parmesan cheese, grated
  (1 cup)
¼ cup whole grain bread
  crumbs
1 tablespoon butter,
  melted

Steam scrubbed whole artichokes until tender, about 30 minutes. Cool, peel, and cube (2 cups). Toss with tofu in a buttered 1½-quart casserole.

Melt butter in a heavy saucepan or in top of a double boiler. Stir in flour and cook for 2 minutes. Very slowly add stock and milk, stirring constantly, to avoid lumping. Cook until thick and smooth, about 10 minutes. Add cheese and cook until melted.

Preheat oven to 350°F. Pour sauce over artichokes and tofu. Mix bread crumbs with melted butter and sprinkle over top of casserole. Bake for 15 minutes, or until top is lightly golden.

4 servings

Linguine á la Tofu

2 tablespoons butter
2 tablespoons olive oil
1 tablespoon soy sauce
2 cloves garlic, pressed or
  minced
1 cup mashed tofu
  (½ pound)

This dish is so simple and quick, it's hard to believe your effort yields such elegance!

Heat butter and olive oil in a heavy skillet. When the foam subsides, add the soy sauce and garlic and cook gently for a moment until the garlic is lightly colored and fragrant. Add the tofu to skillet. Continue to cook over low heat until the tofu is heated thoroughly, about 3 minutes.

Stir in soybeans and toss with sauce to heat thoroughly. When you are almost ready to serve, stir in the parsley.

To serve, spoon over linguine. Sprinkle with Parmesan cheese.

4 servings

1 cup cooked fresh green soybeans

¼ cup minced fresh parsley

1 pound hot cooked whole wheat linguine (4 cups)

¼ to ½ cup grated Parmesan cheese

Onion-Sauced Casserole

The tasty au gratin topping is an added treat to this delicious vegetable combination.

Preheat oven to 350°F.

Butter an 8×13-inch casserole dish and layer in the potatoes, then the tofu. Sprinkle with soy sauce and place the green beans on top.

Over medium heat sauté the onion in the oil until lightly colored, about 5 minutes. Stir in the flour and cook about 1 minute, stirring constantly. Slowly add the stock while stirring and cook until smooth and thickened. Stir in the thyme and nutmeg. Pour over the tofu mixture in the casserole.

Cover and bake until potatoes are almost tender, about 50 minutes.

Uncover; sprinkle with the cheese and then the bread crumbs. Bake until potatoes are tender, about 7 minutes.

4 servings

3 medium-size potatoes, scrubbed and thinly sliced

¾ pound tofu, cubed (2 cups)

2 teaspoons soy sauce

1 cup cut fresh green beans

1 large sweet Spanish onion, sliced

1 tablespoon vegetable oil

3 tablespoons whole wheat flour

1¾ cups Chicken Stock (page 243) or Vegetable Stock (page 244)

1 teaspoon minced fresh thyme leaves or ½ teaspoon dried thyme

⅛ teaspoon ground nutmeg

1 cup shredded Swiss cheese

1 cup fresh whole grain bread crumbs

37

2 tablespoons butter
1 small onion, minced
¾ pound very lean ground
  beef
1 clove garlic, minced or
  pressed
1 tablespoon curry powder
1 pound tofu, cut into
  ½-inch cubes (3 cups)
1 tablespoon soy sauce
3 tablespoons whole wheat
  flour
2 cups milk
½ cup raisins
1½ cups fresh peas or 1
  package (10-ounce)
  frozen
6 cups hot cooked whole
  wheat noodles

Quick and Creamy Curry

This recipe provides an excellent and original way to stretch meat.

Heat the butter in a large skillet. When the foam subsides, add the onion. Cook over medium heat for 1 minute, stirring constantly. Add the ground beef, garlic, and curry powder, and continue to cook, stirring occasionally, until the meat has lost all traces of red color. Add the tofu and sprinkle with the soy sauce. Stir in the flour. Add the milk and raisins and cook gently until the sauce is thickened and the raisins are plumped, about 10 minutes. Add the peas and cook a few minutes more, or until the peas are just heated. Serve over whole wheat noodles.

6 servings

1 cup milk
1½ cups mashed tofu
  (¾ pound)
1 medium-size carrot,
  coarsely chopped
1 scallion, coarsely chopped
½ cup grated Parmesan
  cheese
1 teaspoon dill weed
¼ teaspoon dry mustard
2 tablespoons butter,
  melted
4 egg yolks
3 slices whole wheat
  bread, torn into small
  pieces
4 egg whites, beaten until
  stiff

Quick Blender Tofu Souffle

Preheat oven to 325°F.

Combine the milk, tofu, carrot, scallion, cheese, dill, mustard, butter, egg yolks, and bread in a blender. Puree until smooth and pour into a bowl. Fold in the egg whites. Pour into an oiled 1½-quart souffle dish.

Bake 50 minutes, or until set and golden.

Serve with a tomato or herb sauce. Melted cheese is also very good.

Variation: For a more custard-like souffle, use 3 eggs and only ½ cup milk. This will make a firmer textured souffle that stores well for reheating.

4 to 6 servings

Scalloped Tofu au Gratin

A nice combination of soft and crunchy textures.

Melt 1 tablespoon of the butter in a heavy skillet. Sauté onion and green pepper until tender. Remove from skillet and reserve.

In the same skillet melt 1 tablespoon of the butter and lightly sauté the tofu, about 5 minutes. Reserve.

Melt remaining 2 tablespoons butter in a small saucepan and stir in the flour. Cook lightly for several minutes, stirring constantly, until smooth and bubbling. Slowly stir in milk and cook over low heat, stirring frequently, until thick and beginning to bubble.

Remove from heat and stir in the white pepper, mustard, Parmesan, and ¾ cup of the cheddar cheese.

Preheat oven to 350°F.

Butter a shallow 9-inch ovenproof casserole dish. Layer with half of the tofu, cover with half of the sauce, then half of the vegetables, then the remaining tofu, sauce, and vegetables. Top with the bread crumbs and remaining cheddar cheese. Bake 20 minutes, or until bubbly and browned on top.

4 servings

4 tablespoons butter
1 large onion, thinly sliced
1 small green pepper, thinly sliced
3½ cups ¼-inch cubes tofu
3 tablespoons whole wheat flour
1 cup milk
½ teaspoon white pepper
2 teaspoons dry mustard
¼ cup grated Parmesan cheese
1¼ cups grated cheddar cheese
2 tablespoons soft whole grain bread crumbs

Small Stuffed Tofu Pockets, Scampi Style

2 scallions
¼ cup cooked, coarsely
  shredded crabmeat,
  chicken, or shrimp
1 tablespoon chopped
  fresh dill or parsley
1½ teaspoons soy sauce
1 teaspoon cornstarch
¾ pound block of tofu
2 cloves garlic, minced
¼ cup butter
2 tablespoons vegetable oil
1 lemon
black pepper to taste
4 thick slices Italian bread

Serve these as appetizers, about three per person, or double the recipe and serve as a main course with rice.

Sliver the white part of the scallion, and cut into ½-inch lengths. Chop the green tops and reserve for garnish.

In a small bowl combine half of the white part of the scallions, the crab, chicken, or shrimp, and dill. Sprinkle with soy sauce and cornstarch. Toss to combine.

Cut the tofu into 12⅝ × 1½-inch blocks. By cutting into 2 adjacent sides, hollow a pocket in each square. (Reserve the scooped-out tofu for another use.) Pack about 1 teaspoon of stuffing into each square.

In a medium-size skillet over medium heat, cook the garlic and remaining white part of the scallion in the butter and oil for 30 seconds. Don't let the garlic brown. Add the tofu, cover loosely, and cook for 2 minutes, or until pale gold. Flip squares carefully using kitchen tongs and a small spatula. Reduce heat, and cook, covered, until golden and tofu is very hot, about 5 minutes more. Uncover and squeeze a generous amount of lemon juice over tofu. Sprinkle with pepper and scallion tops. Serve immediately with the butter sauce and a piece of Italian bread.

4 small servings, 12 pieces

Stuffed Pasta Shells with Meat Sauce

Heat 1 tablespoon of the olive oil in a large saucepan and sauté the onion and garlic for a few moments. Add the ground beef and soy sauce. Cook over medium heat, stirring occasionally, until the meat is browned.

Add the tomato paste and cook a few minutes longer over low heat. Add the tomatoes and cook, uncovered, 30 minutes.

Meanwhile, combine the tofu, grated cheese, oregano, parsley, pepper, and remaining olive oil. Spoon this mixture into the cooked shells.

Spread ½ cup sauce in the bottom of an 8-inch square baking dish. Add the stuffed shells and top with the remaining sauce.

Bake at 350°F for 15 to 20 minutes, or until the shells are heated.

4 servings

SAUCE

2 tablespoons olive oil
1 medium-size onion, finely chopped
1 large clove garlic, pressed or minced
½ pound very lean ground beef
1 teaspoon soy sauce
3 tablespoons tomato paste
2 cups crushed peeled fresh or canned tomatoes

STUFFING

1½ cups mashed tofu (¾ pound)
3 tablespoons grated Parmesan or Romano cheese
½ teaspoon dried oregano
2 tablespoons minced fresh parsley
dash of black pepper
5 ounces large whole wheat shell macaroni (24 to 30 shells), cooked

41

Tofu Schnitzel (Stuffed Tofu Cutlet with Mushroom Sauce)

STUFFING

1 medium-size onion,
    finely chopped
4 mushrooms, finely
    chopped
1 clove garlic, minced
1 teaspoon fresh thyme
    leaves or ½ teaspoon
    dried thyme
1½ teaspoons finely
    chopped fresh sage or ½
    teaspoon crumbled dried
    sage
2 tablespoons butter
⅔ cup fresh whole grain
    bread crumbs
1 egg, lightly beaten
⅓ cup shredded
    provolone cheese
¼ cup grated Parmesan
    cheese
black pepper, to taste
milk

TOFU AND BREADING

1 to 1¼ pound block of
    tofu, about 2½ × 5 ×
    2 inches
1 tablespoon soy sauce
⅓ cup whole wheat or
    rye flour
1 egg, lightly beaten with
    1 tablespoon water
⅔ cup fine dry whole
    grain bread crumbs
vegetable oil, for shallow
    frying

This recipe may look complicated, but it is simply an herb bread stuffing sandwiched between thin slices of tofu which are breaded and shallow fried. Set up an assembly line to bread the sandwiches and the work will go quickly. The sauce is optional; you can serve the cutlets with a slice of lemon instead. The cutlets can be breaded and refrigerated a day in advance.

To make the stuffing: In a medium-size saucepan sauté the onion, mushrooms, garlic, thyme, and sage in the butter until onion is tender, about 3 or 4 minutes. Cool slightly. Stir in bread crumbs, egg, provolone and Parmesan cheeses, and pepper. Mix thoroughly. If necessary, moisten with just enough milk to hold stuffing together.

To make the tofu and breading: Slice tofu into 16 squares. Because all tofu is shaped differently it's hard to describe one way to slice it, but the finished slices should be about ¼ × 2½ inches. The thin measurement is the important one; the other dimensions can vary with your tofu.

Spread 2 tablespoons of the stuffing mixture evenly over half of the squares. Press the remaining squares firmly on top of the stuffing to make sandwiches.

Brush the outside of each sandwich lightly with the soy sauce, then flour all sides. When all sandwiches are floured, dip them into the egg and then the bread crumbs to coat the top and bottom of each sandwich.

Heat a thin layer of oil in a large skillet over medium heat. With the skillet loosely covered, sauté the cutlets about 5 minutes on one side until browned. Flip the cutlets carefully to avoid damaging the crumb coating. Add oil if necessary; lower heat slightly, and cook the second side about 5 minutes. When browned, keep warm, on a serving dish in the oven.

To make the sauce: Over medium to high heat, sauté the mushrooms in the butter for 3 minutes. Stir in the paprika and add tomatoes. When mixture boils, remove from heat and allow to cool for a few minutes.

Stir sour cream with a fork until completely smooth. Add sour cream to mushroom mixture. Return to very low heat. Warm sauce, stirring often, but do not let it get too hot.

To serve, spoon a small amount of sauce over each cutlet.

4 servings

SAUCE

8 mushrooms, thinly sliced
1 tablespoon butter
½ teaspoon Hungarian paprika
½ cup diced fresh or canned tomatoes, crushed
¾ cup sour cream

Tofu Arpina

Perfect for a vegetarian entrée. Serve with a steamed green vegetable or fresh salad.

To make the burgers: Combine the bulgur, tofu, eggs, onion, basil, oregano, and Romano cheese. When thoroughly mixed, stir in the flour. With slightly dampened hands, form the mixture into hamburger-sized patties and cook in a skillet in a small amount of oil. You should have 14 to 16 patties. Cooked burgers will keep several days in the refrigerator, or longer in the freezer.

To make the sauce: Heat the olive oil and sauté the onion and garlic for a few minutes until they are softened and fragrant. Stir in the tomato paste and continue to cook for 1 minute more. Then stir in the tomatoes, adding water if the sauce is too thick. Cook uncovered over low heat for 30 minutes.

About 20 minutes before serving, heat the burgers in the tomato sauce. Transfer to a baking dish and top with the mozzarella slices. Bake at 350°F for 15 to 20 minutes, or until the cheese is melted and the dish is thoroughly heated.

4 to 6 servings

BURGERS

3¼ cups cooked bulgur
1 pound tofu, mashed (2 cups)
2 eggs
1 medium-size onion, chopped
1 teaspoon dried basil leaves
¾ teaspoon dried oregano leaves
2 tablespoons grated Romano cheese
2½ cups whole wheat flour
vegetable oil, for frying

SAUCE

2 tablespoons olive oil
1 onion, chopped
1 large clove garlic, pressed
1 can (6-ounce) tomato paste
4 cups chopped peeled tomatoes
¼ to ½ cup water
6 slices (3 ounces) mozzarella cheese

2 cups bulgur
4 cups boiling water
2 tablespoons vegetable oil
2 pounds firm tofu, cut
  into 1-inch cubes (5 to
  5½ cups)
1 large onion, cut in half
  and sliced
2 tablespoons tamari soy
  sauce
3 cups broccoli flowerets
2 tablespoons water

Tofu-Broccoli-Bulgur Dutch Oven

Serve as a side dish or vegetarian main dish.

Add bulgur to boiling water in saucepan and reduce heat to very low. Skim off any chaff that may rise to the surface and cook with cover slightly ajar for 20 minutes. Turn off heat and cover snugly until ready to use.

Meanwhile, in a Dutch oven with a cover, heat the oil and stir-fry the tofu and onion for 2 minutes. Sprinkle with the tamari and stir-fry 1 minute more. Add the broccoli and 2 tablespoons water, stir, and cover. Cook over low heat until broccoli is just tender, about 3 to 5 minutes.

Add the cooked bulgur and heat mixture thoroughly.

4 to 6 servings

Tofu Pockets with Scallions and Ginger

These tofu "sandwiches" are full meals in themselves.

Thinly slice scallions, reserving green tops for garnish. Sauté all but 1 tablespoon sliced white part of scallions, ginger, and half of the garlic in 1 tablespoon of the oil for 2 minutes. Add 1 teaspoon of the soy sauce, carrot, and then the egg. Cook, stirring constantly, until egg is consistency of soft scrambled eggs. Remove from heat and stir in the coriander. Set aside.

Cut the tofu into 8 blocks, approximately ⅝ × 2½ inches. Carefully hollow a deep pocket into one side of each tofu block using a sharp paring knife. Gently force as much stuffing as possible into each pocket. Flour all sides of the tofu especially on the stuffed edge. Shake off extra flour.

In a large skillet heat the remaining 2 tablespoons of oil over medium heat. Sauté the stuffed edge of the tofu blocks first to seal in the stuffing. When lightly crusted, briefly sauté the two sides just long enough to form a light skin, about ½ minute on each side. Remove the tofu from the pan.

Using the same pan, combine the stock, sesame oil, mushrooms, remaining garlic, 1 tablespoon scallion, and remaining soy sauce. Bring mixture to a boil, then reduce heat to low. Stir together the cornstarch and water to make a smooth paste; add to the simmering mixture. Stir until the sauce begins to thicken. Carefully add the stuffed tofu blocks and simmer for 5 minutes, stirring occasionally. (You can add any leftover filling to the sauce.) Serve in shallow bowls with a generous amount of sauce. Garnish with reserved scallion tops.

4 servings

6 scallions
1 tablespoon finely chopped peeled ginger root
1 large clove garlic, minced
3 tablespoons vegetable oil
1 tablespoon soy sauce
1 small cooked carrot, finely chopped
1 egg, lightly beaten
2 teaspoons chopped fresh coriander leaves (optional)
1 to 1¼ pound block tofu
½ cup whole wheat flour
2½ cups Vegetable Stock (page 244) or Chicken Stock (page 243)
1 teaspoon Chinese sesame oil*
4 mushrooms, thinly sliced
3 tablespoons cornstarch
¼ cup water

*Available in Oriental Food Stores, or you may use regular sesame oil.

45

3 cups rich Chicken Stock
  (page 243)
2 teaspoons minced peeled
  ginger root
2 large cloves garlic,
  minced
1 tablespoon soy sauce
3 tablespoons cornstarch
1½ pounds tofu, cut into
  2 × ½ × ½-inch strips
2 cups fresh snow peas

Tofu Strips and Snow Peas with "Chinese Restaurant Sauce"

A traditional Oriental way of serving tofu.

Pour 2½ cups of the stock into a saucepan and add the ginger and the garlic. Place over medium heat and bring to a boil. Reduce heat and simmer 5 minutes.

In a bowl combine the remaining stock with the soy sauce and the cornstarch. Stir until combined. Stir into stock mixture. Cook, stirring, until the sauce has thickened slightly. Add the tofu and snow peas and continue to cook until they are heated through. (Fresh snow peas should still be bright green in color after cooking.) Serve over hot cooked rice or noodles.

6 servings

Tofu Vegetable Dinner
(with Variations)

This full-meal dinner is quick, easy, and adaptable to many variations. Try some of your own ideas.

Add bulgur to boiling water in a saucepan and reduce heat to very low. Skim off any chaff that may rise to the surface and cook with cover slightly ajar for 20 minutes. Turn off heat and keep snugly covered until ready to use.

Meanwhile, toss the tofu with the soy sauce and let marinate until the soy sauce is absorbed.

Heat oil in a large skillet and stir-fry the tofu and onion for 3 minutes. Add the broccoli, 1¾ cups of the stock, and the vinegar. Stir and cover the skillet. Cook over low heat until broccoli is just tender, about 3 to 5 minutes.

Combine the cornstarch with the remaining ¼ cup of the cooled stock and add to the skillet. Cook, stirring, until sauce is thickened. Serve hot over the bulgur.

4 to 6 servings

Variations

Danish Dinner: Substitute green beans for the broccoli and place thin slices of Muenster cheese (or other mild cheese) on the bulgur before spooning on the tofu and vegetables.

Russian Dinner: Substitute cabbage for the broccoli and add ½ teaspoon dried dill weed. Be careful not to overcook the cabbage. Serve over hot cooked kasha (buckwheat groats).

1 cup bulgur
2½ cups boiling water
1 pound tofu, cut into
    ¾-inch cubes (3 cups)
4 teaspoons soy sauce
1 tablespoon vegetable oil
1 onion, cut in half and
    sliced
2 cups broccoli flowerets
2 cups Vegetable Stock
    (page 244)
1 tablespoon wine vinegar
2 tablespoons cornstarch

Tofu Zucchini Quiche in Three-Grain Pressed Crust

2 tablespoons vegetable oil
3 cloves garlic, minced
1 medium-size onion,
    coarsely chopped
2 small zucchini, cut into
    ¼-inch slices
½ teaspoon dried thyme
½ teaspoon dried chervil
1 cup mashed tofu
    (½ pound)
1 cup heavy cream
2 eggs
¼ cup yogurt
1 Three-Grain Pressed
    Crust (recipe follows)
2 cups shredded sharp
    cheddar or Swiss cheese
    (about 8 ounces)

Nice main dish for a brunch menu.

Heat oil in a large skillet. Add garlic, onion, and zucchini; cook until onion is transparent and zucchini is tender, about 10 minutes. Turn off heat. Add thyme and chervil and mix well. Set aside.

Preheat oven to 450°F.

Purée tofu, cream, eggs, and yogurt in blender or food processor until smooth.

Spread sautéed vegetables evenly over bottom of pie crust. Sprinkle cheese over vegetables. Pour tofu mixture over all.

Bake for 5 minutes. Reduce heat to 375°F and bake for 15 minutes, or until filling is set. Serve warm or cold.

8 servings

NOTE: You may also make this quiche using the Whole Wheat Piecrust on page 242.

THREE-GRAIN PRESSED CRUST

1 cup whole wheat flour
¼ cup brown rice flour
¼ cup oat flour*
¼ cup potato flour**
4 tablespoons butter
2 tablespoons vegetable oil
2 to 3 tablespoons ice
    water

*Finely ground oats may be used.
**Available in gourmet shops or natural foods stores.

Combine wheat, rice, oat and potato flours. Cut in butter until mixture resembles coarse cornmeal. Add oil and mix lightly. Add ice water and form into a ball, handling as little as possible.

Preheat oven to 450°F.

Press crust into the bottom of a 13 × 9 × 2-inch dish.

Bake for 10 minutes, or until edges are golden brown.

1 13 × 9 × 2-inch crust

Top-of-the-Stove Casserole

A refreshing change from plain potatoes or rice.

Steam the potatoes and carrots until just tender, about 5 minutes.

Cut cheese into 5 thin slices and reserve. Break remaining cheese into pieces, and place in a blender with the tofu, milk, water, cornstarch, and oil. Blend until mixture is smooth. Pour mixture into a large, heavy saucepan and heat, stirring, until the cheese is melted and the sauce is hot.

Drain any water from the vegetables. Combine the sauce and the vegetables in the saucepan, and sprinkle the wheat germ on top. Place the slices of cheese on top of the wheat germ. Cover and heat very gently until the cheese is melted.

4 servings

4 large potatoes, shredded
6 large carrots, shredded
6 ounces cheddar cheese
¼ pound tofu, cubed
½ cup milk
½ cup water
1 teaspoon cornstarch
1 teaspoon vegetable oil
¼ cup wheat germ

Frozen Tofu Main and Side Dishes

Beefy Chunks and Onions

A quick, tasty way to use up frozen tofu.

Cut tofu into cubes.

Sauté onion in oil until soft and transparent, about 10 minutes.

To make the marinade: In a bowl combine tamari, vinegar, garlic, honey, water, parsley, and basil. Add tofu and toss until marinade is completely absorbed.

Add marinated tofu to sautéed onion and cook over medium heat until tofu is slightly brown, about 5 minutes. Serve over brown rice, bulgur, buckwheat, or buttered noodles.

2 to 3 servings

12 ounces frozen tofu, thawed, and well-drained
1 large onion, thinly sliced
2 tablespoons safflower oil
Marinade
3 tablespoons tamari soy sauce
3 tablespoons wine vinegar
1 teaspoon minced garlic
½ teaspoon honey
2 tablespoons water
1 teaspoon chopped fresh parsley
1 teaspoon dried basil

Chicken-Fried Tofu Cutlets

You won't believe these cutlets are meatless!

1 pound frozen tofu,
  thawed and well-
  drained
¼ cup red wine vinegar
¼ cup soy sauce
¼ cup water
2 cloves garlic, minced
1 teaspoon dried basil
1 tablespoon chopped
  fresh parsley
1 teaspoon black pepper
1 cup cornmeal, for
  dredging
vegetable oil, for frying

Cut tofu into slices about ½ × 2 inches.

In a bowl combine vinegar, soy sauce, water, garlic, basil, parsley, and pepper. Add tofu pieces and toss gently. Set aside until marinade is completely absorbed, about 3 hours.

Coat tofu slices with cornmeal.

In a heavy skillet heat about ¼ inch oil. Fry breaded tofu until golden brown on both sides, adding more oil as needed. Drain on absorbent paper.

Serve hot with rice and steamed vegetables and your favorite sauce or Gravy (page 239). Or serve cold as appetizers: Spear a piece of tofu and a piece of pimiento on each toothpick.

4 servings

Tofu and Apples

An excellent sweet and sour combination. Serve with cooked rice or buttered noodles.

1 pound frozen tofu,
  thawed and drained
¼ cup cider vinegar
2 tablespoons soy sauce
½ teaspoon ground ginger
1 clove garlic, minced
½ teaspoon dried basil
2 tablespoons water
2 tablespoons vegetable
  oil, for shallow frying
1 large tart apple, cored
  and coarsely chopped
1 large onion, thinly sliced

Cut tofu into 1-inch cubes. In a bowl combine vinegar, soy sauce, ginger, garlic, basil, and water. Add tofu and toss until the marinade is well absorbed, about 3 hours.

In a heavy skillet heat oil. Sauté apple and onion in hot oil about 7 minutes, or until onions are fairly soft. Add tofu and any remaining marinade. Cook for about 8 minutes, stirring constantly, or until heated.

4 servings

Tofu Meatballs I

A light spicy Italian meatball. Except for the pale color of tofu meatballs, the flavor and texture are very similar to ground beef.

Lightly sauté the onion and garlic in 2 tablespoons of the olive oil. Remove from heat and stir in the tofu, oregano, soy sauce, tomato paste, and egg. Mix to combine well. Form the mixture into 16 small balls.

Sauté until browned in the remaining olive oil. Simmer for 15 minutes in your favorite tomato sauce or Tomato Sauce (page 241).
4 servings

1 medium-size onion,
   finely chopped
2 cloves garlic, minced
¼ cup olive oil
8 ounces frozen tofu,
   thawed, drained, and
   crumbled
1 teaspoon dried oregano
½ teaspoon soy sauce
2 teaspoons tomato paste
1 egg, lightly beaten

Tofu Meatballs II

These meatballs are slightly richer and a bit herbier than the above meatballs.

Mix tofu in a bowl with soy sauce and garlic. Allow to stand 3 minutes. Combine with remaining ingredients except oil and mix well.

Form mixture into meatballs. If mixture is too dry, add another egg. If too wet add a tablespoon of whole wheat flour.

Fry meatballs in hot oil in skillet until nicely browned on all sides. Serve on whole grain bread with lettuce and tomato or simmer gently in Tomato Sauce (page 241) and serve with pasta.
4 servings

1 pound frozen tofu,
   thawed, drained, and
   crumbled
2 tablespoons soy sauce
1 teaspoon minced garlic
1 teaspoon dried oregano
1 teaspoon dried basil
½ teaspoon dried thyme
2 tablespoons chopped
   fresh parsley
⅓ cup grated Parmesan
   cheese
½ cup whole grain bread
   crumbs
1 egg
2 tablespoons olive oil

2 tablespoons vegetable oil
1 large onion, diced
1 green pepper, diced
3 cups tomato puree
3 to 4 cloves garlic, minced
1 teaspoon dried oregano
½ teaspoon dried basil
¼ cup chopped fresh
   parsley
3 tablespoons olive oil
3 tablespoons soy sauce
1 large eggplant, cut into
   ¼-inch rounds
4 medium-size potatoes
1 pound frozen tofu,
   thawed, drained, and
   coarsely crumbled
Cheese Sauce (page 127)

Tofu Moussaka

This deceptively rich and filling dish greatly reduces the calories, fat, and cholesterol of its traditional counterpart.

In a large heavy skillet heat 2 tablespoons oil. Sauté onion and pepper until soft. Add tomato puree and stir. Cook over low heat about 20 minutes, stirring occasionally.

Stir the garlic, herbs, olive oil, and soy sauce into tomato puree. Simmer gently for 5 minutes.

Steam eggplant slices for about 12 minutes, or until slightly tender. Steam potatoes for about 25 minutes until tender but not soft. Slice cooled potatoes into ¼-inch rounds.

Preheat oven to 350°F.

In the bottom of a 13 × 9 × 2-inch oiled dish, layer ⅓ (1 cup) of the tomato sauce, half of the tofu, and half of the eggplant. Cover with half of the potatoes. Repeat the layers, ending with tomato sauce.

Bake in oven for 40 minutes.

Pour Cheese Sauce evenly over the top of casserole and reduce heat to 300°F. Bake 20 minutes longer. Allow to cool about 15 minutes before serving.

8 servings

Soups and Salads

Korean Hot Beef Soup

This soup is delightfully fragrant. Although it is spicy hot, it is more subtle than the fiery Chinese hot-and-sour soup. If your chili oil is mild, or your heat tolerance high, you may want to fortify this soup by adding a small dried hot pepper while it simmers.

Combine shiitake mushrooms and warm water. Set aside.

Combine garlic, ginger, mustard, sesame oil, 1 teaspoon of the chili oil, and soy sauce. Cut meat into paper-thin slices across the grain, and then to 1-inch lengths. Toss in the marinade mixture, coating the meat evenly. Set aside.

When the shiitake mushrooms are soft, drain off and reserve the liquid. Remove and discard the stems. Slice the mushrooms into ¼-inch pieces.

Bring stock and mushroom water to a boil. Add cabbage, the shiitake and fresh mushrooms, vinegar, and half of the scallions. Reduce heat and simmer for 10 minutes.

Meanwhile, sear beef and tofu in remaining hot pepper oil. Add to soup along with any pan juices. Cook 3 minutes more. Garnish with remaining scallions and sesame seeds.

6 servings

NOTE: This soup can be reheated, but will need an additional flourish, such as thickening the soup with a little cornstarch and drizzling a beaten egg into it.

3 dried shiitake
  mushrooms*
¼ cup warm water
2 cloves garlic, minced
1 teaspoon minced peeled
  ginger root
1 teaspoon dry mustard
1 tablespoon Chinese
  sesame oil*
2 teaspoons chili oil*
1 tablespoon soy sauce
½ pound partially frozen
  flank steak
4 cups Beef Stock (page
  243)
2 cups shredded Chinese
  cabbage
8 fresh mushrooms,
  quartered
3 tablespoons rice wine
  vinegar*
10 scallions with tops,
  thinly sliced
¼ pound tofu, cut into
  ½-inch cubes
1 teaspoon sesame seeds

*Available in Oriental food stores.

4 large scallions
¼ cup sesame seeds
4 cups Chicken Stock
   (page 243)
½ teaspoon crushed red
   pepper or 1 small dried
   chili, seeded and
   chopped
2 large cloves garlic,
   pressed
2 tablespoons soy sauce
3 tablespoons cornstarch
¼ cup water
¾ pound tofu, cut into
   cubes (2¾ cups)
1 tablespoon rice wine
   vinegar

Seoul Tofu Soup

*If you like this combination of flavors, you can also serve it as a sauce over rice.
Simply decrease the chicken stock to 2 cups.*

Chop scallions, reserving green tops for garnish.

Toast the sesame seeds over low heat in a heavy dry skillet, stirring frequently, until they are golden brown, about 2 minutes. Cool slightly and crush lightly with a mortar and pestle or blend in a blender.

Heat the stock in a large saucepan, adding the sesame seeds, white part of scallions, pepper flakes, and garlic. Bring to a boil and reduce heat to low.

Meanwhile, combine soy sauce, cornstarch, and water. Add to the simmering broth and stir. Add the tofu and vinegar and simmer gently for 10 minutes. Stir in the scallion tops right before serving.
6 servings

SALAD

½ pound tofu, cut into
   ½-inch cubes (1½ cups)
1 teaspoon soy sauce
3 to 4 cups chopped
   cabbage
1 cup cooked elbow
   macaroni
½ cup shredded carrots
2 scallions, chopped
1 to 2 tomatoes, cut into
   bite-size pieces
2 tablespoons toasted
   sunflower seeds

Broadway Salad

Toss the tofu with the soy sauce. Place the cabbage, macaroni, carrots, scallions, tomatoes, and tofu in layers in a large bowl. Chill until serving time.

Gently whisk together the yogurt, mayonnaise, lemon juice, and bleu cheese.

Drizzle the dressing over salad or toss with the salad to coat all at once. Serve chilled. Sprinkle with sunflower seeds before serving.

8 to 10 servings

DRESSING

½ cup yogurt
¼ cup mayonnaise
½ teaspoon lemon juice
2 tablespoons crumbled bleu cheese

Cabbage, Beet, Barley, and Tofu Salad

Steam beets until tender, about 30 to 60 minutes. Peel and cut into ½-inch cubes. Reserve.

Chop cabbage coarsely and steam for 7 to 10 minutes.

While cabbage is cooking, make dressing: In a large bowl combine vinegar, honey, soy sauce, garlic, parsley, chervil, and oil. Add tofu cubes and mix to coat well.

Add steamed cabbage to marinated tofu and toss again. Add cubed beets and barley, and toss to coat all ingredients well. Chill for 1 hour before serving.

10 servings

2 medium-size beets
1 small head of red cabbage
⅓ cup cider vinegar
1 tablespoon honey
2 tablespoons soy sauce
1 tablespoon minced garlic
2 tablespoons chopped fresh parsley
2 tablespoons dried chervil, basil, or thyme
¼ cup safflower oil
½ pound firm tofu, cut into ½-inch cubes (1½ cups)
1½ cups cooked barley

10 to 12 ounces firm tofu,
 cubed (2 cups)
1 stalk celery, chopped
1 carrot, cut into julienne
 strips
2 tablespoons minced
 onion
3 cloves garlic, minced
2 tablespoons soy sauce
2 tablespoons chopped
 fresh parsley
1 tablespoon curry powder
2 tablespoons mayonnaise
2 tablespoons yogurt
2 tablespoons cider vinegar
¾ cup fresh pineapple
 chunks or 1 can (5¼-
 ounce) pineapple
 chunks, drained

Curried Tropical Salad

Combine all ingredients and toss together well. Chill for 3 hours. Serve on lettuce as salad or in pita bread with alfalfa sprouts. Salad can be refrigerated for up to 4 days.

4 to 6 servings

2 pounds tofu, mashed
 (4 cups)
1½ teaspoons dried celery
 flakes
1 teaspoon dried dill weed
freshly ground pepper, to
 taste
2 tablespoons finely
 minced onion
½ cup chopped celery
½ cup mayonnaise

Roxy Salad

This simple salad is especially good for people who like the taste of fresh tofu—homemade or very fresh tofu is the best for this.

Combine the ingredients, in the order listed. Chill 2 hours before serving. Serve on a lettuce leaf or as a filling for pita bread.

6 servings

Sunrise Salad

A colorful luncheon salad or appetizer.

In a saucepan sprinkle the gelatin over the water and allow to soften. Place over low heat and stir until the gelatin dissolves. Stir in the honey until it dissolves. Remove the saucepan from heat and stir in the orange juice, orange rind and the lemon juice. Chill until gelatin mixture has the consistency of raw egg whites.

Combine the tofu and the sour cream, mixing well. Stir thickened gelatin mixture into tofu mixture. Turn into a 1-quart mold and chill until firm. Garnish with orange segments.

4 servings

1 envelope unflavored gelatin
½ cup water
2 tablespoons honey
1 cup orange juice
1 teaspoon grated orange rind
1 tablespoon lemon juice
1 cup mashed tofu (½ pound)
⅓ cup sour cream
orange segments

Taste of Spring Salad

Add the bulgur to the boiling water and reduce heat to very low. Skim off any chaff that may rise to the surface, and cook with cover slightly ajar for 20 minutes. Remove cover and allow to cool until warm, and then refrigerate until cold.

Just before serving, add the tuna, peas, tofu, scallions, soy sauce, and mayonnaise to the bulgur and mix thoroughly. Serve cold.

6 servings

1½ cups bulgur
3 cups boiling water
1 can (6½ ounces) water-packed tuna, broken into chunks
2 cups fresh peas or 1 10-ounce package frozen peas, thawed
12 ounces tofu, cut into small cubes
¼ cup finely chopped scallions, with tops
1 teaspoon tamari soy sauce
⅓ cup mayonnaise

2 cups fresh peas or 1
   package (10½-ounce)
   frozen peas
1 cup (4 to 5 ounces)
   ½-inch cubes firm tofu
¼ cup mayonnaise
¼ cup yogurt
1 teaspoon French-style
   mustard
1 tablespoon grated
   Parmesan cheese
2 teaspoons crumbled
   dried dillweed or 1
   tablespoon minced fresh
   dill

Tofu, Peas, and Yogurt

Steam peas until tender but firm, about 7 minutes. Chill. Combine with remaining ingredients and toss well. Chill. Serve on a bed of lettuce.

3 to 4 servings

8 ounces firm tofu, cut
   into ½-inch cubes (1½
   cups)
¼ cup mayonnaise
¼ cup yogurt
2 tablespoons creamed
   horseradish
2 teaspoons soy sauce
¼ teaspoon cayenne
   pepper
1 stalk finely chopped
   celery
1 tablespoon chopped
   fresh parsley
¼ cup finely chopped
   carrot

Tofu with Horseradish Dressing

In a small bowl combine all ingredients. Toss well. Chill before serving.

3 to 4 servings

Dips and Sauces

Dill Tofu Spread or Dip

This dairy-free spread is prepared using a technique similar to the blender method for preparing mayonnaise. It is best to refrigerate spread overnight to blend the flavors.

In a bowl beat the egg yolks with a wire whisk until they begin to thicken. Whisk in ¼ cup of the olive oil, drop by drop, beating constantly with the wire whisk. The mixture should be smooth and have the consistency of mayonnaise. Transfer to a blender.

Add the garlic, dill, parsley, paprika, and mustard. With the blender on low, gradually add the remaining oil in a thin stream. When the oil is completely incorporated into the mixture, slowly add the soy sauce, lemon juice, and tofu. Blend until smooth and refrigerate.

Yields 1⅓ cups

NOTE: If your mayonnaise should thin out or separate, warm a glass or stainless steel bowl and a wire whisk in hot water. Dry thoroughly.
Beat 1 egg yolk lightly in the bowl. Gradually, drop by drop, beat in the broken mayonnaise.

4 egg yolks
½ cup olive oil
2 cloves garlic, coarsely chopped
1 tablespoon minced fresh dill or 1 teaspoon dried dillweed
2 tablespoons finely chopped fresh parsley
½ teaspoon paprika (Hungarian, if available)
½ teaspoon dry mustard
½ teaspoon soy sauce
2 tablespoons lemon juice
¾ cup mashed soft tofu (½ pound)

Garlic Herb Cheese

4 cloves garlic, coarsely
  chopped
2 tablespoons chopped
  fresh parsley
2 tablespoons coarsely
  chopped mixed fresh
  herbs (chervil, lemon
  thyme, tarragon, dill,
  sorrel, chives, scallions,
  basil)
1 cup mashed tofu (about
  ½ pound)
4 ounces cream cheese,
  softened
¼ cup butter, softened
2 tablespoons sour cream
  or yogurt
freshly ground black
  pepper or additional
  chopped fresh herbs

Serve this aromatic cheese as an appetizer with crackers or as a sandwich spread.

On a cutting board combine the garlic, parsley, and herbs and mince together.

Coarsely chop the tofu and wrap the pieces in a clean cotton towel. Wring the moisture out of the tofu.

Combine the parsley mixture, tofu, cream cheese, butter, and sour cream in a large bowl. Beat until smooth with an electric mixer. Chill until firm. The cheese may now be shaped as desired and rolled in the pepper or herbs to garnish. Refrigerate overnight before serving to blend the flavors.

Yields 1 cup

Pesto Tofu Cheese

1 large clove garlic
½ cup loosely packed
  fresh basil leaves
1 tablespoon finely
  chopped fresh parsley
¼ cup sunflower seeds or
  pine nuts (pignoli)
1 tablespoon lemon juice
2 tablespoons sour cream
  or yogurt
¾ cup mashed tofu (about
  6 ounces)
¼ cup grated Parmesan
  cheese
2 tablespoons finely
  chopped sunflower
  seeds or pine nuts
  (pignoli)

Serve this flavorful herbed cheese as an appetizer with crackers.

On a cutting board combine the garlic, basil, parsley, and sunflower seeds and mince together. Combine the lemon juice and sour cream in a blender. Add the garlic-herb mixture and blend briefly, 4 or 5 seconds.

Wrap the tofu in a clean cotton towel. Wring the moisture out of the tofu. Add the tofu and cheese to the blender. Blend until smooth. Pour into bowl and chill until firm. The cheese may now be shaped as desired and rolled in the chopped sunflower seeds to garnish. Refrigerate overnight to blend the flavors before serving.

Yields 1 cup

Tofu Cheese Sauce or Fondue

As a sauce, this recipe is especially good over cooked julienne-sliced root vegetables, such as carrots, potatoes, turnips. As a fondue, serve French bread and raw vegetables to dip into the sauce.

Place tofu in blender and add milk, soy sauce, oil, and tomato puree. Blend until pureed. Sprinkle with cornstarch. Break the cheese into small chunks and add to blender. Process until smooth.

Pour tofu mixture into a saucepan or fondue pot. Add chili powder and oregano and heat gently over low heat, stirring until smooth and bubbly. Serve over hot vegetables or put fondue pot over flame to keep warm.

Yields 2 cups

½ pound tofu, mashed (¾ cup)
1 cup milk
2 teaspoons soy sauce
1 teaspoon vegetable oil
3 tablespoons tomato puree
1 tablespoon cornstarch
4 ounces sharp cheddar cheese
1 teaspoon chili powder
½ teaspoon dried oregano

Tofu Dipping Sauces for Parties

A party is a good place, I find, to introduce friends to the culinary delights of tofu with some of these tangy dipping sauces. Served with a tray of bite-size pieces of fresh tofu, they make a wonderful appetizer. You can also serve these sauces with a batch of Chicken-Fried Tofu Cutlets (page 50) cut into small cubes for a more filling appetizer. These sauces are easily made by blending ingredients in an electric blender, food processor, or by hand until smooth. Serve the sauces in small dip bowls. The yield for each is about ¼ to ½ cup.

SESAME-MISO SAUCE

3 tablespoons miso; 2 tablespoons vinegar; 2 teaspoons honey; 2 tablespoons sesame oil; pepper, to taste; 1 tablespoon mashed tofu; ⅛ teaspoon ground ginger

MUSTARD SAUCE

4 teaspoons prepared mustard; 1 teaspoon honey; 2 tablespoons vegetable oil; 2 to 3 tablespoons white wine vinegar; 2 tablespoons mashed tofu

(Sauces continued on overleaf)

SHELLFISH SAUCE

2 tablespoons vegetable oil; 1 tablespoon lemon juice; ¼ teaspoon paprika; 2 to 3 tablespoons white wine vinegar; ½ teaspoon minced garlic; 1 tablespoon mashed tofu; ½ cup shrimp, crab meat, lobster meat, or cooked clams, chopped (stir in after blending other ingredients); pepper, to taste

TAHINI SAUCE

2 tablespoons tahini (sesame butter); 2 tablespoons mashed tofu; 2 tablespoons yogurt; 3 tablespoons water; ½ teaspoon garlic powder; pepper, to taste

WALNUT-BASIL SAUCE

2 tablespoons vegetable oil; 2 tablespoons soy sauce; 2 tablespoons water; 1 tablespoon vinegar; 1 teaspoon honey; 1 teaspoon homemade catsup; pepper, to taste; 1 tablespoon mashed tofu; 1 tablespoon chopped fresh basil or 1 teaspoon dried basil; ½ cup black or English walnuts, finely chopped (stir in after blending other ingredients)

WINE VINEGAR-GARLIC SAUCE

1 tablespoon olive oil; 2 cloves garlic, minced; ¼ cup red wine vinegar; pepper, to taste; 1 tablespoon mashed tofu

Dried-Frozen Tofu Main Dishes

Herbed Dinner Loaf

Stir the dried-frozen tofu into the water and let it stand for about 30 minutes. Stir occasionally. Drain off any remaining liquid.

Preheat oven to 350°F.

Combine tofu, rice, basil, parsley, whole wheat flour, pimientos, and soy sauce in a bowl and mix well. Stir in eggs.

Sauté onion in oil over medium heat for about 5 minutes. Stir into the tofu mixture and pack into an oiled loaf pan, or shape into free-form loaf on a well-oiled baking sheet.

Bake for about 45 minutes, or until nicely browned. Serve with a parsley, onion, or tomato sauce.

4 to 6 servings

1 cup dried-frozen tofu
1 cup very hot water or whey
1½ cups cooked brown rice
1 tablespoon chopped fresh basil
1 tablespoon fresh parsley, chopped, or 1 teaspoon parsley flakes
1 tablespoon whole wheat flour
½ cup chopped pimientos
1 tablespoon soy sauce
3 eggs, beaten
1 medium-size onion, chopped
2 tablespoons vegetable oil or butter

DOUGH

1 tablespoon yeast
¼ cup warm water
2 to 2¼ cups whole wheat
flour
¾ cup warm milk
2 tablespoons olive oil

MARINADE AND TOFU

½ cup tomato juice (or
broth drained from
canned tomatoes)
1 tablespoon soy sauce
½ teaspoon hot pepper
flakes
1 teaspoon crushed anise
seed
2 garlic cloves, minced
3 2½ × 2½ × ¾-inch
slices (about 2 ounces)
freeze-dried tofu

FILLING

3 tablespoons olive oil
1 small red onion, chopped
1 small sweet red pepper,
seeded and chopped
10 mushrooms, thickly
sliced
½ teaspoon dried oregano
1 cup ricotta cheese
1 cup cubed mozzarella
cheese

Italian Calzone

To make dough: Dissolve yeast in warm water.

Place 2 cups of flour in a bowl; make a well in flour. Pour yeast mixture, warm milk, and oil into the well. Stir to form a smooth dough. Turn out on a smooth floured surface and knead for about 10 minutes, until dough is smooth and elastic.

Place dough in an oiled bowl, turning once to oil top. Cover and let rise at 70°F until double in size. (The dough is easier to handle when slightly cool.)

To make marinade: Combine marinade ingredients in a saucepan large enough to hold the tofu in a single layer. Bring to a simmer, add tofu, cover and cook until liquid is absorbed, about 10 minutes. Remove tofu from pan and chop into small pieces.

Add oil to another saucepan and saute onions, peppers, and mushrooms until slightly wilted, about 10 minutes. Add tofu and oregano, and cook 1 minute longer. Cool, and stir in ricotta and mozzarella cheese.

Punch down dough and knead briefly. Divide into 4 pieces. Shape into balls, then roll out into 8-inch circles on a lightly floured surface. Spread ¾ cup filling over ½ of each circle, leaving ½ inch of the outside bare. Moisten the edge of the dough with water, and fold plain side over the filling. Crimp edges together. Place filled dough on lightly oiled cookie sheets, and cut slash in the center of each.

Preheat oven to 425°F.

Let calzone rise until puffy, about 20 minutes, then bake until lightly browned, about 25 minutes.

Makes 4 calzones

Oriental Meatball Hors d'Oeuvres
with Dipping Sauce

Serve these as an appetizer or as a main dish with vegetables and rice or potatoes.

Mix together the meat and tofu, onion, egg, bread crumbs, mustard, pepper, garlic, and ginger until mixture is very smooth. Shape into walnut-size balls and fry in oil until browned.

Serve on toothpicks with the following Dipping Sauce.

Dissolve cornstarch in water and add meat or vegetable stock.

Add soy sauce, garlic, and honey to the mixture, blend, and heat until thickened. Taste and correct seasonings; it should be fairly sweet.

Serve the meatballs as an hors d'oeuvre with the sauce or as a main dish along with bowls of steamed brown rice and a green vegetable.

Yields about 2 cups

MEATBALLS

2 cups ground meat and
   rehydrated dried-frozen
   tofu (see page 20),
   mixed
¼ cup onion, finely
   chopped
1 egg, beaten
¼ cup whole grain bread
   crumbs
1 teaspoon prepared
   mustard
pepper, to taste
1 teaspoon minced garlic
½ teaspoon finely
   chopped, peeled ginger
   root
vegetable oil, for frying
Dipping Sauce (recipe
   follows)

DIPPING SAUCE

2 tablespoons cornstarch
½ cup cold water or whey
1½ cups rich Beef Stock
   (page 243) or Vegetable
   Stock (page 244)
2 teaspoons soy sauce
1 teaspoon minced garlic
1 tablespoon honey

¾ cup Vegetable Stock,
(page 244) or Chicken
Stock, (page 243)
2 teaspoons soy sauce
2 2½ × 2½ × ¾-inch
slices freeze-dried tofu
(about 1½ ounces)
1 cup cooked chopped
spinach (10 ounces
fresh)
6 eggs, lightly beaten
3 tablespoons butter
2 tablespoons coarsely
chopped fresh basil
1 cup shredded provolone
cheese
1 tablespoon chopped
fresh parsley

Spinach Frittata

Bring stock and soy sauce to a boil in a medium-size saucepan. Add tofu, cover, and remove from heat. Let stand until liquid is absorbed, about 20 minutes. Chop tofu into small pieces.

Squeeze the spinach gently to remove excess water. Stir spinach into eggs. Preheat broiler.

Place a 10-inch ovenproof skillet over medium heat and add 1 tablespoon of the butter. When hot, add tofu and sauté 2 minutes. Add basil and remaining butter. When foaming subsides, add eggs and shake pan to distribute ingredients evenly.

Cook until bottom is set, about 3 minutes. Place skillet under broiler and cook until top is lightly browned, about 10 minutes. Loosen edges of frittata from pan and slide onto warm platter. Top with shredded cheese and parsley. Cut into wedges and serve hot, warm, or cold.

4 to 6 servings

Desserts and Other Treats

Almond-Banana Pudding

8 ounces tofu
1 ripe avocado
1 ripe banana
2 to 3 tablespoons honey
½ teaspoon almond
extract
¼ cup milk if using a
blender
kiwi fruit wedges

Smooth and richer tasting than it really is, this dessert is best served as soon as it is chilled. Its bright emerald color fades after one day of storage.

If using a food processor, combine tofu, avocado, banana, honey, and almond extract in the processor bowl. Purée until smooth.

If using a blender, combine tofu, avocado, banana, honey, almond extract, and milk in a bowl. Process in blender in small quantities until smooth.

Serve chilled in individual glass dishes. Garnish with wedges of kiwi fruit.

4 servings

Buckwheat Almond Pancakes

An excellent dairy-free pancake with the old world flavor of buckwheat.

Combine flours, almonds, and baking powder. In a bowl mix together tofu, 1 cup of the soymilk, honey, and egg yolks. In another bowl beat egg whites until stiff.

Combine flour and tofu mixture until just evenly mixed. Fold in beaten egg whites. Add remaining soymilk, if necessary. Batter should be thick but pourable.

Ladle batter, ¼ cup at a time, onto heated buttered skillet. Cook until pancakes appear slightly dry around edges and bubbles come up through pancakes and break. Flip and cook until other side is browned.

Makes 16 to 20 4-inch pancakes

¾ cup whole wheat flour
¾ cup buckwheat flour
½ cup finely chopped almonds, toasted*
1½ teaspoons baking powder
1 cup mashed firm tofu
1 to 1½ cups soymilk
2 tablespoons honey
2 large eggs, separated

*To toast almonds: Spread them on a baking sheet and place in a 350°F oven. Cook until golden brown, about 10 minutes.

Carob Tofu Pudding

Children will love the creamy smooth texture, rich flavor and color of this healthful dessert.

Purée tofu, soymilk, bananas, carob, and vanilla until smooth in a blender. Serve well chilled.

4 to 6 servings

2 cups 1-inch cubes soft tofu
½ cup cold soymilk or dairy milk
3 medium-size frozen bananas*, cut into 2-inch pieces
4 tablespoons carob powder
1 teaspoon vanilla extract

*It is best to peel the bananas before freezing.

Pastry for 1 Whole-Wheat
    Piecrust (page 242)
1 pound tofu, mashed
½ cup honey
1 teaspoon vanilla extract
½ cup carob powder
½ teaspoon ground
    cinnamon
¼ cup butter, melted
¼ cup milk

Deep and Dark Carob Pie

Preheat oven to 350°F.

Stir together all filling ingredients in a large bowl and then purée in 2 batches in a blender. Pour into the prepared crust and bake for 25 to 30 minutes, or until filling is just set.

Makes 1 9-inch pie

1 pound tofu, mashed
    (2 cups)
1 cup light cream
½ cup honey
1 teaspoon vanilla extract
1 teaspoon mint extract
natural green food coloring
    (optional)
4 teaspoons unflavored
    gelatin
½ cup water
1 cup heavy cream
1 Brownie Piecrust (page
    71) plus 2 tablespoons
    additional cookie
    crumbs

Grasshopper Pie

Purée half of the tofu and light cream in a blender until very smooth. Reserve. Purée the other half of the tofu until smooth. Blend in the honey, vanilla, and mint extracts. Add food coloring slowly, if using, until a pale green color is obtained.

Sprinkle gelatin over water in saucepan. Let stand 1 minute. Heat over low heat until gelatin is completely dissolved. Remove from heat. Slowly whisk about 1 cup of the tofu mixture into the gelatin. Stir until smooth. Stir this thoroughly back into the other tofu mixture.

Beat heavy cream until stiff. Whisk half of the cream into the tofu mixture. Fold in the remaining whipped cream. Chill until almost firm. Pile high into prepared pie shell, swirling the top. Sprinkle center of pie with cookie crumbs.

Makes 1 9-inch pie

Ice Box Cake

This "cake" is fun to make. Sweetened, flavored tofu is layered with cookies and fruit. It can be made without fruit by using a smaller pan.

Purée the tofu, cheese, maple syrup, lemon juice, and peanut butter in a blender in small batches using just enough of the soymilk to process easily. If using a food processor, these ingredients can all be puréed together.

Place a layer of cookies in the bottom of a 9-inch spring form pan. Use broken cookies to fill in the spaces. Top with one-third of the fruit and then 1⅓ cups of the tofu mixture. Repeat the cookie, fruit, and tofu layers so that there are 3 layers of tofu. Top with a cookie layer. If you prefer, the last layer of cookies may be crumbled and sprinkled over the tofu.

Cover and refrigerate at least 6 hours before serving. Loosen edges of cake with a knife before removing sides of pan. Slice and serve as is or top with whipped cream.

Makes 1 9-inch cake

NOTE: This cake can be made dairy-free. Just substitute tofu for the cheese and add another ¼ cup maple syrup.

1 pound tofu, mashed (2 cups)
7½ ounces farmer cheese or dry cottage cheese or ½ pound more tofu
½ cup maple syrup
juice of one lemon
3 tablespoons peanut butter
½ to ¾ cup soymilk
2½ to 3 dozen whole grain cookies
2½ to 3 cups sliced bananas, peaches, strawberries or pineapple

Maple-Walnut Pie

To make the crust: Combine the granola with the softened butter and maple syrup. Blend thoroughly, then press into a 9-inch deep-dish pie plate. Set aside.

To make the filling: Combine the tofu, melted butter, maple syrup, yogurt and eggs in a large bowl, then blend until smooth in two batches in a blender. Stir in ⅓ cup of the walnuts and pour into the prepared crust. Sprinkle the remaining ⅓ cup walnuts over the top.

Bake at 325°F for 45 minutes, or until just set.

Makes 1 9-inch deep-dish pie

CRUST

2 cups granola
2 tablespoons butter, softened
1 tablespoon maple syrup

FILLING

1 pound tofu, mashed (2½ cups)
¼ cup butter, melted
½ cup maple syrup
⅓ cup yogurt
2 eggs
⅔ cup finely chopped walnuts

Morningstar Muffins

Serve hot for breakfast with butter and jam.

1 cup millet, coarsely
   ground in a blender or
   grain mill
1 cup whole wheat flour
3 teaspoons baking
   powder
¼ cup mashed tofu
¼ cup vegetable oil
3 tablespoons maple syrup
   or honey
1 cup milk

Mix together the ground millet, flour, and baking powder in a bowl. In blender container, combine the tofu, oil, maple syrup, and milk. Blend until mixture is smooth, then pour over the dry ingredients. Stir gently, just until all ingredients are moistened. Fill greased muffin tins ¾ full and bake at 425°F for 12 to 15 minutes, or until lightly brown.
Makes 10 muffins

Rich Eggnog Mousse

1 or 2 eggs
1 cup mashed tofu
1 cup soymilk or dairy
   milk
¼ cup honey
½ teaspoon freshly
   ground nutmeg
1 teaspoon unflavored
   gelatin
2 tablespoons cold water
1 teaspoon vanilla extract
1 cup heavy cream,
   whipped
¼ cup slivered almonds,
   toasted

Blend eggs, tofu, milk, honey, and nutmeg. Pour into a heavy-bottomed saucepan and bring nearly to a boil, stirring constantly. Sprinkle gelatin over cold water; let stand 1 minute. Add to the hot mixture and stir well. Remove from heat and stir in vanilla.

Return the mixture to the blender and blend for a few seconds until smooth. Chill in a bowl in the refrigerator. When the pudding is cooled and set, whip until foamy with an electric beater and fold in the whipped cream.

Spoon the mixture into a mold or into individual serving dishes and chill. Serve plain or with chopped fresh fruit or a fruit sauce. Sprinkle toasted almonds over mousse before serving.
4 servings

NOTE: For a lighter mousse omit the eggs or whipped cream or both.

Sunflower Brownie Drops

Cream together butter and honey until very fluffy, about 3 to 5 minutes with an electric beater. Add tofu and blend well on high speed for about 3 minutes. Blend in vanilla.

Using low speed, very slowly blend in carob powder, adding a little at a time. When all the carob is added, beat on high speed for about 2 minutes.

Sift rice and soy flours and baking powder through a fine sieve into a separate bowl. Stir in wheat flour. Using a wooden spoon mix thoroughly into carob mixture. Stir in sunflower seeds.

Preheat oven to 350°F.

Dough should be soft but not sticky. Roll teaspoonfuls of dough into balls. Place on unoiled baking sheet 2½ inches apart. Flatten them with your fingers or with the bottom of a flat glass into 2-inch rounds. Bake about 15 minutes, or until cookies no longer feel soft and doughy when gently pressed. Remove from baking sheet and cool on wire racks.

Makes 3½ to 4 dozen

⅓ cup butter, at room temperature
⅓ cup honey
⅓ cup mashed tofu
1 teaspoon vanilla extract
¼ cup carob powder, sifted
⅓ cup brown rice flour
3 tablespoons soy flour
1 teaspoon baking powder
½ cup whole wheat flour
¼ cup sunflower seeds

Brownie Piecrust

Crush enough cookies to yield 1½ cups very fine crumbs. Mix the crumbs with the butter and press firmly into a 9-inch pie plate. Add desired filling or bake pie crust at 350°F for 7 minutes.

Makes 1 9-inch piecrust

2 to 2½ dozen Sunflower Brownie Drops (above)
2 tablespoons butter, melted

Tofu and Pineapple Topping or Pastry Filling

This delicious rich filling contains no eggs or dairy products. Use it as a topping for fruit puddings, or as a filling for layer cakes, pies, or cream puffs.

Purée tofu, pineapple, almonds, soymilk, and cinnamon in a blender until it reaches a creamy consistency. Chill.

Yields 2 cups

1½ cups mashed tofu
1½ cups coarsely chopped, dried pineapple
½ cup almonds, ground
3 to 6 tablespoons soymilk
¼ teaspoon ground cinnamon

FILLING

1 pound firm tofu, mashed
  (3 cups)
½ cup maple syrup
½ cup cashews, ground
¼ cup safflower oil
¼ cup soymilk or water

TOPPING

¼ cup orange or apple
  juice
1 tablespoon cornstarch
2 cups fresh blueberries

PASTRY

1 cup whole wheat flour
¾ cup granola
¼ cup butter
2 tablespoons vegetable oil
1 tablespoon maple syrup
  or honey

Tofu Blueberry Cheese Pie

The cashews give this pie an added dimension of sweet creaminess.

To make the filling: Blend all filling ingredients in a blender or food processor until smooth. Reserve.

To make the topping: Mix juice and cornstarch in a saucepan. Stir to dissolve cornstarch. Add blueberries. Heat slowly until mixture is thickened, about 10 minutes. Cool.

To make the pastry: Mix all crust ingredients. Press into 9-inch pie plate. Bake at 450°F for 10 to 15 minutes. Cool slightly.

Pour tofu mixture into cooled crust. Spread blueberries on top.
Makes 1 9-inch pie

Tofu, Carob, and Raisin Pastry Filling

2/3 cup raisins
2/3 cup water
1⅓ cups mashed tofu
2½ teaspoons carob
  powder
½ teaspoon vanilla extract
¼ teaspoon ground
  cinnamon
¼ teaspoon ground
  nutmeg

A nice combination of carob and spices. Use also to top fruit or fill cakes.

Combine raisins and water in a saucepan. Simmer uncovered over medium-high heat for 15 to 20 minutes. Transfer to a blender and purée well.

Add the tofu, carob, vanilla, cinnamon, and nutmeg and blend well until very smooth. Chill.
Yields 2 cups

Tropical Carob Pie

A creamy sweet dessert—great for kids. Substitute soymilk for the dairy milk for a dairy-free dessert.

Preheat oven to 375°F.

To make the crust: Mix the granola, 2 tablespoons of the butter and the honey thoroughly and press into the bottom and sides of a buttered 9-inch pie plate. Bake until lightly browned, about 10 to 12 minutes. Set aside.

To make filling: Combine all the filling ingredients in a large bowl and purée in two batches in a blender. Pour into the prepared crust. Chill completely before serving.

Makes 1 9-inch pie

CRUST

2 cups granola
6 tablespoons butter, melted
2 tablespoons honey

FILLING

1 pound tofu, mashed (2 cups)
2 bananas
½ cup maple syrup or honey
1 teaspoon vanilla extract
½ cup carob powder
⅓ cup milk

CRUST

1¼ cups ground almonds
¼ cup dried unsweetened
  coconut
¾ cup whole wheat pastry
  flour
¼ cup vegetable oil
2 tablespoons honey
½ teaspoon vanilla extract

FILLING

2½ cups unsweetened
  pineapple juice
1 cup dried, unsweetened
  coconut
2 tablespoons unflavored
  gelatin
2 tablespoons water
1 cup chopped dried
  unsweetened pineapple
½ cup chopped dried
  unsweetened papaya
2 tablespoons honey
2 pounds firm tofu,
  crumbled (about 4 cups)
6 tablespoons vegetable oil
2 teaspoons vanilla extract
2 tablespoons lemon juice
¾ cup mashed ripe
  banana

DECORATION

thinly sliced dried papaya
  and pineapple
sprigs of mint or blossoms

Tropical Tofu Cheesecake

Rich as it tastes, this elegant dessert contains no eggs or dairy products.

To make crust: Combine almonds, coconut, and flour and set aside. Combine oil, honey, and vanilla and add the dry ingredients using a pastry blender or your hands. Mix well. Press into an oiled 9 × 3-inch springform pan ⅔ up the side. Bake at 400° for 8 to 10 minutes, or until lightly toasted. Cool.

To make filling: Bring juice and coconut to a boil in a saucepan. Reduce heat, cover, and simmer 5 minutes. Pour mixture into a blender. Start at the lowest setting and gradually raise it to the highest. Blend about 30 seconds. Strain mixture well through a jelly bag, doubled cheesecloth, or very fine sieve. The coconut can be saved for use in other recipes or for toasting.

Stir gelatin into water. Bring coconut-pineapple milk back to a boil. Stir in gelatin until dissolved, then add dried fruit and remove from the heat. Stir in honey.

Combine tofu, oil, and vanilla. Stir lemon into banana and add this along with the dry fruit and juice mixture to the tofu. Stir together well. Blend one-third of the mixture at a time, starting on low speed and gradually working to the highest speed. Blend until very smooth, thick and creamy. Pour blended portions into another bowl and mix together well.

Pour filling into prebaked crust. If you intend to decorate the cheesecake, do it now with the dry fruit, placing the slices in an attractive fashion. Chill overnight, preferably 24 hours. Remove from pan and garnish with mint or blossoms.

Makes 1 9-inch cheesecake

Okara Dishes

Armenian Stretched Bread

This bread is called a flatbread, but is really rather puffy and about 1½ inches thick. Eat the bread while still warm or reheat it. Leftover bread can be torn into pieces and used with dips as you do with pita bread. The dough can also be used to make pizzas or Italian bread.

Since this recipe makes 2 loaves, instructions for two different toppings are included, one with sesame seeds and the other with herbs.

To make the dough: Combine honey and water. Sprinkle yeast into the mixture. Set aside to dissolve.

Place three cups of the flour in a large bowl. When the yeast has dissolved, pour it into the center of the flour. Add the oil and okara. Stir with a spoon until stiff enough to knead.

Using as little of the remaining flour as possible, knead the dough to form a smooth soft dough. It should be slightly sticky. Form dough into a ball, place in a lightly oiled bowl, cover with a damp cloth, and set in a warm place to rise.

When almost doubled in bulk after 45 to 50 minutes, punch dough down, knead briefly, and divide in half. Shape dough into balls and then into slightly flattened ovals. Let rest 10 minutes.

Gently stretch and press dough into 2 long flat loaves, about 1 inch thick. Dangling the dough by one end will help it to stretch. The stretch marks should remain visible. Place loaves on a buttered baking sheet, leaving 2 inches between the loaves. Poke indentations into the loaves all over with a fingertip at 1½-inch intervals. Let rise just until light, another 15 to 20 minutes. (It is important to prevent unsalted bread from over rising.)

To make the sesame seed topping: Beat the egg and milk together. Brush egg mixture gently on one loaf. Sprinkle with sesame seeds. Bake both loaves immediately in a preheated 400°F oven.

To make the herb topping: Stir together the butter, oil, garlic, parsley, rosemary, and thyme. When top crust of plain bread begins to form, after baking about 15 minutes, spoon herb topping over the loaf and return to bake until edges of breads are golden brown, another 5 to 10 minutes.

Cool partially on wire racks before serving.

Makes 2 loaves

DOUGH

1 tablespoon honey
1½ cups warm water
1 tablespoon dry yeast
3½ to 4 cups whole wheat flour
2 tablespoons olive oil
1 cup fresh okara

SESAME SEED TOPPING

1 egg
1 tablespoon milk
3 tablespoons hulled sesame seeds

HERB TOPPING

2 tablespoons butter, melted
2 tablespoons olive oil
1 or 2 cloves garlic, minced
¼ cup finely chopped fresh parsley
1 teaspoon chopped fresh rosemary leaves or ½ teaspoon dried rosemary
1 teaspoon fresh thyme leaves or ½ teaspoon dried thyme

75

1¼ cups cornmeal
¾ cup whole wheat flour
1 tablespoon baking
  powder
1 teaspoon chili powder
2 eggs
2 tablespoons honey
1¼ to 1½ cups milk*
2 tablespoons butter,
  melted
¾ cup fresh okara
¼ cup grated Parmesan
  cheese
½ cup shredded cheddar
  cheese

*If the okara is very moist use
 1¼ cups milk; if it is drier use
 1½ cups milk.

Cheese Cornbread with Okara

To make a sweet cornbread, omit the cheese and chili powder, increase the honey to ¼ cup, and decrease the milk by ¼ cup.

Preheat oven to 425°F.
Sift together the cornmeal, flour, baking powder, and chili powder.
In a separate bowl beat the eggs lightly. Mix in the honey, then the milk, butter, and okara.
Stir the egg mixture into the dry ingredients until just mixed. Stir in the Parmesan and cheddar cheeses. Pour batter into a buttered 8-inch square baking pan.
Bake until lightly browned around the edges, about 20 minutes. Serve warm with butter.
8 to 10 servings

¾ cup dried okara* (page
  30)
½ cup dry whole grain
  bread crumbs
1/3 cup grated Parmesan
  cheese
½ teaspoon garlic powder
½ teaspoon onion powder
2 teaspoons mixed dried
  Italian herbs, such as
  basil, oregano and
  thyme or 1½ teaspoons
  chili powder

*If okara is not fine, grind it
 briefly in a blender.

Dried Okara Breading Mix

Use this breading to coat oven-baked chicken or pan-fried vegetables.

Combine all ingredients in a plastic bag. To use, shake meat or vegetables in bag until coated. If breading does not stick to a dry vegetable such as eggplant, dip the vegetable first in milk or beaten egg.
Yields 1 1/3 cups breading mix

Ground Beef and Okara Patties or Meatballs

This is a tasty way to stretch your ground beef.

In a medium-size bowl mix together ground beef, okara, onion, garlic, eggs, soy sauce, Worcestershire sauce, and hot pepper sauce. Mix well and form into 6 patties or 24 small meatballs. Broil or panfry until done. Use about 2 tablespoons oil or butter if pan frying.
6 servings

1 pound ground beef
2 cups fresh okara, packed
¼ cup finely chopped onion
2 cloves garlic, minced
2 eggs, beaten
2 teaspoons soy sauce
2 teaspoons Worcestershire sauce
2 drops hot pepper sauce

Mushroom and Pimiento Spread

In a small covered saucepan over medium to low heat, cook the onion, carrots, mushrooms, garlic, and sage in the butter until onion begins to get tender, but carrots are still firm, about 7 minutes. Cool slightly.

In a medium-size bowl, with a fork or electric mixer, beat together the cream cheese, lemon juice, mayonnaise, and pepper. Top this with the okara, celery, pimiento, parsley, and cooked vegetables. Mix together thoroughly but gently. Fold in the eggs, trying not to mash them. For a fancy presentation, the spread can be packed in a small buttered loaf pan or 1-quart mold. Chill thoroughly. Dip pan in hot water before unmolding. The spread can also be served from a glass bowl. Serve with crackers or thin slices of bread.
Yields 3½ cups

1 small onion, finely chopped
2 small carrots, diced
6 mushrooms, chopped
1 clove garlic, minced
5 fresh sage leaves, finely chopped, or ½ teaspoon crumbled dried sage
2 tablespoons butter
½ cup cream cheese, at room temperature
1 tablespoon lemon juice
¼ cup mayonnaise
freshly ground black pepper, to taste
1½ cups fresh okara
1 small stalk celery, finely chopped
¼ cup chopped canned pimiento
1 tablespoon finely chopped fresh parsley
2 hard-cooked eggs, coarsely chopped

2 cups fresh blueberries
¼ cup date sugar
½ cup ground dried
okara (page 30)
2¾ cups whole wheat
   pastry flour
3 teaspoons baking
   powder
½ cup honey
1¼ cup sour cream
½ cup butter, softened
3 eggs
1 teaspoon vanilla extract
2 tablespoons date sugar
½ cup ground almonds
2 tablespoons butter,
   melted

Okara Blueberry Coffee Cake

This cake is great any time—breakfast, brunch, dessert, or snack time. The dried okara can be easily ground in a small electric coffee mill or crushed with a rolling pin.

In a medium-size bowl stir together blueberries and ¼ cup date sugar. Set aside. In another medium-size bowl sift together okara, flour, and baking powder. Add honey, sour cream, ½ cup butter, eggs, and vanilla. Mix well.

Butter a 13 × 9 × 2-inch baking pan. Pour in half of the batter, top with half of the blueberry mixture. Top with the remaining batter, then with the remaining blueberries. Sprinkle the top with 2 tablespoons date sugar and nuts. Drizzle with 2 tablespoons melted butter.

Bake at 350°F for 40 to 45 minutes until top is golden brown and cake tests done. Serve warm.
Makes 1 13 × 9 × 2-inch cake

Okara Cheese Crackers

¼ cup butter
5 tablespoons whole wheat
   flour
⅛ teaspoon cayenne
   pepper
½ teaspoon paprika
¼ teaspoon caraway seeds
2 tablespoons grated
   Parmesan cheese
⅓ cup grated cheddar or
   Swiss cheese
½ cup fresh okara
2 teaspoons sesame seeds
   (optional)

Cut the butter into the flour in a medium-size bowl.

Add the cayenne, paprika, caraway, Parmesan and cheddar cheeses. Knead lightly to combine ingredients.

Add the okara and knead until well combined. The mixture should be uniformly colored. If it is too sticky add a bit more flour. Cover and chill for at least 1 hour.

Preheat oven to 400°F.

Roll the dough out on a floured board to approximately ⅛ inch thick. Sprinkle with the sesame seeds. Lightly press the seeds into the dough. Cut the dough into desired shapes and place on a lightly oiled cookie sheet.

Bake until lightly browned, about 6 to 10 minutes.

Remove crackers from cookie sheet and cool on a wire rack.
Makes 2 dozen 1 × 2-inch crackers

Okara Loaf

The okara loaf may be seasoned in a variety of ways. Try allspice, caraway, cayenne, celery seed, cinnamon, cumin, curry, dry mustard, fennel, nutmeg, onion, oregano, and sage.

Slice and fry leftover loaf in oil or slice thinly and bake as for melba toast. Chunk and use in casseroles also.

Combine flour, wheat germ, garlic, oregano, basil, savory, and black pepper in a large bowl. Mix well.

In another bowl combine the okara, oil, soy sauce, honey, vinegar, and soymilk. Mix well.

Combine the flour and okara mixtures and mix well. Form the mixture into a loaf and place in an oiled 9 × 5 × 3-inch loaf pan. Cover with aluminum foil. Steam on a rack over boiling water for about 60 minutes. Cool in pan on wire rack. Remove from the pan. Wrap and store in the refrigerator for up to a week or in the freezer for six months.

Makes 1 9 × 5-inch loaf

2½ cups whole wheat flour
½ cup toasted wheat germ
1 large clove garlic, minced
½ teaspoon dried oregano
1 teaspoon dried basil
½ teaspoon dried savory
¼ teaspoon black pepper
2½ cups fresh okara
⅓ cup vegetable oil
3 tablespoons soy sauce
2 tablespoons honey
2 tablespoons vinegar
½ cup soymilk

Okara Patties with Variations

1 small onion, finely
  chopped
1 stalk celery, finely
  chopped
1 large clove garlic, minced
2 tablespoons butter
1 medium-size carrot,
  grated (about ½ cup)
2 tablespoons finely
  chopped fresh parsley
1 cup soft whole grain
  bread crumbs
1 cup fresh okara
1 tablespoon tomato paste
  (optional)
juice of 1 lemon
2 eggs, lightly beaten
⅛ teaspoon white pepper
½ teaspoon dry mustard
vegetable oil, for frying

Sauté onion, celery, and garlic in butter until tender. Transfer to a large bowl.

Stir in the carrot, parsley, bread crumbs, okara, tomato paste, lemon juice, eggs, pepper, and mustard. Add seasoning variation (see below), if desired. Press mixture firmly into 24 small patties.

Heat oil in a skillet. Fry patties over medium heat in an oiled skillet until browned on each side.

4 to 5 servings

Variations

Add any of the following seasoning combinations to the above recipe: *Italian Patties:* ¼ cup grated Parmesan cheese, 1 teaspoon dried basil, 1 teaspoon dried summer savory, ½ teaspoon dried thyme. *Peanut Patties:* 4 to 6 teaspoons tamari soy sauce, 1 cup raw peanuts, ground, ¼ to ½ teaspoon ground ginger. *Cheddar Cheese Patties:* ¼ cup wheat germ, ½ teaspoon cayenne pepper, ¼ teaspoon ground cumin, ½ cup grated cheddar cheese.

Okara Pecan Crumb Crust

¼ cup butter
3 tablespoons maple syrup
¾ cup dried okara (page
  30)
½ cup rolled oats
1 cup coarsely ground
  pecans
¼ teaspoon vanilla extract
  or ½ teaspoon ground
  allspice

Melt butter with maple syrup in a 1-quart saucepan. Quickly stir in the okara, oats, and pecans. Stir until thoroughly mixed. Add vanilla or allspice, whichever is more compatible with your pie filling.

Pat crumbs firmly and evenly into a 9-inch pie plate, making sure that the top edge is as thick as the sides.

If pie filling will be baked, prebake pie shell for 10 minutes in preheated 350°F oven. If filling will not be baked, the shell should be baked about 15 minutes in preheated 350°F oven until golden brown.

Makes one 9-inch pie shell

Okara Pudding with Raisins and Cinnamon

This is a tasty, high-fiber breakfast cereal. The dried okara acts as a thickening agent and provides protein and iron.

Combine okara and 1¾ cups of the milk in a 1-quart saucepan. Simmer over medium heat, stirring frequently, for 20 minutes.

Beat egg with honey. Add some of the hot milk mixture to the egg and honey, then slowly pour egg mixture into hot milk, stirring constantly.

Cook over low heat until thickened and almost ready to boil. Thin with remaining milk if desired. Remove from heat. Stir in vanilla, cinnamon, and raisins. Pour into serving dishes. Serve hot or cold.

4 to 6 servings

½ cup finely ground dried okara
2 cups milk
1 egg, beaten
2 tablespoons honey
½ teaspoon vanilla extract
½ teaspoon ground cinnamon
½ cup raisins

1 tablespoon dry yeast
1 cup warm water
6½ cups whole wheat
    bread flour,
    approximately
1 cup warm milk
¼ cup dark molasses or
    Barbados & blackstrap
    mixed together
1 medium-size onion,
    minced
⅓ cup butter
2 teaspoons caraway seeds
1½ cups fresh okara or
    reconstituted dried
    okara (page 30)
¾ cup chopped walnuts
melted butter, for brushing

Walnut Onion Okara Bread

This is a standard country bread from France to which we have added okara for moistness and fiber.

Dissolve the yeast in ¼ cup of the warm water. In a large bowl mix 3 cups of the wheat flour, ¾ cup water, milk, and 2 tablespoons of the molasses. After the yeast foams, add it to the flour mixture. Beat until the batter is completely smooth. Cover the bowl and let it stand in a warm place for about 20 minutes to proof. The batter should be bubbly and light.

Meanwhile, cook the onion in the butter over low heat until tender, about 10 minutes. Add onion mixture, the caraway seeds and the remaining molasses to the proofed mixture.

Stir in the okara and enough wheat flour to make dough kneadable. Knead dough adding just enough wheat flour to make the dough manageable. The dough will remain slightly sticky. Continue to knead until the dough feels smooth and elastic. Work in the walnuts. Form the dough into a ball, and place it in a large oiled bowl, turning once. Cover bowl and let rise in a warm place until doubled, 40 to 50 minutes.

Punch down dough, turn out onto a floured surface and knead again briefly. Shape into 2 free-form round loaves, and place on lightly buttered baking sheets.

Cover and let rise to double in a warm spot, about 20 to 30 minutes.

Preheat oven to 350°F.

Slash tops with a large X ¼ inch deep using a sharp knife. Bake 30 minutes. Brush tops of loaves with melted butter and return to oven for 5 to 10 minutes more, or until loaves sound hollow when rapped on bottom. Remove from pans and cool on wire racks.

Makes 2 loaves

The Lotus Cafe, Rochester, New York

The 60-seat dining room of the restaurant, specializing in vegetarian soyfoods cuisine, is filled with wicker chairs, natural maple tables, stained glass designs, and plants. The warm decor evokes a light, airy, garden-like feeling. It's hard to imagine that the premises of the Lotus Cafe in Rochester, New York, were originally a tuxedo shop.

The Lotus Cafe, Rochester, New York. Owners display a freshly made sampling of their "gourmet approach to soyfoods."

Despite its polished trendy appearance and its gourmet approach to soyfoods, the Lotus Cafe comes from humble beginnings. "In the early seventies, cooks from the Rochester Zen Center would make monthly trips to nearby Toronto to bring back fresh tofu for the Center's hungry staff," remembers Greg Weaver, one of the cafe's owners. "Very few Americans had heard of tofu back then, but some of the first may have been the bewildered Customs officials we dealt with at the United States-Canada border! In the summer of 1976, a small traditional tofu-making shop was built in the basement of the Zen Center. The shop produced only a 24-pound batch—enough for one staff meal."

The business soon increased its tofu production, and 2 years later the Tofu Shop, a soy deli, was born. The menu included such enticing features as the Tempeh Reuben, Tofu Spinach Pie, and Banilla Shake. Three years later the take-out deli expanded into the elegant Lotus Cafe Restaurant.

In addition to the all-soy favorites from the original Tofu Shop, the Lotus Cafe features dairy and non-dairy soups, entrées, and desserts, including a soft soy ice cream.

"Although vegetarians remain the core of our clientele, an estimated 70 percent of our meals go to non-vegetarians," Greg says. "Meat eaters are constantly surprised to find that meatless fare can be as delicious and as satisfying as more traditional meals. People come not only from Rochester's suburbs, but from all of upstate New York to try us out. Families with school-age children find the Lotus Cafe ideal—our meals are the perfect antidote to the junk food so many parents must battle." The clientele includes local professionals who find the vegetarian fare the perfect light lunch for active schedules.

Greg Weaver is confident the good taste, low cost, high nutrition, and high versatility are what make soyfoods and soyfoods restaurants a potent new force in today's food market.

Tempeh

In the colorful marketplaces of Bali, tempeh cakes wrapped in banana leaves are a common sight. Indonesians have long savored fragrant cakes of tempeh with its rich meatlike flavor and unique chewy, but tender texture. Westerners are just beginning to discover this delicious fermented food that originated in Indonesia centuries ago.

Natural foods restaurants often offer some of the most creative tempeh dishes. That is how I first sampled this unusual and appealing food. I ordered the Tempeh Reuben, not sure what to expect. The baked tempeh on a bed of sauerkraut atop a warm open-face whole wheat bun—all smothered with a velvety mustard sauce—was marvelous. The winning combination prompted me to make some of my own creations with this tasty ingredient.

I can make a nice light meal of a tempeh, the Spicy Baked Tempeh, Breakfast Tempeh, or even the Corn Chowder, for example. But, I especially like tempeh for my more filling winter meals. Instead of the Tempeh Reuben with its highly salted sauerkraut, we offer Debra Deis' very inspired alternative—Broiled Tempeh with Mustard Sauce.

Tempeh is as versatile and as nutritious as tofu, but is made in a quite different way—by inoculating cooked, hulled soybeans with a beneficial mold that binds the beans into a solid compact cake. The mold, which is related to mushrooms, is responsible not only for the pleasant changes in flavor and aroma, but also for some noteworthy added nutrition.

Tempeh can serve as a satisfying main course dish or dozens of side dishes. Besides versatility, tempeh has other features. You get a third more protein in tempeh than in an equal-size serving of soybeans or tofu, along with more riboflavin, thiamine, and niacin. Because it has fiber, tempeh is a more complete food than tofu. Most tempeh is rich in vitamin B-12, a nutrient that tends to be lacking in strict vegetarian diets. An average serving (about 3½ ounces) is apt to contain from 1½ to 3 times the adult recommended daily allowance of B-12. Finally, tempeh has an attractive calorie-protein ratio: A 3½-ounce serving provides 19 grams of protein with only 157 calories; the same amount of hamburger gives 24.2 grams of protein with 286 calories (see Nutrient Content of Soyfoods and Other Foods, page 3).

Tempeh's flavor is distinct; it is different from any food in our culture, ranging from mild to very strong. At its mildest tempeh can resemble the earthy flavor of mushrooms, or it might suggest the mild sweetness of chicken or veal. A little bit stronger tempeh may have the musty flavor and aroma of yeast bread. At its strongest tempeh's flavor becomes sharp—reminiscent of a very sharp cheese. Its strength of flavor depends on several factors, mainly the behavior of the mold used in fermenting, and the length of time the beans are incubated. Tempeh makers learn the habits of the mold through experience and are able to control the final product. In general, the longer the beans are incubated, the more rampant the mold growth, thus the stronger the fermenty taste and aroma. Some people prefer it that way, while others prefer the milder flavors of shorter incubation periods.

I find tempeh's appearance is as unique as its flavor. It is a light moist springy cake. If you hold it in your hands it feels a little firmer than firm tofu, but it crumbles and breaks just as easily. White cotton-like filaments appear throughout most tempeh. Like the mold clusters in blue cheese you may see some blackish or grey-green spots where mold sporulation has occurred. These clusters do not indicate any spoilage. As a rule, the more of these blackish spots present the stronger the flavor of the tempeh will be.

The mold (*Rhizopus oligosporus*) is what makes tempeh the most wondrous of all the soyfoods. It performs the alchemy of converting soybeans into a completely new food. Besides causing a significant rise in the B vitamins and protein level, inoculation with the mold makes the beans much more digestible by producing enzymes that partially break down or digest the soy proteins and oils.

Actually the mold that transforms soybeans into tempeh with its unique nutrition and flavor is no more mysterious than the molds that ripen many dairy cheeses, the bacteria culture that changes milk to yogurt, or the yeast used to raise bread dough or to brew beer. In East Asia and in many other countries, molds are used extensively in altering many foods. In fact, tempeh can be made with many other grains and legumes besides soybeans, and each type has its own unique flavor. Chick-peas, okara, peanuts, dried peas, rice, or wheat can all be used alone or in combination to make delicious tempeh. When tempeh is made with a grain and a legume that complement each other protein-wise, the product is especially nutritious.

Buying and Storing Tempeh

You can find tempeh in natural foods stores and some supermarkets in the refrigerated or frozen food sections. It is usually sold in cake form (about $6 \times 7 \times 1$ inches), packaged in an inner and an outer sealed plastic bag. Tempeh does not spoil easily, but like tofu, its flavor diminishes in storage, so try to buy tempeh that is freshly made, and to use it as soon as possible. Tempeh has no dating code so ask the store manager about its freshness.

You should keep tempeh that you buy or make tightly sealed in plastic wrap in the refrigerator or freezer. Refrigerated, you can keep it about seven to 10 days before cooking. In the freezer, wrapped in several layers of plastic, it will keep indefinitely. Cooked tempeh has the same keeping qualities unless it is part of a dish with perishable ingredients. Tempeh that has been frozen has a slight change in texture that you may not notice. However, if you fry it, it may absorb oil more easily, and tend to stick to the pan.

Preparing Tempeh

Tempeh is as easy to prepare as any convenience food. It can even be eaten straight out of the package with no cooking. It can be crumbled, puréed, and made into cold salads or spreads. It retains its shape nicely when deep-fried or lightly sautéed or when breaded and pan-fried. Like tofu it can also be mashed and used in stuffings and casseroles. It can be served in bite-size pieces as an appetizer or skewered with vegetables and broiled. It adds flavor and texture to soups and stews. With only a few minutes of preparatory work, tempeh can be served in such popular forms as burgers, cutlets, sloppy joes, cacciatore, or Parmesan.

Tempeh's flavor is most distinct when it is eaten uncooked. When baked in casseroles or lightly sautéed in oil, its pungency is slightly mellowed. Like tofu, it works in just about any dish, and can stand in for some or all of the meat in recipes. It can become the pork in sweet-and-sour pork, the veal in veal Parmesan, and the beef in Stroganoff. You can give it a beefier flavor, if you like, as you can do with tofu. You can steep tempeh in different marinades, and season it however you like. Its texture is not quite as porous as that of tofu, but it will soak up flavors almost as quickly if left to marinate an hour or two.

One of my favorite things to do with tempeh is to bread it. Simply cut tempeh cakes to any desired size. Dip them in an egg mixture, milk, or a marinade, then coat with bread crumbs, cornmeal, or seasoned flour, and bake or sauté. You can also coat tempeh pieces in a batter, then deep-fry them as you would fritters or tempura.

Making Tempeh

My first homemade tempeh, like my first homemade tofu, did not resemble the perfectly uniform shapes of the store-bought version. But, like tofu too, its flavor was so fresh and remarkable, that I didn't mind its odd appearance. By the time I had incorporated it into many pasta, rice, meat, and vegetable dishes, its shape was truly irrelevant.

There's no doubt about it—the tastiest tempeh is fresh out of the incubator where it was made. Unless you live near a soyfoods' manufacturer you are not likely to purchase such tempeh in stores. But you can experience tempeh at its freshest if you make it yourself in your home. It is as easy to make as tofu, and in some ways even easier.

The method given here to make tempeh eliminates a very time-consuming step. It also cuts the beans' cooking time from 45 minutes to 10 minutes. The short cut is to use roasted soy halves or soy nuts (available in natural foods stores and some supermarkets) instead of whole dry soybeans which require more cooking and need hulling. The short cut costs a little more, but it barely affects the tempeh's nutritional value.

There are a few factors to be aware of before you get started: The mold used to make tempeh is as temperamental as the yeast used to raise dough. The live micro-organisms demand a certain optimum environment in which to thrive. If you have ever made bread, you know that the yeast usually works very well if you provide a warm moist environment. Sometimes it works better than at others, often because of factors you cannot control—weather, altitude, and freshness of ingredients, for example. The same is true of homemade tempeh. The crucial part in making tempeh is first to avoid contamination of the mold. Work with very clean equipment, and do not touch the beans with your hands when mixing or transferring them—use a very clean spoon or spatula instead. Also, you must be sure to provide the optimum temperature in the incubator (which you can make yourself very easily, p. 90) for proper mold growth. The best temperature is just between 92° and 96°F. Slightly above or below this range will not spoil your tempeh, but a great divergence from it may cause the mold to take too long to work or to multiply too quickly.

The following recipe will make one batch of tempeh weighing 1½ to 1¾ pounds. The cake size will depend on the size tray you use.

Equipment Needed
    4-quart pot
    spatula
    colander
    2-quart bowl
    tempeh incubator and trays (see Constructing a Tempeh Incubator and Trays, page 90)
Ingredients
    4 cups dry roasted soy halves (these are actually dehulled and roasted soybeans)
    1 tablespoon of distilled white or rice vinegar
    tempeh starter*
    8 cups of water
Procedure
    Remember, all equipment that you use should be very clean before beginning to make tempeh.

1. Boil 8 cups of water in a 4-quart pot. Add the vinegar to the water. Add the soy halves when the water is at a rolling boil. Stir well so none of the beans stick to the pot. Allow the water to return to a boil, then simmer for 10 minutes, stirring frequently.
2. Drain the soy halves well through a colander. Cool and dry the soy halves by spreading them with a spatula onto a paper towel-lined cookie sheet. Turn them several times with the spatula or spoon to get them fairly dry and to help cool them.

*Tempeh starter is available at natural foods stores or from tempeh manufacturers. See Soyfoods Mail Order Sources, page 247. Use the amount of starter recommended by the manufacturer, or 1 teaspoon for this recipe.

CONSTRUCTING A TEMPEH INCUBATOR AND TRAYS

The following directions will help you construct a tempeh incubator out of easily found materials. Once you have made the incubator you can use it over and over. Just remember to clean it thoroughly after each use.

Materials
1 styrofoam picnic cooler, approximately 16 × 10 × 12 inches
1 ceramic light socket
1 7½-watt clear bulb
1 6-foot extension cord
electrical tape

Procedure
1. With a pencil or similar object, punch a hole in the middle of the cover of the styrofoam picnic basket.
2. Thread the two leads of the ceramic socket through the hole so that the socket can be attached to the underside of the cover.
3. Tape the socket on both sides of the cover.
4. Splice the leads from the socket to the extension cord.
5. Screw the bulb into the socket.

Materials
1 aluminum foil tray 8¾ × 5¾ × 1⅛ inches (available in most hardware and department stores)
aluminum foil sheet to cover the pan bottle
bottle caps or small jar lids

Procedure
1. Perforate the entire bottom of the pan, spacing the holes ¼ inch apart.
2. Perforate enough aluminum foil to cover the top of the pan.
3. The covered pan of inoculated beans should be set on the bottle caps or jar lids inside the incubator. This allows plenty of air to the tempeh on all sides.

3. When the beans have cooled to room temperature spoon them into a 2-quart bowl, and inoculate them with the starter. (If the beans are too hot, too wet, or too dry, the mold will not

grow properly.) Using the recommended amount, mix the mold in well.

4. Fill the incubator tray with the beans, packing them firmly with a spatula. They should form a layer ¾- to 1-inch thick. Cover the trays with the perforated aluminum foil.

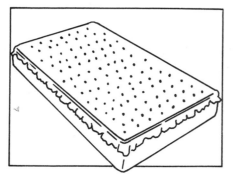

5. Place the trays in the incubator, switch on the light, and incubate the tempeh in a warm spot for 22 to 24 hours at about 85° to 100°F.

Checking The Incubated Beans

After about 12 hours you should see the first visible signs of mold growth—a fine white filament spread throughout the beans. When done, the tempeh cake should be solidly bound with this white mold. There may also be some streaking of grey or black due to sporulation. Tempeh that has turned completely black or smells strongly of ammonia should be discarded. Good tempeh will feel firm and flexible and not crumble easily. If the white mold is not uniform throughout, or if the beans crumble, allow them to incubate a little longer. Cut away any portions that look done, and store them securely wrapped in plastic in the refrigerator or freezer. Store any freshly made tempeh this way if you do not intend to cook it immediately.

TEMPEH VARIATIONS

Try any one of these variations for a different treat in homemade tempeh.

Peanut Tempeh: Substitute 4 cups of coarsely chopped dry roasted unsalted peanuts for the roasted soy nuts.
Yields 1 pound

Soy-Sesame Tempeh: Substitute 3¼ cups roasted soy halves and ¾ cup roasted sesame seeds for 4 cups roasted soy halves.
Yields 1½ pounds

Okara Tempeh: Add 1 tablespoon white distilled vinegar to 2½ cups fresh okara. When cooled to room temperature, inoculate the okara with 1 teaspoon starter and spread in the incubating container. The okara should be no more than ½ inch deep. Incubate for 22 to 24 hours.
Yields 1 pound

Chick-pea Tempeh: Substitute chopped, hulled, canned chick-peas for the roasted soy halves. Chop the chick-peas coarsely. If the chick-peas have been salted, rinse them thoroughly before chopping as salt will inhibit fermentation. To rinse the chick-peas, place them in a colander, and run cold water over them.

DRY-TOASTED TEMPEH

Dry-toasting chopped tempeh removes the moisture and browns the tempeh, giving a nice pungent toasted flavor. These toasted savory bits can be used like bacon bits to add zippy flavor and crunch to salads and salad dressings. They are a nice flavor and texture contrast in creamy-dressed salads, such as potato, chicken, and cole slaw. Use toasted tempeh like nuts, especially in savory baked goods, such as yeasted breads, quiches, and souffles.

You can dry-toast tempeh on the range-top or in the oven. To dry-toast it on the range-top heat a heavy skillet, preferably cast-iron, over medium-low heat. Stir in 2 to 3 cups finely chopped tempeh. Fry the tempeh, stirring and tossing constantly with a metal or wooden spatula to prevent sticking or burning, until well toasted.

Grind finely in a blender or coffee mill.

To dry-toast tempeh in the oven spread the finely chopped tempeh evenly in a jelly roll pan.

Place in a 250°F oven for 30 minutes, tossing every 10 minutes to brown evenly. Store in a tightly sealed container in the refrigerator.

Main Dishes

Baked Barbequed Tempeh

½ cup tomato paste
½ cup water
2 teaspoons soy sauce
½ cup finely chopped
  tomatoes
2 tablespoons cider vinegar
½ teaspoon ground
  cinnamon
1 teaspoon dry mustard
¼ cup finely chopped
  onion
¼ cup finely chopped
  green peppers
2 tablespoons blackstrap
  molasses
2 tablespoons honey
cayenne pepper, to taste
2 cups ½-inch to ¾-inch
  squares tempeh
1 teaspoon butter

A pleasant variation of a popular American dish.

Preheat oven to 375°F.
   In a large bowl combine all ingredients except tempeh and butter.
Mix well. Add tempeh and stir gently to coat pieces with sauce.
   Pour mixture into an oiled ovenproof casserole dish and dot with
butter. Bake uncovered for 35 minutes.
4 servings

Barbequed Tempeh Cheese Burgers

Tempeh squares really soak up this marinade. These burgers are great for picnics—indoors or out.

In a medium-size bowl or a large plastic bag mix together tomato sauce, oil, honey, mustard, Worcestershire sauce, garlic, pepper, and oregano. Add tempeh squares, gently toss to coat with sauce. Marinate at least four hours or overnight in the refrigerator, tossing occasionally to mix.

Broil or grill tempeh, using marinade as a basting sauce, until tempeh is browned on both sides. Top each square with a slice of cheese. Broil until cheese is melted, about 2 more minutes. Top with some remaining marinade if desired. Serve immediately on hamburger rolls.

4 servings

2 cups tomato sauce
¼ cup vegetable oil
¼ cup honey
2 tablespoons prepared mustard
2 tablespoons worcestershire sauce
4 cloves garlic, minced
½ teaspoon black pepper
2 teaspoons dried oregano
½ pound tempeh, cut into 3-inch squares
4 slices provolone cheese
4 whole grain hamburger rolls

Broiled Tempeh with Mustard Sauce

Brush a shallow baking pan with some of the butter. Add the tempeh in a single layer and drizzle with the remaining butter. Broil until lightly browned, about 10 minutes. Turn tempeh, sprinkle with the shallots and broil until browned, about 5 minutes.

Meanwhile, mix together the mustard, heavy cream, and sour cream. Pour the sauce over the browned tempeh and broil a few minutes longer until sauce is lightly browned. Serve on whole grain toast or with cooked brown rice.

4 servings

¼ cup butter, melted
1 pound tempeh, cut into 2 × 3-inch strips
2 tablespoons finely chopped shallots or red onions
¼ cup French-style mustard
½ cup heavy cream
½ cup sour cream

1 pound tempeh, sliced
    into ½-inch slices
vegetable oil, for shallow
    frying
2 cups unsweetened
    applesauce
ground cinnamon
maple syrup or honey
    (optional)

Brunch Tempeh

This is particularly good with grain or grain/soy tempeh.

Blanch tempeh slices in boiling water for 2 minutes. Drain well. Fry tempeh in ½ inch oil over medium-high heat until golden on both sides. Drain well on wire grid or paper towels. Meanwhile, heat applesauce over low heat. Serve tempeh with warmed sauce and shaker of cinnamon. If applesauce is very tart add a drizzle of honey or maple syrup.

6 servings

Chicken and Tempeh ala King

1 cup cubed tempeh
1¼ cups sliced
    mushrooms
¼ cup butter
4 tablespoons whole wheat
    flour
1¾ to 2 cups Chicken
    Stock (page 243)
2 teaspoons tamari soy
    sauce
1 tablespoon finely
    chopped fresh parsley
½ teaspoon dried thyme
1 cup cubed, cooked
    chicken breast

In a large skillet sauté tempeh and mushrooms in 2 tablespoons of the butter until golden brown. Remove and set aside on paper toweling.

Brown flour in remaining butter and slowly add stock, tamari, and thyme. Simmer about 2 minutes. Stir in mushrooms and tempeh, parsley, thyme, and chicken. Simmer 5 minutes more. Serve immediately over toast or rice.

4 servings

India Spiced Rice Casserole

The spices in this dish enhance the winey flavor of tempeh.

Toss tempeh in 1 cup hot oil until browned on all sides. Drain well.

In a large bowl combine rice, shoyu, cinnamon, nutmeg, and cloves. Set aside.

Preheat oven to 375°F.

Sauté onion in ¼ cup oil until tender. Add cashews, soybeans, and a drop of water. Cover and cook 2 minutes.

Mix tempeh and sautéed vegetable mixture with the spiced rice and turn into an oiled 2-quart casserole.

Bake for 15 minutes or until piping hot.

6 servings

12 ounces tempeh, cut into ¾-inch cubes
1¼ cups vegetable oil
4 cups cooked brown rice
1 tablespoon shoyu soy sauce
½ teaspoon ground cinnamon
¼ teaspoon ground nutmeg
pinch of ground cloves
¾ cup chopped onion
1 cup roasted cashews
1½ cups fresh green soybeans

Julie's Sausage and Tempeh Cheese Strata

This recipe is adapted from a recipe in the file of our Rodale Test Kitchen secretary, Julie Mayers. It's her favorite dish to serve to company. It's a good brunch recipe—you can assemble it the night before, then bake in the morning.

In a large skillet heat butter and oil; add sausage, tempeh, pepper, and sage. Cook over medium heat until sausage is browned. Drain and set aside.

Preheat oven to 350°F.

Butter a 13 × 9 × 2-inch baking dish. Fit the bread slices to cover the bottom. Cover the bread with sausage mixture. In a small bowl whisk together the eggs and cream. Pour over the sausage mixture. Top with shredded cheeses.

Bake at 350°F for 40 minutes, or until hot.

6 to 8 servings

1 tablespoon butter
1 tablespoon vegetable oil
1 pound bulk sausage
½ pound tempeh, diced (2 cups)
¼ teaspoon pepper
¼ teaspoon dried sage
6 to 7 slices whole grain bread
3 eggs
1 cup heavy cream
3 cups shredded mixed cheeses, such as provolone and mozzarella

2½ cups cooked brown
   rice
12 ounces cooked tempeh,
   cut into ½-inch cubes
   (3 cups)
2 cups steamed cooked
   vegetables
Sauce
2 tablespoons butter
2 tablespoons whole wheat
   flour
1 cup milk
¼ cup grated mild cheese
   or 2 tablespoons grated
   Parmesan

Leftover Tempeh Casserole

Leftovers are given a second life in this easy casserole. If you have colorful left-over vegetables, this recipe becomes a very attractive presentation.

Preheat oven to 350°F.

Press rice into the bottom of a buttered 2-quart casserole. Top with a layer of tempeh, then a layer of vegetables.

To make the sauce: Melt butter in saucepan over low heat. Add flour, stirring constantly, and cook for 4 to 5 minutes, or until mixture is thick and pasty. Slowly stir in milk, stirring constantly until thickened. Pour the sauce over layers in casserole. Top with cheese.

Bake for about 25 minutes, or until mixture is hot and cheese is melted.

6 servings

NOTE: If you don't have leftover cooked brown rice, tempeh, or steamed vegetables, just cook the amount needed for this recipe.

Miniature Eggplants Stuffed with Tempeh and Raisins

Cut a deep lengthwise slit in each eggplant, being careful not to split the skin on the other side. If using Italian eggplant, hollow out a small pocket. Steam the eggplants on a rack over boiling water until slightly limp and almost tender. (Japanese eggplants take about 12 minutes and Italian eggplants take about 20 minutes.) Let eggplants cool slightly.

Sauté tempeh, onion, celery, and garlic in butter until onion is tender, about 5 minutes. Add raisins, cinnamon, and oregano and cook 1 minute more. Stir in the bread crumbs, and let mixture cool slightly. Add the egg and cheese, mixing well.

Pack the tempeh mixture into pockets in the eggplants. Set eggplants in a baking dish. Add the tomato juice to a depth of 1 inch and bake in 375°F oven until sizzling hot, about 20 minutes. Spoon some of the juice over the eggplants and serve.

4 to 8 servings

¼ cup raisins
½ teaspoon ground cinnamon
½ teaspoon dried oregano
¼ cup fine whole grain bread crumbs
1 egg, slightly beaten
3 tablespoons grated Parmesan cheese
8 Japanese eggplants or small Italian eggplants
1½ cups tomato juice, Beef Stock (page 243), or a combination of the two
¼ pound tempeh, diced
1 small onion, finely chopped
3 tablespoons finely chopped celery
2 cloves garlic, minced
3 tablespoons butter or olive oil

8 ounces tempeh, diced
   (2 cups)
1 cup catsup
¼ cup molasses
¼ cup vinegar
2 teaspoons Worcestershire
   sauce
1 teaspoon soy sauce
½ teaspoon black pepper
2 tablespoons butter
½ cup chopped onion
½ cup chopped green
   pepper
3 cloves garlic, minced
1 pound lean ground beef
8 whole grain hamburger
   buns

Sloppy Joes

Purée tempeh, catsup, molasses, vinegar, Worcestershire sauce, soy sauce, and pepper in a blender or food processor. Set aside.

In a large skillet melt butter and sauté onion, pepper, and garlic until onion is translucent. Add ground beef and sauté until beef is browned. Stir in tempeh mixture and simmer, covered, for 15 to 20 minutes. Serve immediately on hamburger buns.

8 servings

Spicy Baked Tempeh

12 ounces tempeh
1¼ cups thick tomato
   sauce
½ cup vinegar
¼ to ½ cup soy sauce
½ teaspoon curry powder
½ teaspoon ground ginger
¼ cup minced onion

Serve this quickly prepared dish as an entrée with cooked rice and a fresh vegetable salad.

Cut tempeh into bite-size pieces. Set aside.

Combine tomato sauce, vinegar, soy sauce, curry, ginger, and onion and simmer several minutes until thickened. (Cooking time will depend upon how thick the tomato sauce is.)

Put a thin layer of sauce on the bottom of a 1½ to 2 quart baking dish, top with tempeh strips, and spoon on remaining sauce.

Bake at 350°F for about 20 to 30 minutes.

4 servings

Sweet and Sour Tempeh

Serve on a bed of hot rice for a colorful Chinese meal. Pork or chicken cubes can be substituted for all or some of the tempeh for a more traditional variation.

In a medium-size bowl whisk together soy sauce, water, and cornstarch. Stir in honey, eggs, and pepper. Add tempeh, and marinate for 3 to 4 hours in the refrigerator.

Steam carrots for 3 to 5 minutes, or until tender. Set aside.

Dredge tempeh in flour. Heat 1 inch oil in wok. Stir-fry tempeh until nicely browned on both sides, about 2 to 4 minutes. Drain on paper towels.

Remove all but 2 to 3 tablespoons oil, and add carrots, peppers, scallions, and ginger root. Stir-fry over high heat, about 3 to 5 minutes. Add pineapple, Sweet and Sour Sauce, and tempeh. Heat until tempeh is hot, and serve immediately.

6 to 8 servings

½ cup soy sauce
½ cup water
¼ cup cornstarch
2 tablespoons honey
2 eggs, beaten
½ teaspoon black pepper
1 pound tempeh, cut into 1-inch squares
2 carrots, sliced into ¼-inch thick rounds
¾ cup whole wheat flour
corn oil, for frying
2 red or green peppers, diced
4 scallions with tops, cut into 1-inch pieces
2 teaspoons minced fresh ginger root
1 can (20 ounces) unsweetened pineapple chunks, drained
Sweet and Sour Sauce (recipe follows)

SWEET AND SOUR SAUCE

In a small bowl dissolve the cornstarch in water. Set aside.

In a medium-size saucepan combine concentrate, tomato sauce, vinegar, and honey. Bring to a boil. Simmer 10 minutes.

Add cornstarch mixture and simmer about 2 minutes or until sauce thickens.

Yields about 2 cups

2 tablespoons cornstarch
3 tablespoons water
1 can (6 ounces) frozen pineapple-orange juice concentrate, thawed
1 cup tomato sauce (8-ounce can)
½ cup malt or cider vinegar
¼ cup honey

Tempeh and Shrimp Curry in Coconut Milk

1 tablespoon vegetable oil
¾ pound tempeh, cut into
  1-inch squares
1½ cups Coconut Milk
  (recipe follows)
1 tablespoon plus 1½
  teaspoons Chili Paste
  (recipe follows)
¼ pound fresh green
  beans, cut into ¾-inch
  lengths (1 cup)
1 fresh green chili, seeded
  and cut into tiny strips*
½ pound shrimp, shelled
  and deveined
1 tablespoon soy sauce
1 tablespoon honey

*The chili paste is hot, so add
the fresh chili only if you like
very hot foods.

Coconut milk, which is easy to make at home, is essential to the cooking of In-donesia, the original home of tempeh. Unfortunately, many of the other ingredients such as laos, tamarind, salem leaves, and fresh lemongrass are difficult to find here. So, we've borrowed some of the exotic spicy flavors found in Thai cooking for this rec-ipe. The fascinating flavors of Southeast Asia make an excellent combination with tempeh.

Heat oil in a large heavy skillet over medium-high heat. Sauté tempeh until brown on both sides. Remove and reserve.

Place the thick cream of the coconut milk (there should be about 3 tablespoons) in the skillet. Cook, stirring constantly, until it thick-ens and oil begins to separate from the solids. Add chili paste, and cook until color changes slightly and oil is clear, about 2 minutes.

Add coconut milk and bring to a boil. Add beans, cook until ten-der, then add green chili, shrimp, and tempeh. Immediately reduce heat to low. Cook about 2 minutes until shrimp are just cooked. Add soy sauce and honey. Serve in bowls accompanied with rice and plain yogurt.

4 servings

COCONUT MILK FROM DRIED COCONUT

Make the coconut milk at least 12 hours in advance.

Scald milk in a medium-size saucepan. Place coconut in a blender and add milk. Process on low speed for a few seconds. Let cool until lukewarm and process again until the coconut is ground to very small pieces. Let stand until almost cool.

Line a large sieve with a damp linen dish towel or fine-mesh nylon net. Pour mixture through the towel into a bowl. When drained, wrap remaining pulp securely in the towel and squeeze it over the bowl to extract remaining milk. Refrigerate until needed. Do not shake milk because a thick cream will solidify on the surface that is used separately in preceding recipe.

Yields about 2 cups milk, approximately 3 tablespoons cream

2½ cups milk
2 cups shredded
   unsweetened dried
   coconut

CHILI PASTE

This makes a little extra, but it will keep refrigerated in a small glass jar for 2 weeks. It is a very convenient condiment to have on hand.

Grind all ingredients until finely pulverized and slightly moist, using a mortar and pestle or blender.

Yields about 3 tablespoons

1 teaspoon ground
   turmeric
2 teaspoons ground
   coriander
2 teaspoons ground cumin
½ teaspoon ground
   cinnamon
¼ teaspoon ground
   nutmeg
2 teaspoons finely
   shredded lemon rind
2 teaspoons finely
   shredded orange rind
4 small dried hot chilis,
   seeded and coarsely
   chopped
3 cloves garlic, finely
   chopped
2 shallots, chopped

2 cups finely chopped soy
   tempeh
1 onion, finely chopped
1 carrot, finely shredded
1 teaspoon minced garlic
¾ cup toasted wheat germ
½ cup cooked long grain
   brown rice
¼ teaspoon dried dillweed
¼ teaspoon dried basil
2 eggs, lightly beaten
vegetable oil, for frying

Tempeh Burgers

The grain and wheat germ upgrade the protein content in this tasty herbed burger.

Combine tempeh, onion, carrot, garlic, wheat germ, rice, dillweed, basil, and eggs in a large bowl. Mix well. Shape into 12 patties.

Fry in oil over medium heat until a dark golden brown on each side.

4 to 6 servings

Tempeh Chili

1 tablespoon vegetable oil
1 large onion, coarsely
   chopped
1 green pepper, coarsely
   chopped
½ pound lean ground beef
1½ cups ½-inch cubes
   tempeh
2 tomatoes, coarsely
   chopped
1 bay leaf
⅛ to ¼ teaspoon dried
   red pepper flakes
1 to 2 teaspoons chili
   powder
1 teaspoon soy sauce

Heat oil in a heavy skillet over medium heat. Stir in onion and green pepper and sauté until tender. Break up the beef in the pan and brown over medium heat. Drain off extra fat.

Stir in tempeh, tomatoes, bay leaf, red pepper, chili powder, and soy sauce. Mix well and cover. Reduce heat to low and simmer for 10 minutes, stirring occasionally.

4 servings

Tempeh Parmesan

The tempeh takes on a mild sweet flavor and is richly enhanced by the tomato sauce and cheese. Serve with a lightly dressed green salad.

Preheat oven to 350°F.

Dip tempeh first in the egg, then in the bread crumbs. Fry in ¼ inch heated oil until golden brown on both sides. Drain on paper towels.

Spoon about ½ cup tomato sauce on the bottom of a 9-inch square baking dish. Cover with a layer of breaded tempeh. Add a layer of tomato sauce, a layer of grated mozzarella, and another layer of tempeh. Continue layering until tempeh is used, topping with a layer of sauce and mozzarella. Sprinkle Parmesan cheese on top and bake for 15 minutes, or until cheese is melted.

4 to 6 servings

1 pound tempeh, cut into 2-inch squares
2 eggs, beaten
1 to 1½ cups Italian-Seasoned Whole Grain Bread Crumbs (page 239)
vegetable oil, for frying
1 quart Tomato Sauce (page 241)
½ pound mozzarella cheese, grated
¼ cup grated Parmesan cheese

Tempeh Stroganoff

A vegetarian dish that tastes very meaty and rich.

In a large saucepan mix oil, grape juice, shoyu, garlic, ginger, paprika, and pepper. Gently toss tempeh strips in mixture while warming over low heat. Simmer, tossing mixture for 4 to 5 minutes. Remove from heat and set aside.

Melt butter in a large skillet and sauté mushrooms with basil and nutmeg until mushrooms are tender, about 5 minutes. Add tempeh mixture and simmer until hot. Reduce heat to warm and stir in sour cream. Serve over noodles.

6 to 8 servings

¼ cup vegetable oil
1 cup white grape juice
⅓ cup shoyu soy sauce
1 clove garlic, minced
½ teaspoon ground ginger
½ teaspoon paprika
freshly ground black pepper, to taste
1 pound tempeh, cut into 2 × ½ × ¼-inch strips (3 cups)
2 tablespoons butter
1 pound mushrooms, halved
½ teaspoon dried basil
freshly grated nutmeg to taste
1 cup sour cream
12 ounces hot spinach noodles, cooked

Tempeh-Stuffed Chard in Herbed Tomato Sauce

An exotic meatless version of stuffed cabbage. Serve with a crusty Italian or French bread or with any cooked whole grain.

SAUCE

2 tablespoons olive oil
1 cup sliced mushrooms
1 small onion, chopped
1 clove garlic, minced
1/3 cup minced fresh
  parsley
1/4 teaspoon dried
  rosemary, crushed
1/4 teaspoon dried sage,
  crumbled
2 cups tomato sauce
Tabasco and shoyu soy
  sauce, to taste

To make the sauce: Heat oil in a large saucepan. Add mushrooms, onion, garlic, parsley, rosemary, and sage. Sauté vegetables until tender. Add tomato sauce and simmer for 1 hour. Add Tabasco and shoyu to taste. Set aside.

STUFFING

3/4 pound tempeh,
  chopped
1/4 cup finely chopped
  onion
2 tablespoons minced
  fresh parsley
1/2 teaspoon dried thyme
1/2 teaspoon dry mustard
1 clove garlic, mashed
dash of cayenne pepper
1 to 2 tablespoons shoyu
  soy sauce
2 tablespoons vinegar
1 tablespoon honey
10 large Swiss chard leaves
freshly grated Parmesan
  cheese

To make the stuffing: Steam tempeh for 10 minutes. Then mash tempeh and combine with onion, parsley, thyme, mustard, garlic, and cayenne.

In a small saucepan heat shoyu, vinegar, and honey just until honey is melted. Combine with tempeh mixture.

Steam Swiss chard leaves for 3 minutes to soften them. Cut away tough part of leaves if necessary. Place about 2 tablespoonfuls of filling at the base of each leaf, roll up and seal. Place rolls seam-side down in an oiled baking dish and cover with sauce.

Bake at 350°F until leaves are tender, about 20 minutes. Serve with Parmesan cheese.

4 servings

Tempeh-Stuffed Peppers

Slice the tops off peppers and remove seeds. Reserve tops. Steam pepper shells until barely tender, 5 to 7 minutes. Core and finely chop green pepper tops. Set aside.

Preheat oven to 350°F.

Heat oil over medium heat in a large skillet. Sauté garlic, onion, celery, and mushrooms until wilted. Add tomatoes and cook over medium heat, stirring frequently, until liquid evaporates. Stir in chervil and basil.

Stir in the tempeh and chopped green peppers. Sauté 10 minutes more. Add more oil if necessary.

Remove from heat and stir in ½ cup of the cheese. Season with black pepper. Stuff peppers with tempeh mixture and place in an oiled, shallow baking pan or dish. Pour puréed tomato around the peppers, but not on top. Top peppers with the remaining cheese.

Bake for 30 minutes, or until peppers are tender.

4 servings

4 medium-size green peppers
3 tablespoons vegetable oil
1 clove garlic, minced
¾ cup finely chopped onion
¾ cup finely chopped celery
1 cup coarsely chopped mushrooms
1 cup finely chopped tomatoes
1 teaspoon dried chervil
1 teaspoon dried basil
1½ cups finely chopped tempeh
¾ cup grated colby longhorn cheese
black pepper
1 cup puréed tomatoes

Soups and Side Dishes

Corn Chowder

2 cups fresh or 1 package
(10-ounce) frozen corn
4 cups Chicken Stock
(page 243) or Vegetable
Stock (page 244)
2 cups diced, unpeeled
potatoes
1 cup fresh green soybeans
¾ cup chopped onion
1 clove garlic, minced
½ teaspoon ground
coriander
½ teaspoon ground
turmeric
½ pound tempeh, cut into
½- to ¾-inch cubes
(2 cups)
1½ to 2 cups milk or
heavy cream

Combine corn, stock, potatoes, soybeans, onion, garlic, coriander, and turmeric in a large soup pot. Bring to a boil and simmer about 10 minutes.

Add tempeh cubes and simmer another 10 minutes. The chowder will be very thick and potatoes will begin to disintegrate. Add milk and heat until very hot, but do not boil. Serve immediately.

8 servings

Fruit and Tempeh Stuffing

½ cup finely chopped
dried pineapple
½ cup raisins
1 cup water
1 tablespoon soy sauce
1 cinnamon stick (2-inch)
½ cup unsweetened dry
coconut

Combine the pineapple, raisins, water, soy sauce, and cinnamon in a 2-quart saucepan. Simmer uncovered until the liquid is reduced to about 1 tablespoon. Remove from the heat and transfer to a 2-quart mixing bowl. Remove the cinnamon stick and stir in the coconut. Set aside.

Melt the butter in a skillet and sauté the tempeh and onion until lightly browned. Add the sautéd tempeh to the fruit mixture. Stir in the bread crumbs, cumin, and cardamom and mix well. Use this stuffing for chicken, fish, or vegetables. Freeze any leftover stuffing.

Yields 3½ cups

TEMPEH

2 tablespoons butter
2 cups ¼-inch pieces soy-sesame tempeh*
1 large onion, finely chopped
1 cup day-old bread crumbs
½ teaspoon ground cumin
pinch cardamom

*Soy tempeh may be substituted for soy-sesame tempeh.

Green Salad with Walnuts, Goat Cheese, and Tempeh Croutons

Serving this salad while the croutons are still warm is currently popular, but if you prefer ice cold salads chill the tempeh before serving.

Cut the tempeh into 1½-inch squares, and cut each square in half diagonally. Dip each piece briefly in the soy sauce and then dredge lightly with the flour, shaking off any excess flour. Sauté tempeh in hot vegetable oil until both sides are brown and crisp. Drain on paper towels.

Meanwhile, crush the garlic in a salad bowl using a wooden spoon. Rub garlic around the bowl, and discard it. Add lettuce and toss with the walnut oil until all the leaves are coated. Add lemon juice and herbs, and toss again. Arrange lettuce on individual salad plates. Surround with warm tempeh croutons.

Cut cheese into slices roughly the same shape as croutons (you may want to trim the rind off the cheese first, taste it, and decide). Place a slice on each crouton. Sprinkle lettuce with walnuts and black pepper and serve.

4 servings

¼ pound tempeh, about 4½ × 6 inches
2 tablespoons soy sauce
¼ cup whole wheat pastry flour
vegetable oil for shallow frying
1 clove garlic
2 heads boston lettuce, torn into bite-size pieces
¼ cup walnut or olive oil
2 tablespoons lemon juice
2 teaspoons chopped fresh herbs, such as thyme, chervil or chives
¼ pound chèvre (a creamy, strong-flavored cheese)
½ cup coarsely chopped walnuts
black pepper

Mushrooms Stuffed with Tempeh, Herbs, and Cheese

16 large mushrooms
1 small onion
3 tablespoons vegetable oil
¼ pound tempeh, diced
1½ teaspoons fresh thyme
    or ¾ teaspoon dried
    thyme
1½ teaspoons fresh
    rosemary, chopped, or
    ¾ teaspoon dried
    rosemary, crumbled
2 tablespoons chopped
    fresh parsley
4 ounces cream cheese, at
    room temperature
⅔ cup shredded Swiss
    cheese
⅛ teaspoon freshly
    ground black pepper
1 tablespoon lemon juice

Serve as an appetizer or as an accompaniment to a light main dish.

Preheat oven to 375°F.

Trim mushrooms and gently twist out stems. Chop stems with the onion.

Add 2 tablespoons of the oil to a large skillet. Sauté the mushroom caps over medium-high heat, turning to coat all sides with the oil, for 4 minutes.

Transfer mushroom caps to a lightly oiled baking dish. Add remaining oil to the skillet, reduce heat to medium, and add mushroom stems, onion, tempeh, rosemary, and thyme. Cook, stirring occasionally and breaking up the tempeh, until onion is tender, about 8 minutes. Let mixture cool to lukewarm.

Add the parsley, cream cheese, half of the Swiss cheese, pepper, and lemon juice. Stir to thoroughly combine.

Pile filling into mushroom caps, and sprinkle with remaining Swiss cheese. Bake until sizzling hot and lightly browned, about 20 minutes.

4 servings

Appetizers

Blue Cheese Tempeh Spread

This spread is particularly good on toasted black bread.

Steam tempeh 10 minutes. Cool slightly.

Mash or blend the tempeh with butter, onion, Worcestershire, mustard, and horseradish. Use some of the cooking liquid from steamer, if necessary, to make a smooth mixture. Crumble and blend in 4 ounces of the cheese and taste, adding more cheese if desired. Stir in parsley. Chill.
Yields 1½ cups

½ pound crumbled
  tempeh (2 cups)
2 tablespoons butter
¼ cup minced onion
1 tablespoon
  Worcestershire sauce
1 tablespoon prepared
  mustard
horseradish (optional)
4 to 8 ounces blue cheese
1 tablespoon minced fresh
  parsley

Sandwich Spread Normandy

Serve this savory spread on small triangles of toasted bread as an appetizer. Derived from a French recipe using Camembert cheese, this spread has the ripe flavor of tempeh instead.

Steam tempeh over boiling water for 6 minutes. Cool slightly and chop finely.

Combine tempeh with remaining ingredients, using a spoon, electric mixer, or food processor. Pack into a crock or wide-mouth glass jar. Cover tightly and refrigerate for 1 day to allow flavors to blend.
Yields 1½ cups

¼ pound tempeh
½ pound muenster cheese,
  shredded
¼ cup mayonnaise
2 tablespoons apple juice
2 tablespoons red wine
  vinegar
3 tablespoons French-style
  mustard

111

2 eggs, separated
¼ cup to 5 tablespoons
   whole wheat flour
½ teaspoon baking soda
1 tablespoon milk
¼ teaspoon black pepper
½ cup frozen corn
½ cup diced tempeh
3 to 4 tablespoons butter

Corn and Tempeh Fritters

These pan-fried fritters are similar to pancakes.

In a small bowl beat egg whites until stiff. Set aside.

In a medium-size bowl mix together egg yolks, flour, soda, milk, and pepper. Add corn and tempeh. Fold in egg whites.

Melt 3 tablespoons butter in a large skillet. Drop batter by heaping tablespoons into skillet. Sauté over medium-low heat until fritters are golden brown. Flip over and brown the other side. Add more butter to skillet if necessary. Serve immediately with warm maple syrup.

2 to 3 servings

Tempeh Tempura

1 cup whole wheat pastry
   flour
1 cup cold water
¼ cup lemon juice
1 tablespoon honey
1 egg, beaten
1 teaspoon baking powder
½ pound tempeh, cut into
   1½ × 2-inch pieces
¼ cup lemon juice
½ cup whole wheat flour
vegetable oil, for frying

In a medium-size bowl whisk together 1 cup flour, water, ¼ cup lemon juice, honey, egg, and baking powder. Set aside.

Dip tempeh into ¼ cup lemon juice, then dredge in ½ cup flour.

Heat a wok with 3 inches oil. Dip floured tempeh into batter and fry until golden. Any leftover batter can be dropped by teaspoons into the oil and fried until done. Serve immediately.

4 to 6 servings

Baked Goods

Pumpkin-Tempeh Bread

Serve this spicy loaf warm with sweet butter and fruit preserves.

Preheat oven to 350°F

Beat together oil, honey, and syrup with a wire whisk. Alternately beat in eggs and pumpkin.

In a separate bowl combine flour, baking powder, baking soda, cinnamon, allspice, and cloves. Gradually beat into liquid mixture. Stir in tempeh and raisins.

Pour mixture into a 9 × 5 × 3-inch greased and floured loaf pan and bake at 350°F for 1 hour. Reduce heat to 325°F, cover top with foil and bake 15 minutes more.

Cool on wire rack.

Makes 1 loaf

½ cup peanut oil
⅓ cup honey
⅓ cup sorghum syrup or
   Barbados molasses
2 eggs
1½ cups mashed cooked
   pumpkin
2 cups whole wheat flour
1 teaspoon baking powder
1 teaspoon baking soda
1½ teaspoons ground
   cinnamon
⅛ teaspoon ground
   allspice
⅛ teaspoon ground cloves
¾ cup Dry Toasted
   Tempeh (page 93)
½ cup raisins

1 cup tempeh, diced
2 tablespoons butter
3 medium-sized apples,
  cored and sliced
1 tablespoon ground
  cinnamon
1 tablespoon date sugar
3 cups whole wheat pastry
  flour
3 teaspoons baking
  powder
½ cup honey
1½ cups milk
¾ cup butter, melted
3 eggs
¼ cup date sugar
1 tablespoon whole wheat
  pastry flour
2 tablespoons butter,
  softened
1 cup coarsely chopped
  nuts

Tempeh Apple Crumb Cake

In a medium-size saucepan sauté tempeh in 2 tablespoons butter until crispy. Drain on paper towels and cool.

In a small bowl mix together apples, tempeh, cinnamon, and 1 tablespoon sugar. Set aside for filling.

In a medium-size bowl stir together 3 cups flour and baking powder. Add honey, milk, ¾ cup butter, and eggs. Mix well.

Butter a 13 × 9 × 2-inch baking pan. Pour in half of the batter and top with half of the filling. Pour remaining batter on top, then remaining filling.

Combine ¼ cup sugar, 1 tablespoon flour, 2 tablespoons butter, and nuts. Sprinkle on top of filling.

Bake at 350°F 40 to 45 minutes, or until cake tests done. Best served warm.

Makes 1 13 × 9 × 2-inch cake

Tempeh Piecrust

1 cup whole wheat flour
½ cup finely ground Dry-
  Toasted Tempeh (page
  93)
6 tablespoons butter,
  softened
3 to 4 tablespoons ice
  water

Use this piecrust for quiches or for fruit, custard, cream, and other dessert fillings.

Combine flour and tempeh and mix well. Cut in butter until crumbs form. Sprinkle mixture with water while mixing with a fork, adding just enough water to make crumbs cling together and form a ball. Knead together for a few seconds. Press into a buttered 9-inch pie plate. Fill and bake according to filling directions. If filling does not require baking bake crust at 425°F for 8 to 10 minutes.

Makes 1 9-inch piecrust

Soymilk

If you have ever made tofu you have surely tasted fresh soymilk. It is the creamy, slightly nutty-tasting liquid from which tofu is made. Soymilk is rich in protein and comparable to dairy milk protein. Although its mild flavor does not really resemble that of dairy milk, soymilk can often replace dairy milk in cooking and baking. Soymilk is slightly darker in color—a creamy almond instead of pure white. Because it lacks the butterfat of dairy milk, soymilk has a thinner consistency much like skim milk. Soymilk can be enriched with honey and butter or oil to bring its fat and carbohydrate content up to that of dairy milk.

In Japan and China the use of soymilk is so widespread that at least 6 subtly different types are commonly used, ranging from light to rich. In fact, soy drinks are much more popular there than the ever-present colas are here. They are served at all times of day and in many different ways. In the morning soymilk may be savored as a spicy hot soup. Throughout the day it may be drunk as a hot or cold beverage, seasoned and flavored in many different ways. I have tasted a popular Japanese soy beverage sweetened with barley malt. The tetra-pak drink brought back from Japan by Richard Leviton (see Japanese Soyfoods, page 144) was lightly sweet and refreshing.

To the Western palate plain soymilk is likely to taste flat, but to some Westerners plain dairy milk or cream tastes that way, too. But who could not resist the temptations of a dreamy cream dessert such as ice cream or custard, or a rich cream soup or sauce. Soymilk is a useful substitute for the dairy milk in these rich foods because it is much lower in calories, fat, and carbohydrates, and has no cholesterol. Yet most of its other nutrients except for calcium and some B vitamins, are comparable to dairy milk.

Soymilk's mild taste is very adaptable to numerous flavorings. Fresh fruit shakes are quick and easy—banana, strawberry, orange, coconut, pineapple—for a refreshing high-health beverage. Add some nuts, seeds, carob, or raisins and you have a satisfying light meal. Subtler treatments such as a drop of honey or maple syrup and some vanilla flavoring are also satisfying. Warmed, sweetened soymilk, spiced with cinnamon, nutmeg, and cloves is a tasty nighttime or cold weather beverage.

Soymilk is also a perfect base for soups or sauces in place of fat-rich dairy products. You can blend soymilk with any pureed vegetable and season it as you like for a low-calorie hot or cold soup. Soymilk can stand in for the cream in most cream soups when meat, fish, or vegetable flavorings are used. The Spicy Cream of Broccoli Soup is one of my favorite examples. You can also add soymilk to meat loaves, casseroles, or baked goods for nutritious enrichment; just substitute it for some of the liquid called for in these recipes.

Sauces made from all soymilk are generally light and mild-tasting and not as filling as dairy-based sauces. You may thicken soymilk the same way you thicken dairy milk—with egg yolks, flour, cornstarch, or gelatin. As with dairy milk, you must apply the same precautions when thickening over heat to avoid lumping or scorching. You can concentrate or reduce soymilk for a richer product by gently heating it in an uncovered saucepan. An acidic ingredient such as tomatoes, lemon juice, or soy sauce adds a nice tanginess to soymilk sauces or soups, but add these slowly to prevent curdling.

Soymilk can be used in most desserts. With a few exceptions, the same principles used to make dairy products into souffles, custards, puddings, and pie fillings can be applied to soymilk. Desserts made with soymilk will be less rich and have fewer calories—something their rich and filling taste may seem to contradict. Try the heavenly Almond Custard for such a paradox.

Because soymilk is low in fat it will not whip like dairy cream, but it can be mixed with heavy cream to make desserts less rich and more nutritious. When substituting soymilk for dairy milk you may do so cup for cup.

When heating soymilk, it is best to heat it slowly in the top of a double boiler to avoid overheating or boiling it. It is a little less stable than dairy milk, and will curdle or stick to the saucepan when overheated.

Buying and Storing Soymilk

You can purchase pure soymilk in bottles or in covered plastic containers in most natural foods stores, which usually make their own, or from a soy dairy. You may also come across a soymilk product that is canned or bottled. It is thickened and highly sweetened with sucrose so its texture is more like that of dairy milk. This type of soymilk is not recommended for use in any of the recipes in this book and is best avoided for its higher cost and excessive sweetness.

Soymilk should be refrigerated as you would store dairy milk. Its color is naturally off-white. Like tofu it is freshest and most flavorful when first made. In storage its subtle flavor diminishes quickly, but it always blends well with other ingredients. Ask the store manager when the soymilk is made so you can buy it at its freshest. Better yet, consider making your own for only pennies and for less work than it takes to make tofu (see Making Soymilk, page 118).

Soymilk has a longer storage life than dairy milk. Covered tightly and stored in the refrigerator soymilk will keep for about ten days *from the day it was made.* During storage a light sediment may form on the bottom of the soymilk container. This sediment is simply the very fine okara not strained out during production. You can easily blend this into the soymilk by shaking the container. These extra solids, in fact, can make the milk richer and creamier.

Clabbered Soymilk

Soymilk will sour the same as dairy milk, even under refrigeration. It will smell faintly sour and form a light yellow curd in a clear yellow whey. Its consistency will resemble that of a soft custard. Clabbered soymilk has many uses in cooking and baking. You can substitute it cup for cup for buttermilk. It can also be used to prepare a lighter sour cream, cream cheese, and cottage cheese (see recipes, page 127). Clabbered soymilk has a tangy flavor similar to that of yogurt. It can be used in much the same way—on baked potatoes, with fresh fruit, or in baking.

When frozen, soymilk separates into curds and whey. If you wish to freeze soymilk this curdling can be avoided by blending a little sweetener into the soymilk before freezing it. Use about two tablespoons of honey per quart. Partially thawed soymilk makes a great base for a slushy drink. Mix it in a blender with fresh or frozen fruit and vanilla or other natural flavorings.

Making Soymilk

I must admit it only occurred to me to use soymilk in place of dairy milk in recipes when I was asked to do this cookbook. The Raspberry Chiffon Pie, Kiwi Custard Pie, and the Fruit and Nut Roll were born of my quest to create unique, exciting roles for soymilk. These and other successful desserts and main dish recipes whetted my interest, and soymilk acquired well-deserved space in my refrigerator. The soymilk from soy dairies is generally quite pure and good, but here is a simple formula for a delicate creamy homemade version you may want to try.

The soymilk you produce when making tofu is slightly different from the soymilk recipe we give below. The higher protein content of the traditional soymilk recipe produces a higher yield when making tofu. However, the traditional soymilk also has a beany flavor that some people find undesirable without heavy flavoring. The recipe below yields what is considered a much better tasting soymilk, requiring much less flavoring. Therefore this recipe is good for a soymilk that is to be used as a beverage base or in recipes where few flavoring ingredients are added.

If you go on to make tofu from this soymilk (and you can), the yield will be about half that of tofu made from the traditional recipe, and it will not clabber as will the traditionally made soymilk.

Two popular production techniques have been developed by soyfoods experts to reduce soymilk's characteristically beany flavor caused by lipoxidase, an enzyme released when beans are ground in cool water. Cornell University has developed a method referred to as the hot grind technique. Another method, called the preblanch enzyme inactivation process, has been developed at the University of Illinois. The method given below combines both these techniques to produce the best-tasting soymilk in a home kitchen.

The following recipe yields 6 cups of soymilk and may be doubled.

Equipment Needed
    3-quart pot with lid
    colander
    electric blender (with a steel or glass bowl and a top—do not use plastic blender bowls)
    2- to 3-quart pot
    forming box cloth (see Tofu Equipment, page 22)
    1 2-quart container or 2 1-quart containers
Ingredients
    11 cups water
    ¼ teaspoon baking soda
    1 cup whole dry soybeans

1. In the 3-quart pot bring 4 cups water to a full rolling boil. Stir in baking soda while water is boiling.
2. Add the soybeans to the boiling water, then remove pan from the heat. Cover the pot and let beans soak at room temperature 8 to 16 hours.
3. Drain and rinse the soaked beans in a colander.
4. Bring 7 cups water to a boil. While waiting for water to boil, warm the blender with hot tap water. It is important that the beans and water be near boiling when blended. Prewarming the blender helps maintain heat and will also help prevent breakage of the blender bowl (if a glass one is used).
5. Blend the soaked beans and hot water in several batches. For each batch add 1 cup beans and about 2 cups hot water. Keep the remaining water near boiling. As soon as you add the water, cover the blender and turn it on at low speed, increasing the speed quickly as the mixture blends. Blend at top speed for 1 minute. Do not overblend. As each batch is blended put it into a container until all beans and water are used.
6. Dampen the forming box cloth and place it in the colander, then place the colander over the second pot. Pour the cooked soy purée into the cheesecloth to separate out the soymilk. You may have to stir the soy purée or fold the cheesecloth over it and apply pressure with a plate to force the liquid through the cloth.
7. Put the strained soymilk into a container with a cover and refrigerate. Reserve the okara in the cheesecloth for use in recipes (see Okara, page 29).

119

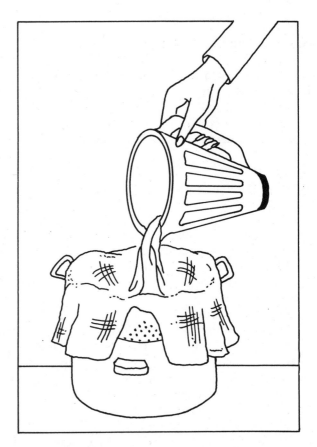

Main Dishes

Fancy Seafood

Shrimp, monkfish, and mushrooms mingle in a sauce with a deceptively rich texture. The sauce and fish may be prepared a day ahead and baked just before serving. Snow peas are an excellent accompaniment to this.

Clean and devein shrimp, placing shells in a small saucepan. Cover shells with stock. Add bay leaves, peppercorns, and fennel seeds. Cover and simmer slowly for 20 minutes.

Meanwhile, in a large skillet over medium-high heat, stir-fry shrimp in oil until opaque, about 2 minutes. Place shrimp and any liquid in a bowl. Reduce heat to medium, and add butter to skillet. Sauté the monkfish, mushrooms, tofu, red pepper, onion, and garlic until monkfish becomes firm and opaque, about 7 minutes. Stir carefully so tofu doesn't break up.

Stir in the grape juice, scraping the bottom of the pan. Reduce heat to medium-low. Strain the shrimp-shell stock through a fine sieve into the skillet.

In a small bowl mix the cornstarch and water to a smooth paste. Add shrimp, soymilk, and paprika to the skillet. Stir in the cornstarch paste. Stir slowly until sauce bubbles slightly and thickens to the consistency of heavy cream. Stir in the lemon juice, soy sauce, and dill. Serve the seafood over or beside rice or toast points. Or for a fancier presentation, place fish and sauce in a shallow casserole or individual casseroles. Top with cheese and broil until a slight crust forms, 5 to 10 minutes. Garnish with chives and serve.

4 to 6 servings

½ pound medium-size shrimp, in their shells
1 cup Chicken Stock (page 243)
2 bay leaves
¼ teaspoon whole peppercorns
½ teaspoon fennel seeds
1 tablespoon vegetable oil
3 tablespoons butter
1 pound monkfish fillet, cut into bite-size pieces
8 mushrooms, thinly sliced
½ cup ½-inch cubes tofu
½ sweet red pepper, finely chopped
1 medium-size onion, finely chopped
1 clove garlic, minced
¼ cup white grape juice
4 tablespoons cornstarch
4 tablespoons water
½ teaspoon paprika
1 cup soymilk
2 teaspoons lemon juice
2 teaspoons soy sauce
1 tablespoon chopped fresh dill
4 cups hot cooked brown rice or 8 pieces whole grain bread, toasted and cut into triangles
1 cup shredded Swiss or provolone cheese (optional)
½ teaspoon fresh chive, thinly sliced (optional)

1 tablespoon tomato paste
1 teaspoon Worcestershire
    sauce
dash of Tabasco sauce
1½ cups shredded cheddar
    cheese or Jarlsburg (or
    Gruyere for a stronger
    flavor)
Thick White Sauce (page
    126)
4 eggs, separated, at room
    temperature
1 tablespoon chopped
    fresh basil, dill, or
    chervil
¼ teaspoon cream of
    tartar

CRUST

2½ to 3 cups cooked
    brown rice
2 teaspoons minced fresh
    parsley
1 teaspoon dried basil
1 teaspoon dried tarragon
1 tablespoon soy sauce

FILLING

½ pound mushrooms,
    sliced (3 cups)
1 medium-size onion,
    diced
2 to 3 cloves garlic, minced
2 tablespoons vegetable oil
1 pound spinach, steamed
    and chopped (2 cups)
Parsley Sauce (recipe
    follows)

Cheese Souffle

This showy souffle is moist and flavorful.

Preheat oven to 425°F.

Stir tomato paste, Worcestershire sauce, Tabasco sauce, and cheese into the white sauce. When sauce is cool enough to touch, beat in egg yolks, one at a time. Add basil.

In a separate bowl beat egg whites until frothy; sprinkle with cream of tartar. Continue beating until whites form soft peaks.

Fold egg whites into cheese mixture. Do not overmix. Pour into a buttered 1½-quart souffle dish.

Bake for 15 minutes. Reduce heat to 350°F and bake until top crust is nut-brown and a thin knife inserted through a crack in the crust comes out very hot, about 25 minutes. Serve immediately.

4 servings

Vegetable Brown Rice Pie with Parsley Sauce

Mix rice, parsley, basil, tarragon and soy sauce and press firmly into a 9-inch pie plate.

Sauté mushrooms, onion, and garlic in heated oil until onions are transparent. Mix in spinach and saute for 5 minutes or until most of the liquid has evaporated. Pour mixture into brown rice crust, top with Parsley Sauce, and bake at 350°F for 20 minutes.

4 to 6 servings

PARSLEY SAUCE

Heat oil in top of a double boiler or in a heavy saucepan. Add flour, stirring to form a paste. Very slowly stir in soymilk and then stock into the roux, stirring constantly, to avoid lumping. Cook sauce until thick enough to coat a spoon, about 15 minutes. (The sauce may appear curdled at this point, but it will quickly smooth out when the egg is added.)

Then add 2 to 3 tablespoons of the hot sauce slowly to the beaten egg and stir well. Add this back to the sauce and stir in. Do not boil or the egg will curdle. Add parsley and cook 3 minutes longer. Remove from heat.

Yields about 2½ cups

3 tablespoons vegetable oil
3 tablespoons whole wheat flour
1 cup clabbered soymilk
1 cup Vegetable Stock (page 244) or Chicken Stock (page 243)
1 egg, beaten
2 tablespoons minced fresh parsley

Soups

Clam and Cod Chowder

This creamy but dairy-free thick New England chowder gets its body from nourishing potatoes rather than fattening cream. It is a meal in itself served with toasted whole grain rolls or crisp crackers. This chowder can be successfully reheated the next day or frozen and reheated. It takes less than an hour to prepare.

Place clams and their liquor in a small saucepan. Cover and bring to a boil, reduce heat and simmer for 3 minutes. Remove from heat, strain and measure liquid. Add enough water to liquid to make 2 cups. Reserve. Chop clams finely. Set aside.

Sauté onion and carrot in butter in a 4-quart pot for about 5 minutes. Add bay leaves, pepper, parsley, and reserved clam broth to sautéed vegetables. Cover and bring to a boil over high heat.

Add cod. Return to a boil and stir in soymilk, potatoes, and reserved clams. Reduce heat and simmer chowder, stirring frequently, until warmed. Remove bay leaves and serve.

6 to 8 servings

NOTE: To reheat frozen soup, thaw and cook over low heat, stirring frequently, until just hot enough to serve. Soup will have a curdled appearance that will disappear when heated.

12 chowder clams, shucked and in their liquor*
1 large onion, coarsely chopped
1 carrot, finely grated
4 tablespoons butter
2 bay leaves
¼ teaspoon white pepper
1 tablespoon chopped fresh parsley
1 pound cod steak, trimmed and cut into bite-size pieces
2 to 3 cups soymilk
3 cups unseasoned mashed potatoes

*Any fish market should perform this service for you.

2 tablespoons butter
1 stalk celery, thinly sliced
2 carrots, thinly sliced
1 large onion, coarsely
    chopped
¼ teaspoon dried thyme
2 teaspoons chopped fresh
    parsley
1 cup Chicken Stock (page
    243)
2 cups Thick White Sauce
½ cup chopped cooked
    chicken meat
black pepper, to taste
freshly grated nutmeg, to
    taste

Cream of Chicken Soup

Melt the butter in a 2-quart saucepan. Sauté the celery, carrots, and onion over medium heat until tender. Stir in thyme, parsley, and stock. Cover and simmer, stirring frequently, for 15 to 20 minutes.

Slowly stir vegetable mixture into Thick White Sauce. Season with pepper and nutmeg. Do not allow soup to boil. Serve hot.

4 servings

1 large onion, chopped
3 stalks celery, finely
    chopped
1 green pepper, seeded and
    chopped
1 tablespoon vegetable oil
3 ripe juicy tomatoes,
    coarsely chopped
1 teaspoon fresh thyme
    leaves
1 tablespoon honey
2 teaspoons soy sauce
1 cup Medium White
    Sauce (page 126)
3 scallions with tops,
    thinly sliced
1 tablespoon finely
    chopped fresh parsley
1 cup croutons

Cream of Tomato Soup

This soup is quick and easy to make. The White Sauce can be prepared while the tomatoes simmer.

In a large saucepan sauté onion, celery, and pepper in oil for 4 minutes. Add tomatoes, thyme, honey, and soy sauce. Simmer, covered, until tomatoes are quite soft, about 15 to 20 minutes. Cool slightly.

Purée in a blender or put through a food mill.

Over low heat stir puréed tomatoes into white sauce, a spoonful at a time, and then in a slow stream. If the soup curdles, return to blender and purée. When soup is very hot, but not boiling, add scallions and parsley. Garnish with croutons and serve.

4 servings

Creamy Potato and Leek Soup

Discard roots and tough leaves from leeks. Cut leeks in half lengthwise. Separate the layers and wash thoroughly to remove the sand. Chop into bite-size pieces.

In a large saucepan sauté leeks and celery in butter until leeks begin to soften, about 5 minutes.

Add potatoes, stock, and thyme. Cover and simmer until potatoes are tender, about 20 minutes. Remove from heat.

Purée about half of the soup with soymilk in a blender until smooth. Return to saucepan, add mustard, pepper, soy sauce, and parsley. Heat, stirring occasionally, but do not boil. Top with scallions and serve.

4 to 6 servings

½ pound leeks (2 or 3 medium-size)
2 stalks celery, finely chopped
3 tablespoons butter
4 potatoes, peeled or well scrubbed, cut into ½-inch cubes
1½ cups Chicken Stock (page 243)
½ teaspoon minced fresh thyme or ¼ teaspoon dried thyme
2 cups soymilk
1 teaspoon dry mustard
black pepper, to taste
1½ teaspoons soy sauce
1 tablespoon finely chopped fresh parsley
1 scallion, thinly sliced, or 1 tablespoon finely chopped fresh chives

Spicy Cream of Broccoli Soup

This beautiful pistachio-green soup is easy and quick and makes a very elegant appetizer soup.

Cut broccoli into small flowerets. Cut stems into bite-size pieces. Steam broccoli flowerets and stems until tender-crisp, about 7 minutes.

In a large skillet melt butter and add onion. Sauté until onion is transparent. Add herbs and spices; stir well. Add steamed broccoli to skillet; mix well.

In a blender purée half the broccoli mixture with half the soymilk. Repeat with remaining broccoli and soymilk and place in a 3-quart pot over low heat. Slowly blend in lemon juice. Cook until just heated. Do not boil.

4 servings

1 medium-size head of broccoli (about 2 pounds)
2 tablespoons butter
1 medium-size onion, coarsely chopped
¼ teaspoon each: ground turmeric, cardamom, coriander, cumin, ginger, and cinnamon
3 cups soymilk
2 tablespoons lemon juice

NOTE: Soup may be enriched with a beaten egg by blending a little of the hot soup with the beaten egg in a small bowl and then stir into the soup pot.

Sauces and Dressings

Basic White Sauces

Basic White Sauce, also called béchamel, can be made easily with soymilk. Its consistency is often varied as we have done below. On its own this sauce is bland, but it serves as the basis for other flavorful sauces. White sauce can also be used to bind stuffings, croquettes, and the like and as the base for souffles. When thickening sauces with whole wheat flour, find a flour that is finely ground or use pastry flour. Depending on the flour used, you may have to thin the sauce by adding extra soymilk.

THICK WHITE SAUCE

4 tablespoons whole wheat
   pastry flour
4 tablespoons butter
1 cup soymilk

This sauce is generally used to bind stuffings together and as the base for souffles. It may be used to make very rich soups or sauces.

MEDIUM WHITE SAUCE

3 tablespoons whole wheat
   pastry flour
3 tablespoons butter
1 cup soymilk

This sauce is appropriate as the base for many sauces or soups.

THIN WHITE SAUCE

2 tablespoons whole wheat
   pastry flour
2 tablespoons butter
1 cup soymilk

This sauce is best used as a base for cream soups and in cooked custards with eggs added.

In a small saucepan over medium-low heat, cook the flour in the butter for 2 minutes, stirring constantly. Add the soymilk slowly, stirring constantly with a flat bottomed wooden spoon to prevent lumps. Bring mixture to a boil. Stirring occasionally, cook for 2 minutes.
Yields 1 cup

126

Cheese Sauce

Melt butter in a medium-size heavy saucepan. Add flour, stirring constantly, and cook 2 minutes. Slowly stir in soymilk, whisking constantly to avoid lumping. Cook mixture over medium heat until it is thick enough to coat a spoon. Add cheese and cook 3 minutes longer. Cool slightly and stir in the egg.

Yields 1¾ cups

2 tablespoons butter
2 tablespoons whole wheat flour
1½ cups soymilk or dairy milk
½ cup grated Parmesan cheese
1 egg, lightly beaten

Soymilk Cream Cheese

Combine all ingredients in a large stainless steel pot. Slowly heat until 100° to 102°F. Let stand uncovered in a warm place (85° to 100° F) until curds form, 16 to 24 hours.

Line a colander with muslin or several layers of cheesecloth; slowly pour the mixture through. Bring the ends of the cloth together to form a bag, tie it, and suspend bag from the faucet spout so mixture can drip into the sink. Allow to hang for about 3 hours.

Pack cheese firmly into a square plastic freezer container. Top with another freezer container filled with water to act as a weight. Refrigerate.

Yields 1½ cups cheese

2 cups drained clabbered soymilk
½ cup heavy cream
4 cups milk

Soymilk Sour Cream

Blend soymilk and cheese together in a blender until smooth and creamy. Taste and add lemon juice if soymilk is not tart enough.

Yields 2½ cups

1¾ cups drained clabbered soymilk
1 cup farmer's cheese
2 tablespoons lemon juice (optional)

Basil Tomato Sauce

1 tablespoon tomato paste
1 cup Medium White
    Sauce (page 126)
1 tablespoon finely
    chopped fresh basil

Use this tangy sauce for delicate white fish, for vegetables or egg dishes.

In a small saucepan over medium-low heat, add the tomato paste to the hot sauce, stirring well. Add the basil just before serving. Serve hot.
Yields 1 cup

Mustard-Cheese Sauce

½ teaspoon dry mustard
    or 1 teaspoon prepared
    mustard
½ teaspoon
    Worcestershire sauce
1 cup Medium White
    Sauce (page 126)
¼ cup soymilk
½ cup shredded cheese
    (muenster, Swiss or
    Gruyere)
dash of Tabasco sauce
¼ teaspoon ground
    turmeric
freshly grated nutmeg, to
    taste

This sauce goes well with strong-flavored vegetables such as broccoli, cauliflower, or asparagus. Try it over plain eggs or omelets, too.

In a small saucepan over medium-low heat, add mustard and Worcestershire sauce to white sauce. Add soymilk and cheese at the same time. Stir until cheese is melted, and sauce is smooth. Add hot sauce, turmeric, and nutmeg. Serve hot.
Yields 1½ cups

Peanut Butter Sauce

Over low heat warm the peanut butter and honey. Stir in the soymilk, a spoonful at a time, until the sauce is smooth and pourable.

Serve hot as a dessert topping, or cool to room temperature and swirl into homemade ice cream.

Yields ½ cup

⅓ cup peanut butter
3 tablespoons honey
3 to 5 tablespoons soymilk

White Sauce with Herbs

Choose herbs that complement food to be sauced, and use fresh herbs, if possible. If fresh herbs are out of season, add extra chopped parsley for color. Use this sauce over delicate fish or over vegetables.

Heat sauce until very hot. Add herbs and chives; allow sauce to set for 5 minutes before serving. Thin sauce with soymilk or dairy milk if it has thickened too much.

Yields 1 cup

Medium White Sauce (page 126)
2 teaspoons chopped fresh dillweed, chervil, tarragon, or basil or 1 teaspoon dried herbs*
2 teaspoons finely chopped fresh chives or parsley

*For thyme or rosemary, use half the amount given and add herbs to the butter and flour mixture when preparing the sauce.

129

3 tablespoons drained,
   clabbered soymilk, or
   dairy yogurt
2 tablespoons mayonnaise
2 tablespoons sour cream
1 tablespoon chopped
   fresh dillweed
1 tablespoon cider vinegar
1 teaspoon prepared
   mustard

½ cup drained clabbered
   soymilk
2 tablespoons mayonnaise
2 teaspoons cider vinegar
2 teaspoons tomato paste
½ teaspoon Hungarian
   paprika
2 teaspoons finely
   chopped fresh parsley
2 tablespoons finely
   chopped pickle or pickle
   relish*

*If using a sour pickle, add 1
teaspoon of honey.

Creamy Dill Dressing

This zesty salad dressing is also delicious over steamed vegetables.

Stir together soymilk, mayonnaise, sour cream, dill, vinegar, and mustard with a wire whisk until smooth. Toss with salad ingredients. Refrigerate until ready to use.
Yields about ½ cup

Russian Dressing

Try this dressing over a mixture of cooked potatoes, beets, and carrots.

In a small bowl stir together soymilk, mayonnaise, vinegar, tomato paste, and paprika with a wire whisk or a fork until smooth. Stir in parsley and pickle. Refrigerate until ready to use.
Yields about 1 cup

Baked Goods

Crusty French Bread

Stir together the water and honey in a medium-size bowl. Sprinkle yeast on water. Gently stir. Let yeast set about 15 minutes until mixture is foamy.

Place 4 cups of flour in a large bowl. Pour soymilk, lemon rind, soy sauce, and yeast mixture into the center of the flour. Stir until combined.

Knead dough at least 10 minutes, until smooth and elastic, using as little of the remaining flour as possible. The dough should be soft and slightly sticky. Shape into a ball, place in a lightly oiled bowl and turn over to coat with oil. Cover bowl with a damp cloth. Let rise in a slightly warm area (70° to 75°F). French bread is best when handled at a slightly cooler temperature than other yeast breads so it takes longer to rise.

When doubled in bulk, 1 hour or more, knead again briefly and divide dough in half. Shape into 5 $\times$ 15-inch rectangles. Roll up lengthwise, stretching the dough while rolling. Place loaves seam-side down in buttered French bread pans or on buttered baking sheets. Cover and let rise until almost doubled, 30 to 45 minutes.

Preheat oven to 375°F.

Make 3 ¼-inch-deep diagonal slices on each loaf. Bake until lightly browned, about 20 minutes. Quickly and carefully remove loaves from baking pan and return to oven racks. Bake until nut brown, 5 to 10 minutes more. When done, the bottom of the loaves will sound hollow when rapped.

Cool slightly before serving. If storing, cool completely before wrapping.

Makes 2 loaves

½ cup warm water
2 teaspoons honey
2 tablespoons dry yeast
4 to 4¾ cups whole wheat flour
1½ cups clabbered soymilk, undrained, at room temperature
½ teaspoon grated lemon rind
1 tablespoon soy sauce (optional)

131

Fruit and Nut Roll

DOUGH

1 cup soymilk
4 tablespoons butter
2 tablespoons honey
4 teaspoons dry yeast
2¼ to 2¾ cups whole
   wheat flour
1 cup soy flour, sifted
2 eggs

FILLING

1 cup dates
1 cup raisins, dried
   pineapple, apricots,
   papaya, or any dried
   fruit mixture
1 cup soymilk
1 cup finely chopped
   walnuts
1 teaspoon ground
   cinnamon

To make dough: In a small saucepan warm soymilk over low heat. Add butter and honey and heat just until butter is melted. Allow to cool to about 95°F. Add yeast and allow to set in a warm spot for about 15 minutes, or until nice and bubbly.

In a large bowl mix wheat and soy flours together. Add eggs and yeast mixture and mix well. Knead dough for about 10 minutes, adding flour as needed. Dough should be soft and satiny. Shape dough into a ball, place in a greased bowl, and turn over to coat with oil. Cover with a damp towel and allow to rise in a warm place for 1 hour or until doubled in bulk.

To make filling: Combine dates, dried fruit, and soymilk in a saucepan. Place over low heat and cook until very hot but not boiling. Remove from heat. Let stand for about 1 hour.

Drain off excess soymilk from fruit. Then puree fruit in a blender or food processor. Combine with walnuts and cinnamon in a bowl.

Punch down dough and divide in half. Roll out each half to about ¼ inch thickness. Spread each with half the fruit mixture. Roll up like a jelly roll, pinching all openings to avoid leaks. Place loaves on an oiled cookie sheet, seam-side down.

Cover and let loaves rise until almost double, about 25 minutes. Preheat oven to 350°F.

Bake for 25 minutes, or until golden brown on top. Remove from oven and rub tops with butter for a nice soft crust.
Makes 2 loaves

Two-Grain Banana, Bran, and Seed Muffins

Two of these muffins along with a soy-fruit beverage make a nice high-energy breakfast.

Preheat oven to 350°F.

Stir together oil and honey. Add egg, soymilk, and mashed banana and blend well.

Sift together oat flour, soy flour, whole wheat flour, baking powder, and baking soda onto banana mixture. Add to mixture any bran remaining in sifter. Mix to blend. Fold in sunflower seeds and bran. Do not overmix.

Pour batter into 18 greased muffin cups, filling two-thirds full.

Bake 18 to 22 minutes or until muffins test done.

Makes 18 muffins

¼ cup safflower oil
½ cup honey
1 egg
⅓ cup clabbered soymilk (or buttermilk)
3 large or 4 medium-size ripe bananas, mashed (about 1¾ cups)
¾ cup oat flour*
¾ cup soy flour
1½ cups whole wheat flour
1 teaspoon baking soda
1 teaspoon baking powder
½ cup toasted sunflower seeds
1 cup wheat bran

*You can grind oats in your blender to make oat flour.

133

Desserts

Almond Custard

2 cups soymilk
3 tablespoons cornstarch
2 eggs
2 egg yolks
⅓ cup honey
¾ cup blanched, lightly
toasted almonds, finely
chopped
½ teaspoon vanilla extract
¼ teaspoon almond
extract

This is a simple stove-top stirred custard. The recipe also can be used to make a basic custard by omitting the almonds. It can also be made thinner, for use as a sauce by omitting 1 tablespoon of the cornstarch.

In the top of a double boiler, mix ¼ cup of the soymilk with the cornstarch. Warm the remaining soymilk in another pan over low heat.

Beat the eggs and yolks into the cornstarch mixture, mixing well. Then stir in the honey and hot, not boiling, soymilk. Cook over simmering water, stirring with wooden spoon or heat-resistant rubber spatula. If lumps form, break them up with a wire whisk. When sufficiently cooked, the custard steams and a trail will form on top of the custard when stirred. The custard thickens further as it cools. Remove from heat and stir in almonds. When almost cool add vanilla and almond extracts.

Variations: Almond Custard Fruit Pie: Fill a baked piecrust with cooled custard and layer with fresh fruit.

Fruit Custard Cups: Layer custard in glass bowls with fresh fruit and top with whipped cream.

Yields 3 cups custard, enough for a 9-inch piecrust, 4 to 6 servings

Blueberry Dessert

1 tablespoon unflavored
gelatin
¼ cup water
1¼ cups drained clabbered
soymilk (see Index)*
2 tablespoons honey
1 teaspoon vanilla extract
1 cup blueberries or
raspberries

*1 quart of clabbered soymilk
yields 1¾ cup when drained.

Fresh or frozen blueberries can be used, or substitute raspberries for a pretty pink color.

Dissolve the gelatin in water over very low heat. Add the gelatin mixture to the soymilk in a large glass bowl. Mix well.

Refrigerate until the mixture begins to thicken, about 30 minutes. Then beat until foamy. Add the honey, vanilla, and then the blueberries. Whip until mixture is smooth and foamy and the fruit is incorporated into the mixture. Serve cold.

4 servings

Bread Pudding

In a blender combine soymilk, eggs, butter, honey, cinnamon, and vanilla extract; blend until smooth.

Place bread cubes and raisins in a buttered 1½-quart casserole. Pour soymilk mixture over top. Bake at 325°F for 45 to 55 minutes, or until a knife inserted near the center comes out clean. Serve warm.

6 to 8 servings

2 cups soymilk
4 eggs
½ cup butter, softened
2 tablespoons honey
½ teaspoon ground cinnamon
1 tablespoon vanilla extract
3 cups dry whole grain bread cubes
½ cup raisins

Cherry Custard

Heat cherries and apple juice in saucepan over medium heat until mixture comes to a boil. Add honey.

In a small bowl combine cornstarch and water, stirring to make a paste. Add cornstarch mixture to cherry mixture and stir until mixture is smooth and thickened. Remove from heat and reserve.

Lightly beat together eggs and maple syrup. Stir in soymilk, vanilla and almond extracts.

Preheat oven to 325°F.

Place 6 custard cups in a baking pan. Place a spoonful of cherry mixture into the bottom of each cup. Fill cup with egg mixture to within ¾ inch of rim. Add 1 inch of hot water to the baking pan.

Bake until custard is just set in the middle and very lightly browned on top, about 35 minutes. Remove from oven. Top with remaining cherry mixture and almonds. Serve warm or cool.

8 servings

2 cups sweet cherries*, pitted
½ cup apple juice
⅓ cup honey
2 tablespoons cornstarch
2 tablespoons water
3 eggs
⅓ cup maple syrup
2 cups soymilk
1 teaspoon vanilla extract
¼ teaspoon almond extract
¼ cup slivered almonds

*If using sour cherries, increase honey by ¼ cup.

3 whole eggs and 1 egg
  yolk
1/3 cup honey
2 cups soymilk
2 teaspoons vanilla extract
1/2 teaspoon grated orange
  rind
1 unbaked Whole Wheat
  Piecrust (page 242)
2 kiwi fruits, peeled and
  thinly sliced

Kiwi Custard Pie

*This delicious custard pie can be topped with any kind of fruit or a combination
of fruit.*

Preheat oven to 400°F.

Lightly beat eggs and yolk. Add honey and stir until well mixed.
Stir in milk, vanilla, and orange rind.

Bake piecrust for 10 minutes, then fill with egg mixture.

Bake for 15 minutes. Reduce heat to 325°F and bake until custard
is just barely set, and top begins to brown, about 40 to 45 minutes.
(A knife inserted near the center of the pie will come out clean.) Cool
pie on a rack.

Top with overlapping kiwi slices and refrigerate.

Makes 1 9-inch pie

Peaches and Cream Rice Pudding

1 can (16 ounces) sliced
  peaches
1 cup brown rice
2 eggs
1 cup soymilk
2 teaspoons vanilla extract
1/4 cup honey
1/4 teaspoon ground
  cinnamon
1/4 teaspoon ground ginger
1 cup heavy cream

Drain peaches, reserving juice. Add enough water to reserved liquid to equal 2 cups.

Cook rice in 2 cups reserved liquid, until done, about 45 minutes.

In a blender blend eggs, soymilk, vanilla, honey, cinnamon, ginger, and cream. Pour into a 1½-quart casserole. Stir in rice and
peaches.

Bake at 325°F for about 1½ hours, or until there is a soft spot
about 2 inches in diameter in the center. Serve warm.

6 to 8 servings

Raspberry Chiffon Pie

Light, airy, and a beautiful rose color.

Purée raspberries in a blender along with soymilk, honey, and vanilla.

In a small saucepan sprinkle gelatin over water; let stand 1 minute. Cook over low heat, stirring constantly, until dissolved. Blend into raspberry mixture. Cool completely.

Whip cream until stiff. Fold whipped cream and raspberry mixture together.

Beat egg whites until very stiff. Fold into raspberry mixture. Pour into piecrust, cover loosely and chill until set, about 6 hours.

8 servings

1½ cups fresh raspberries
¾ cup soymilk
⅓ to ½ cup honey
1 teaspoon vanilla extract
1 tablespoon unflavored gelatin
¼ cup water
1 cup heavy cream
3 egg whites
1 10-inch Crumb Piecrust (page 212)

Orange Ice Milk

This dairy-free frozen dessert has a very creamy feel, and the flavor of those creamy, frozen orange-and-vanilla treats from childhood. Without the last 1¾ cups of soymilk the cooked custard base can be used as a cake filling or layered with fruit. For a richer ice cream, replace one or two of the last cups of the soymilk with heavy cream. While this ice milk is best made in an ice cream maker, it can be frozen in a home freezer. To put on sticks, just pour the custard into molds and freeze for at least four hours.

Heat 3 cups of the soymilk until hot (but do not boil). In a separate 2-quart saucepan beat the eggs with a wire whisk until slightly thickened. Whisk in the honey and oil. Slowly stir in the hot soymilk. Stir ¼ cup of the cold soymilk into the cornstarch and add this to the saucepan. Place over medium-low heat, stirring constantly, until the mixture bubbles slightly. Remove from heat.

Place pan in a sink of ice water, stir occasionally to cool mixture.

When mixture is cold, stir in the remaining 1¾ cups soymilk, vanilla, orange juice concentrate, and orange extract. If using an ice cream freezer, prepare ice milk following manufacturer's directions. Or place mixture in a stainless steel or plastic bowl, cover and freeze. Beat ice milk at 1 hour intervals, using a portable electric mixer. Return to freezer after each beating and continue until frozen. Let the container stand at room temperature for 15 to 20 minutes before serving.

Yields 1½ quarts

5 cups soymilk
2 eggs
½ cup honey
2 tablespoons vegetable oil
¼ cup cornstarch
2 teaspoons vanilla extract
1 can (12 ounces) orange juice concentrate, thawed
¼ teaspoon orange extract

1 quart clabbered soymilk
  (see Index)
½ cup mild honey
1 cup heavy cream
1 cup milk
1½ teaspoons vanilla
  extract

Vanilla Ice Cream

This ice cream has an added tang, like frozen yogurt from the thick clabbered soymilk. This is a basic vanilla recipe that is good with nuts, fruit syrups, or pureed fresh fruits swirled through the ice cream after it is frozen. Peanut Butter Sauce (page 129) is particularly good on plain vanilla version.

Drain clabbered soymilk in cheesecloth for 1 hour. Mix together drained soymilk, honey, heavy cream, milk, and vanilla. Beat until smooth.

Freeze mixture according to manufacturer's directions in an ice cream freezer.

Store ice cream in freezer containers. If desired, drizzle favorite sauce over the ice cream and fold it into the ice cream with a narrow metal spatula. Stir as little as possible.

Freeze about 2 hours before serving. If the ice cream isn't eaten at this point it will get quite hard, like all homemade ice creams, and should stand at room temperature for 15 minutes before serving.

Yields 6 cups

¾ cup soymilk
2 tablespoons butter
⅓ cup honey or maple
  syrup
1 cup walnuts
4 large eggs, separated, or
  3 eggs, separated, plus
  ⅓ cup crumbled tofu

Walnut Souffle

A nice light dessert when served alone, this souffle can be topped with some whipped cream for a richer treat.

In a small heavy saucepan warm soymilk slightly. Stir in butter and cook just until melted. Stir in honey. Allow to cool to almost room temperature.

Grind walnuts in a blender. Add cooled soymilk mixture and egg yolks or combination of egg yolks and tofu. Blend well.

Preheat oven to 325°F. Beat egg whites until they form stiff but moist peaks. Fold into blended walnut mixture. Pour into ungreased 1-quart souffle dish.

Bake at 325°F for 30 to 40 minutes, or until top forms a golden crust, and a knife inserted in the center comes out clean.

4 to 6 servings

Beverages*

Carob-Banana Shake

Combine soymilk, bananas, honey, carob, and vanilla in a blender and purée well. Serve chilled.
Yields about 4 cups

2 cups soymilk
4 very ripe medium-size
 bananas
2 tablespoons honey
2 teaspoons carob powder
1 teaspoon vanilla extract

Coconut Soymilk

Combine soymilk, coconut, and honey in a small saucepan. Bring to a boil over medium heat, stirring frequently. Remove from the heat and cool.

Puree cooled mixture in a blender, and then strain out the solids through a fine-meshed strainer. Chill.
Yields 2 cups

3 cups soymilk
1½ cups unsweetened dry
 coconut
3 tablespoons honey

Honeyed Soymilk

Combine soymilk, honey, and vanilla and mix well. Serve chilled.
Yields about 4 cups

4 cups soymilk
¼ cup honey
1 teaspoon vanilla extract

*Soymilk beverages should be prepared daily because they tend to darken
 when stored overnight.

139

Maple Soymilk

4 cups soymilk
¼ cup maple syrup
1 teaspoon vanilla extract

Combine soymilk, maple syrup, and vanilla and mix well. Serve chilled.

Yields about 4 cups

Piña Colada Shake

2 cups soymilk
1 cup dried pineapple
    chunks
Coconut Soymilk (page
    139)
about ½ cup pineapple
    juice

Combine the soymilk and dried pineapple in a small saucepan. Bring to a boil over medium heat, stirring frequently. Remove from heat and chill.

Purée pineapple-soymilk mixture in a blender. Add coconut soymilk and blend well. Thin to desired consistency with pineapple juice.

Yields 5 cups

Strawberry-Banana Drink

2 cups soymilk
2 cups fresh or frozen
    strawberries
1 very ripe medium-size
    banana
5 tablespoons honey
1 teaspoon vanilla extract

Combine the soymilk, strawberries, banana, honey, and vanilla in a blender and purée well. Serve chilled.

Yields about 4 cups

Strawberry Slush

There are two approaches to making slushy frozen fruit drinks. You may freeze either the liquid or the fruit. The result will be the same, so do whatever is most convenient.

2 cups soymilk
3 tablespoons maple syrup
1 teaspoon vanilla extract
2 cups frozen or fresh
   strawberries

If using frozen berries: Combine soymilk, maple syrup, and vanilla in blender and blend until smooth. Add frozen strawberries. Purée until mixture is thick and smooth. Serve immediately.

If using fresh berries: Combine soymilk and 2 tablespoons of the maple syrup. Freeze at least 12 hours.

Partially thaw soymilk so that it is about half ice and half liquid. Combine fresh strawberries, remaining syrup, and vanilla in a blender. Drain liquid into blender and purée. Add remaining frozen mixture and purée until mixture is thick and smooth.

Makes about 3½ cups

141

Brightsong Light Foods, Petaluma, California

"Brightsong Light Foods started as a cliche," says owner Dick Rose, "two hippies in the hills of Mendocino County, Northern California, making tofu by hand in their garage." With tofu's ascending popularity the shop moved into a commercial building in town where the present owners bought it. Using their business acumen and a personal interest in soyfoods, the new owners sought to improve production efficiency, product diversity, and widen the distribution area.

Brightsong Light Foods, Petaluma, California. Fresh, creamy soymilk, plain or flavored, is one of Brightsong's popular convenience soyfoods.

Dick and Sharon Rose eventually opened the Real Food Tofu Shop, serving people who were the mainstream of the population, who wanted to better their diets, and use more tofu. These customers happily savored the Roses' tofu cream pies, salads, desserts, and soy beverages. Then the Roses offered their soyfoods cheesecakes, burgers, and sandwiches at a benefit concert and the response was gratifying. The Roses decided to take advantage of the public acceptance of their convenience soyfoods.

During the following 3 years they produced and experimented with 70 soy products. Dick recalls, "We moved from being just a tofu shop toward being a company that produces high-protein, low-calorie convenience foods that happen to contain tofu and other soyfoods."

Although soyfoods is a successful business for them, the Roses feel it is important to remain close to "the craft of tofu-making and our spiritual and social values in relation to the corporate culture we are developing. Our tofu method is traditional—handmade with open cauldron, stonemills, and natural *nigari*," Dick Rose proudly explains.

Today Brightsong's owners sponsor a food booth and a cooking contest at the local county fair and harvest fair. They go to many other fairs "where we give away as much food as we sell," says Sharon. "The best way to sell our products is to have folks sample them." Their current line of soyfoods includes: fresh and marinated tofu, soymilk, Honey-Nilla soymilk, Maple-Maple Soymilk, Cottage Salad, Missing-Egg Salad, Almond Lite and Creamy, Chocolate Lite Mousse, Amaretto-Almond Lite and Creamy, Soy-Nog, Pumpkin and Mincemeat (meatless) Pie. They are all lower in calories than similar products, but high in protein, cholesterol-free and most important, they taste great.

After several years in their successful soyfoods business, the Roses have developed a fitting slogan: Brightsong . . . where good taste and nutrition come naturally!

Japanese Soyfoods

by Richard Leviton

Richard Leviton is founder, editor, and publisher of Soyfoods Magazine, *and former executive director of Soycrafters Association of North America. Mr. Leviton, who helped found the New England Soy Dairy (now Tomsun Foods), lectures on soyfoods in the United States, Canada, and Europe. During his many travels he has spent time in Japan investigating the soyfoods cuisine there. In his report, he takes us inside Japanese supermarkets, restaurants, and soyfoods plants to reveal just a sampling of the deep-rooted soyfoods culture of that country.*

The Japanese, who consume 100 million cakes of fresh tofu daily, also regard dozens of other soyfoods as a fixed part of their eating culture. This deep-rooted trend is reflected in Japanese supermarkets, where shelves and dairy cases exhibit at least 60 different types of soyfoods—some familiar to Americans, many not. Tofu pouches, deep-fried tofu cutlets, yuba rolls, dried-frozen tofu wafers, *natto* miso, *kinako* powder, flavored soymilk, and other soyfoods pass through Japanese supermarkets as swiftly as bread and milk pass through ours.

Deep-Fried and Grilled Tofu Treats

Japanese manufacturers commonly transform *momen,* their version of firm tofu, into feather-light brown slabs and puffs that somewhat resemble homemade potato chips. Pouches, cutlets, and burgers are three traditional deep-fried products made from *momen* that may appear familiar to many American tofu shoppers.

Deep-fried tofu pouches, called *age* (AH-gay), are made by deep-frying thinly sliced, firm-pressed two-inch squares of tofu until they puff up and expand, forming a pouch similar to pita bread. The dense slab of tofu undergoes a remarkable transformation after a 15 minute immersion in the boiling vegetable oil, changing into an amber-hued hollow pouch. Freshly fried pouches have a mild taste, and a light chewiness. Pouches are stuffed with minced vegetables, grains, cheese, fruits, even sautéed tofu.

Deep-fried tofu cutlets are made from larger slabs of tofu, measuring perhaps ½ inch thick and 3 inches square, and sometimes up to 10 ounces in weight. These slabs are pressed free of water, and deep-fried. A crust forms on the outside, and the inside remains succulent and mildly seasoned. Cutlets called *atsuage* (AHT-soo-ah-gay) are also available in the United States. Tofu cutlets may be marinated, steamed, or baked instead of deep-fried.

The third variety of deep-fried tofu popular in Japan is tofu burger, or *ganmo*. To make *ganmo* firm tofu is mashed, then mixed with sesame seeds and various land and sea vegetables. The mixture is shaped into patties (about 4 ounces each) and deep-fried until the outer surface becomes crisp. Tofu burgers have caught on as a lunchtime favorite in this country and are often available in natural foods stores.

In Japan soft- and firm-style tofus are grilled also, and called *yaki* (YAH-kee), or burned-skin tofu. To make *yaki* thin slices of tofu are grilled, often by a handheld blow torch, until the outer surface is a rich brown color. This creates a barbecued or charcoal-broiled texture on the tofu, leaving the inside section moist and unaltered.

Another very tasty tofu product originally developed in China is *doufu-gan* (DOH-fu-gahn). An extra-firm piece of tofu is marinated in rose hips, shoyu, peppers, and spices until the flavors permeate the tofu. Also called spicy tofu, this variation found in stores in Asian communities is very dry and chewy.

Just as in the most streamlined American convenience store one always finds cheese, milk, cream, and margarine; in Japan, this quintet of deep-fried and grilled tofu preparations is always on hand.

Tofu Haute Cuisine

A lunchtime visit to *Sasa-No-Yuki*, Tokyo's 280-year-old tofu restaurant, provides one with a marvelous and elaborate presentation of Japanese tofu haute cuisine. This world-famous gourmet tofu restaurant specializes in eight-course tofu meals. Diners are comfortably ensconced on soft floor mats, next to ankle-high tables. Becalmed by sake and green tea, one is served bowl after bowl of tofu, smothered in sauces, garnished with greens, and sprinkled with shoyu.

Sasa-No-Yuki's fare makes it perfectly clear that the Japanese treasure the light, sweet taste of silken tofu (produced in the restaurant's ground floor tofu shop). For a typical meal, patrons may expect to receive any or all of the following tofu variations: tofu with shoyu, leeks, and ginger root; tofu with *yuzu* (a fragrant fruit) simmered in miso; a sweet tofu pudding with shoyu, eggs, oil, and *mirin*; silken tofu steamed with eggs in a lemon-shoyu sauce; tofu scrambled with vegetables and sesame seeds; tofu with miso soup, called *miso shiru* (containing leeks and mushrooms); tofu blended with ground meat or chicken; tofu simmered in sweet yuba rolls; tofu with shoyu and slabs of fish. In each guise tofu's simple taste is counterpointed by the stronger flavors of fish, fowl, vegetables, and sauce.

Another major variation on tofu preparation is dried-frozen tofu, called *kori* tofu (CORR-ree). Making *kori* tofu was once a local cottage industry throughout the cold, mountainous regions of central Japan. Traditionally in the cold winter months, homesteaders would string up slices of tofu outside to freeze, then either preserve the tofu in the frozen state, or thaw then dry it in a warm shed. The freezing process, followed by drying, greatly modifies the tofu's texture, rendering it sponge-like.

Today in Iida, surrounded by mountains and ample river water, Asahimatsu Kori Tofu Company turns out one million pieces of dried-frozen tofu each day. In a 25-day period Asahimatsu transforms soybeans into beige dried-frozen tofu wafers packed in cellophane or colorful boxes. To make this style of tofu, firm tofu is frozen, and stored frozen for 20 days, after which it is thawed, pressed under heavy rollers, doused with baking soda (which helps it to swell during cooking), pressed again, then dried in hot air tunnels, and packaged. In the supermarket, one is likely to find a dozen varieties of packaged dried-frozen tofu. It appears in red and yellow cartons or simple cellophane sacks, with the wafers varying in size from tiny squares to 2-inch square slabs.

Wine-fermented tofu (also called *sufu, toufu-ru,* and other names), originally a Chinese soyfood, is another unique preparation of tofu. It has a soft, creamy consistency with an aroma and taste similar to ripe Camembert cheese. Cubes of tofu are inoculated with a mold, incubated for 3 days, placed in pint bottles filled with a brine of rice wine, salt, red chilies, and other seasonings, then allowed to ripen for

2 months. This cheeselike fermented tofu can be a key ingredient in blended dips, dressings, spreads, or casseroles and in stir-fried dishes or sauces. Wine-fermented tofu can be found in Asian specialty shops under the names wet bean curd and preserved bean curd.

Delights of Soymilk and Yuba

The dairy case of most Japanese supermarkets displays a festive collection of cartoned soymilks. Soymilks in flavors including chocolate, orange, coffee, vanilla, strawberry, and plain are a favorite refreshment in Japan. Often using barley malt as the sweetener, the Japanese soymilks have a rich, creamy, smooth and dairylike consistency with the pleasant flavor of malt—not too sweet, not too beany.

Yuba (YOO-bah), made from soymilk, is a rich-tasting and hearty soyfood not well known in the U.S. *Yuba* was developed centuries ago in China where the vegetarian lifestyle of the Buddhists prompted the quest for new foods. Also called by the evocative names bean oil skin and tofu robes in the Orient, *yuba* is the delicate film that forms on heated soymilk, and is scooped up to stretch dry in sheets or rolls. *Yuba* contains up to 52 percent protein, 24 percent natural oils, 11 percent natural sugars, and only 8.7 percent water. With its high levels of protein and fat, *yuba* is a calorically rich food, nearly a meal in itself.

At the *yuba* plant, *Yuba Han,* soy craftsmen use about 100 pounds of soybeans every day and sell their day's production by nightfall. Using a sawdust-fired oven, the shop heats steel basins of thick simmering soymilk. The *yuba* master uses bamboo skewers to scoop up the delicate films, hanging them to dry. He often obtains as many as 22 skins from one shallow basin of soymilk.

The Chinese Buddhists developed an astonishing application for this otherwise dry, crinkly, and brittle *yuba* sheet. They discovered that when fresh yuba is wrapped up with spices and flavorings and steamed for about 40 minutes, it congeals into a chewy meatlike uniform roll, remarkably smooth, and easily sliced like cold cuts. Steamed, basted, and baked yuba can be fashioned into a number of meat analogs—sausages, drumsticks, rolled meats, plucked hens, ducks, roosters, even fish. At holiday time the Japanese proudly display such fabrications, dubbing them Buddha's Duck and Buddha's Chicken.

At *Yuba Han* our host served us steaming fresh *yuba* with shoyu and a plate of deep-fried yuba balls for a rich memorable breakfast. In the supermarket, one is likely to find large *yuba* sheets or tidy *yuba* coils packed in colorful decorated boxes with a cellophane window. *Yuba* can be crumbled in soups and simmered, and it soon takes on the chewy consistency of mozzarella cheese. You can use *yuba* also as a cracker, or egg roll skin. Oriental specialty stores in the United States often market *yuba* labelled with the misleading title bean curd wrapper or dried bean curd.

Natto, Miso, and Savory Soy Condiments

Natto (NAH-toe) is another Japanese soyfood largely unknown outside Asian-American communities in this country. Its sharp taste, like that of strong-flavored cheeses, is less appealing to Americans than the mild taste of tofu and other soyfoods. *Natto,* which is a cake of fermented, sticky soybeans, was developed in Japan about 1000 years ago and today is made in over 1000 shops throughout the island nation.

To make *natto* whole soybeans are cooked, inoculated with a bacteria (*Bacillus subtilis*), then incubated for about 18 hours. Finished *natto* has a sticky, slippery surface of fine filaments that hold the beans loosely together. *Natto* has a strong mustard-like taste that makes it ideal for use as a seasoning. The Japanese customarily use *natto* as a rice or noodle topping, adding it to wok-fried dishes or to soups. In America cooks have found *natto* to be a lively seasoning blended with mayonnaise, vegetables, and spices and in Italian-style entrées, French onion soup, burgers, and even as a topping for baked potatoes.

With 17 percent protein, 10 percent fat, 10 percent carbohydrate, and 2 percent fiber, snappy-tasting *natto* makes for a nutritionally superior condiment.

Hamanatto (HAH-mah-nah-toe), or savory soy nuggets, can be traced back 2000 years to China. Related to *natto,* but milder-tasting, *hamanatto* is today a delicacy in many Japanese Buddhist temples. Whole soybeans are soaked, steamed, inoculated with a mold (*Aspergillus oryzae*), incubated for 2 days, then packed in a salt brine with spices and aged for several months. Finally, the soybeans are sun-dried to impart the characteristic black color. Black and chunky, the nuggets resemble plump chocolate-covered raisins with a taste reminiscent of strong miso. Soy nuggets contain 28 percent protein and 2900 milligrams salt, and are available in the United States in Oriental food shops in jars often labelled Chinese black beans, fermented soybeans, or salted black beans. Because of their high salt content, these nuggets are most often used in small amounts to season dishes.

Thua nao, a soyfood from Thailand, is a fermented product also similar to *natto* and made from the same bacterial culture. However, after a 2-day incubation, the fermented soybeans are mashed into a paste with salt, garlic, onion, and red pepper. The paste is wrapped in banana leaves and cooked. The paste, containing 16 percent protein, is sometimes formed into small balls, then pressed into chips which are sun-dried. *Thua nao,* like *natto* and *hamanatto,* is used to season foods.

Miso in Japan is as ubiquitous as coffee in the West. Japanese supermarkets provide a large space for this pastelike condiment. Miso is readily available in this country, but not in the plethora of hues, flavors, and consistencies of the miso products in Japan. Three favorite styles are especially popular.

Natto miso, made from whole soybeans, barley *koji,* slivered *kombu* seaweed, ginger root, and a natural grain sweetener can be enjoyed straight from the container, used to make a sweet broth, or used as part of a vegetable topping. Finger Lickin' Miso (carrying a Westernized name) is made from finely chopped salt-pickled vegetables and soybeans, and a large amount of *koji,* to make a light brown, chunky miso with a consistency like applesauce. Sweet simmered miso is made from miso, a sweetener, sake, nuts, seeds, minced vegetables, seafoods, and is lightly simmered during the blending. Often peanuts, roasted sesame seeds, and sometimes raisins are used. *Natto miso* and Finger Lickin' Miso are sometimes available in bulk containers at the larger natural foods stores in the United States.

And Still More . . .

Scattered throughout the Japanese supermarket one notes an abundance of other intriguing soyfoods: cooked soybeans in a film-wrapped styrofoam tray, cooked soybeans with *wakame* seaweed, dry soybeans in a pouch-pack, soy sprouts packed in a sausagelike clear tube, green soybeans in the pods, *kinako* powder (a flour made from dry roasted soybeans, used as a base for confections or nut butters), a half-dozen variations on freeze-dried instant miso soup powder, boxes of instant silken tofu powder (just add water and stir), and dry meat sauces for tofu.

Perhaps as Americans grow fonder of soyfoods, more of these soy products will be stocked in our food stores.

Whole Dry Soybeans

Why bother with the whole dry soybean, you may ask, when one can enjoy it processed into a more concentrated source of protein as tofu or soymilk, or in another more flavorful and easily cooked form such as tempeh? It's true that the Eastern world has made soybeans infinitely more interesting by processing the bean into these meat-, cheese-, and milklike foods. But soybeans are also an excellent ingredient in many dishes when used simply as a legume.

Whole dry soybeans can be used in classic dishes prepared with white beans, pinto beans, kidney beans, chick-peas, or dried lima beans. Some of these classic international dishes include: pasta fagiole, chili con carne, Brazilian black beans and rice, and hummus—to name just a few. When you substitute soybeans for the beans in any of these dishes, you work some wonderful flavor and nutritional changes.

Like other dried beans, soybeans are best when combined with zesty flavored foods such as tomatoes, onions, chilies, cheeses, or meats. In fact, like its derivative tofu, the nutty slightly sweet taste of soybeans is compatible with just about any food. Soybeans taste good when seasoned heartily with curry or chili, or you can keep them mild if you prefer.

Soybeans add taste and texture to salads—hot or cold. Unlike other dried beans, soybeans keep their firmness and do not become mushy even when slightly overcooked. Try adding some soybeans (as you may do with chick-peas) to fresh vegetable salads for a pleasant variation. Because soy protein complements that of grains, soybeans are an excellent addition to pasta, whole grain salads, or casseroles. They will also blend right in with any vegetable or meat-based soup or stew.

When you mash or purée cooked soybeans, you extend their versatility even further. You can easily blend puréed soybeans into meat or vegetable stuffing mixtures, meat loaves, meatballs, bread doughs, and other baked goods. You can also season puréed soybeans to make a savory vegetable pâté or vegetable patty.

SOY NUTS

People who like to munch between meals will be happy to know that whole dry soybeans can be turned into a very nutritious snack. Soy nuts (page 173), which you can also purchase in supermarkets and natural foods stores, are a crunchy, tasty treat made by roasting soybeans in much the same way you roast other nuts. You can season the roasted nuts and eat them as a snack, much lighter and lower in calories than peanuts and other nuts. Or you can add them to baked goods, cereals, and granola or sprinkle them on top of casseroles.

A Nutritional Feast

Though physically different from tofu, tempeh, and soymilk, you will find that soybeans can easily be the foundation of many appetizing meals. And like these other soyfoods, they are equally responsible for a notable nutritional boost in meals where they appear.

Soybeans rank high as an important protein source (especially in meatless and low-meat diets), and they have a much lower carbohydrate content than other dried beans (see Nutrients in Soybeans and Other Dried Beans, page 152). Soybeans are the only vegetable protein source containing all the essential amino acids. They are deficient in two amino acids (the same two that beef lacks). To compensate for this deficiency, I try to include grains, dairy foods, or nuts and seeds as part of the same meal with soybeans.

Nutrients in Soybeans and Other Dried Beans
(Dried, Uncooked, 100 g)

Bean	Water (g)	Food energy (calories)	Protein (g)	Fat (g)	Carbohydrate Total (g)	Carbohydrate Fiber (g)	Ash (g)	Calcium (mg)	Phosphorus (mg)	Iron (mg)	Sodium (mg)	Potassium (mg)	Vitamin A (IU)	Thiamine (mg)	Riboflavin (mg)	Niacin (mg)	Ascorbic acid (mg)
Black	11.2	339	22.3	1.5	61.2	4.4	3.8	135	420	7.9	25	1,038	30	.55	.20	2.2	—
Chick-peas	10.7	360	20.5	4.8	61.0	5.0	3.0	150	331	6.9	26	797	50	.31	.15	2.0	—
Lentils	11.1	340	24.7	1.1	60.1	3.9	3.0	79	377	6.8	30	790	60	.37	.22	2.0	—
Lima	10.3	345	20.4	1.6	64.0	4.3	3.7	72	385	7.8	4	1,529	Trace	.48	.17	1.9	—
Mung	10.7	340	24.2	1.3	60.3	4.4	3.5	118	340	7.7	6	1,028	80	.38	.21	2.6	—
Peas, whole	11.7	340	24.1	1.3	60.3	4.9	2.6	64	340	5.1	35	1,005	120	.74	.29	3.0	—
Pinto	8.3	349	22.9	1.2	63.7	4.3	3.9	135	457	6.4	10	984	—	.84	.21	2.2	—
Red	10.4	343	22.5	1.5	61.9	4.2	3.7	110	406	6.9	10	984	20	.51	.21	2.3	—
Soybeans	10.0	403	34.1	17.1	33.5	4.9	4.7	226	554	8.4	5	1,677	80	1.10	.20	2.2	—
White	10.9	340	22.3	1.6	61.3	4.3	3.9	144	425	7.8	19	1,196	0	.65	.22	2.4	—

The soybean, the prince of legumes, is higher in protein and lecithin-rich oil, and lower in carbohydrates than any other dried bean.

Unlike red meat, cheese, and most dairy products, which owe a large percentage of their calories to fat, whole dry soybeans are only 5 percent fat by weight. Nearly all that fat is unsaturated—the kind of fat associated with low cholesterol. The oil in soybeans is also rich in lecithin, which is associated with limiting cholesterol build-up in the circulatory system.

Happily for many, whole dry soybeans—though a tasty and filling carbohydrate food—are not high in calories. A 3½-ounce serving, providing a noteworthy 11 grams of protein, has only 130 calories. Soybeans also contain a good dose of fiber—a substance sadly lacking in many of the highly refined foods Americans eat today. Studies have shown high-fiber diets to be positively correlated with a low incidence of some types of cancer and other so-called modern-day diseases.

Though they've had a low profile for years, soybeans have been in this country since the early nineteenth century—a fairly recent discovery when you consider that the Chinese have known about them since about the ninth century A.D. For many years we grew soybeans as a rotation crop or for foraging. Today we are the world's number one exporter of soybeans. We export thousands of tons of soybeans annually and process most of those we keep for the oil.

Though you are probably most familiar with the light cream-colored soybean, there are many varieties ranging in colors from beige to gray, brown, and black. Black soybeans are the ones used in making fermented black beans often used in Chinese cooking.

Buying and Storing Soybeans

Natural foods stores have long been a reliable source for soybeans, but the increasing popularity of soybeans makes it easier to find them in regular supermarkets. In general, it is cheaper to buy soybeans in bulk when possible. They keep fairly well when stored properly, so it is worth buying large quantities to keep for up to a year. If you buy them pre-packaged, make sure you can examine the product you are buying. Good soybeans should have a smooth, creamy tan surface. They should be uniform in size, as mixed sizes result in uneven cooking. Seed coats should be clean and smooth without cracks or wrinkles. Visible defects such as shriveled seed coats, too much foreign material, and signs of insect damage indicate low quality.

Store soybeans—as you should all dried beans—in a sealed container well-protected from moisture and insects. If you store them in

153

a canister, seal them tightly in a plastic bag first, and keep in a cool dry place. Sealed in airtight plastic containers or jars in the refrigerator or freezer is an even better way to store soybeans.

Rehydrating and Cooking Soybeans

As a dried food, soybeans must be rehydrated before you cook them. Rehydration takes several hours if you use the preferred long method below, but remember, the beans do this on their own time. You simply place them in the water and do other things while they soak. If you prefer the quicker method, you can greatly reduce rehydration time.

It is not uncommon for little stones or other debris to stay with dried beans and grains after initial cleaning. Therefore, it is a good idea to sort through the beans before cooking them to remove this foreign material. An easy way to do this is to spread the beans out on a clean dishcloth, or in a wide shallow pan. Also look for and remove any cracked, shriveled, or otherwise deformed beans. Rinse the sorted beans under cold running water to remove any surface dust, and drain them in a colander.

Then place the dry beans to soak in cold water that is three to four times their volume. You can place the beans directly in the pot in which you will cook them or in a large bowl. The beans should soak for at least 6 to 8 hours to fully expand in the water. A good time to soak them is overnight. It is best to refrigerate the soaking beans, otherwise they may sour in the water and produce an off-taste.

When the beans have fully rehydrated, they will have absorbed most of the soaking water. If they have absorbed all the water, add enough fresh water to cover the beans by about ½ inch. The beans are now ready to be cooked.

If you are concerned about the flatulence that sometimes occurs after eating beans, you can drain the beans of any remaining soaking water, rinse them well, and add fresh water to cover them for cooking. If time permits change the beans' water two or three times during their soaking period. The more you change the water, the more you lessen the presence of the oligosaccharides—the culprits of flatulence. (Sprouting soybeans is another way to lessen their presence, see Soy Sprouts, page 182). Some water-soluble vitamins are lost with each rinse, but you can compensate for the loss by adding nutritious ingredients later.

To cook soybeans, cover the pot, and allow them to a simmer over low heat. There is no need to stir soybeans during the cooking. You may check them occasionally to make sure they have not absorbed all the water. If they have, add hot tap water just to cover them again.

For the best results in flavor and texture, soybeans should be cooked slowly and fully. It will take about 3 hours over low heat to cook them properly. This time may vary slightly depending on where the soybeans were grown, their age, and the hardness of the water in which they are cooked. So it is best to taste a few soybeans to see if they are done after about 2½ hours of cooking. When fully cooked, soybeans will be firm but tender; their texture will be buttery smooth and their taste nutty and sweet—something akin to that of sweet potatoes.

Stirring during cooking is not necessary. You need only be sure the soybeans have not absorbed all the cooking water before they are done. If you notice the soybeans' skins bursting as they cook, the heat is probably too high.

You can add baking soda to the cooking water if you wish to hasten the beans' cooking time. The soda helps soften the beans, and reduces cooking time by as much as half, depending on how old the beans are. However, you should know that baking soda destroys some of the B vitamins. Also, the beans will be smaller in size, and their color slightly darker. A slight flavor difference is barely noticeable, especially if the beans are mixed with other ingredients. To use baking soda in cooking soybeans, add ½ teaspoon for every pound of beans to the water at the beginning of the cooking period.

TIMESAVING SOAKING METHOD

If time is limited you can shorten the soybeans' soaking time with this method. Boil the amount of water you would normally use to soak the beans. Drop in the beans slowly so as not to interrupt the boil. Let the beans boil, uncovered, for 2 minutes, then remove the pot from the heat, and let the beans set for an hour or more before proceeding with cooking as above. The boiling ruptures the hard shells of the beans so they swell more quickly. It is not known whether the overnight soaking preserves more nutrients, however, we prefer it, if only for reasons of aesthetics. The slowly swollen beans are more appealing.

PRESSURE-COOKER METHOD

You can greatly reduce the cooking time of soybeans by using a pressure cooker. Total time for this preparation method is only 55 minutes, and the beans have a wonderful texture and delicious flavor. When soybeans are cooked using this method, the foam does not clog the vent.

First, sort and wash 1 cup of dry soybeans. Parcook the beans by placing them in a 6-quart pressure cooker with 2 cups of cold tap water. Close the lid securely. Place pressure regulator over vent pipe. Bring the pressure cooker up to 15 pounds pressure. When the rocking motion of the pressure regulator begins, remove cooker from heat and wait until the pressure drops. When you are sure it has dropped, remove the lid and drain the beans.

Place drained beans in a stainless steel bowl that fits loosely inside the pressure cooker. The rim of the bowl should not be more than 3 inches below the top edge of the pressure cooker when placed on the rack in the cooker. Add 1 cup cold tap water to the drained beans. Be sure that beans do not fill bowl more than two-thirds full. Cover bowl tightly with foil. Place 2 cups water and a rack inside the pressure cooker. Top with covered bowl. Close lid securely. Place pressure regulator over vent pipe. Bring up to 15 pounds pressure and cook for 15 minutes. Time the cooking from the point that the regulator begins rocking. Remove cooker from heat and let pressure drop of its own accord.

Drain beans by removing them from the bowl with a slotted spoon or empty them into a colander.

Storing Cooked Soybeans

If you do not intend to serve cooked soybeans immediately, drain, and store them in well-sealed plastic or glass containers in the refrigerator or freezer. You can store them in the refrigerator for about 4 to 5 days. If you intend to use them in salads add a little vinegar—about one teaspoon per cup—to keep them from souring. In the freezer cooked soybeans will keep well indefinitely. Thaw them in the refrigerator or at room temperature.

If cooked soybeans begin to sour you can freshen them the same way you do souring tofu. Drop soybeans gently into enough boiling water to cover them, remove the pot from the heat, and allow beans to remain in the water for 15 minutes. Drain and use.

Main Dishes

Baked Soybean Purée with Pepper Strips

This is rich, savory, and satisfying. Serve as a main course with a salad.

Soak soybeans according to preferred method (see Rehydrating and Cooking Soybeans, page 154).

Drain and simmer soaked beans, onion, garlic, and bay leaves in water and oil until beans are almost tender, about 1 hour. Remove bay leaves and add soy sauce.

Process mixture in a blender or food processor until almost puréed. The mixture should be thick but pourable.

Melt butter in an 8-inch square casserole in the oven while it preheats to 350°F. Stir the bean purée and the pepper into the butter.

Bake mixture until the beans are slightly browned around the edges, about 1 hour. Top with cheese and bake until cheese is melted, about 10 minutes.

6 servings

¾ cup dry soybeans
1 large onion, coarsely chopped
3 cloves garlic, chopped
2 bay leaves
2½ cups water
1 tablespoon peanut oil
2 teaspoons soy sauce
¼ cup butter
1 fresh chili, seeded and cut into 1-inch long julienne strips
1½ cups shredded muenster cheese

Barbequed Pork and Beans

These beans are sweet and perfect for picnics. They are excellent reheated. Freeze any leftover beans in smaller serving-size portions.

In a large skillet brown pork in hot oil. Drain and place pork in a 3-quart casserole.

Add soybeans, onion, tomato juice, catsup, molasses, honey, mustard, and pepper. Mix together thoroughly.

Bake, covered, at 350°F for 1 hour. Uncover and bake about 1½ hours longer, stirring occasionally, until pork is tender and sauce is thickened.

16 to 20 servings

1½ pounds boneless pork, cut into bite-size pieces
2 tablespoons vegetable oil
7 cups cooked soybeans (1 pound or 2½ cups, uncooked)
1 medium-size onion, chopped
1 cup tomato juice
1¼ cup catsup
⅓ cup Barbados molasses
½ cup honey
1 tablespoon prepared mustard
½ teaspoon black pepper

Bean and Sausage-Filled Enchiladas

The bean and pepper mixture, with or without the sausage and potatoes, makes a fine main course. You can also make this recipe without the sausage and potatoes and serve as a side dish.

BEAN FILLING

½ pound sausage, bulk form or removed from casing

1 large onion, diced

2 green peppers, chopped

1 3- to 4-inch fresh red chili pepper, seeded and finely chopped, or ⅛ teaspoon cayenne

2 tablespoons peanut oil

1½ cups cooked soybeans

2 cloves garlic, minced

1 teaspoon finely chopped fresh marjoram or ½ teaspoon dried marjoram

2 cooked red potatoes, peeled and diced

CHILI SAUCE

2 tablespoons peanut oil

2 tablespoons whole wheat pastry flour

¾ cup Beef Stock (page 243) or water

2 medium-size tomatoes, finely chopped

½ teaspoon ground cumin

1 very small fresh red chili, seeded and finely chopped

1 tablespoon lemon or lime juice

To make the filling: Sauté sausage in a large frying pan, breaking the meat up into small chunks. When thoroughly cooked, drain off fat and transfer meat to a bowl.

In the same pan over medium heat, sauté onion, peppers, and chili in the oil for 5 minutes. Reduce heat to low.

Add soybeans, garlic, and marjoram. Cover and cook until onion is tender, about 10 minutes.

Add sausage and potatoes; heat thoroughly. Cover and keep warm until ready to use.

To make the sauce: Heat oil in a 7-inch saucepan. Cook flour in oil over low heat until flour turns a slightly deeper shade of brown, about 5 minutes. Slowly add stock, stirring constantly, to keep sauce smooth.

Add tomatoes, cumin, and chili. Cover pan if tomatoes are not juicy. Simmer until sauce is the consistency of thick soup. Stir in lemon juice. Set aside but keep sauce warm until ready to use.

To make the enchiladas: Warm a large baking dish in a 200°F oven.

In a skillet just larger than the tortillas, heat about ¼ inch oil until a tortilla dipped in the oil sizzles.

Fry a tortilla briefly on both sides. The tortilla should blister slightly but not get crisp. Drain on a paper towel to remove excess oil.

Dip one surface of tortilla in sauce. Place sauce-side up in baking dish. Spread about ¼ cup of filling over half of the tortilla. Sprinkle lightly with cheese and fold in half.

Repeat with remaining tortillas, lining them up neatly in baking dish. Spoon on a little additional sauce and bake at 350°F for about 10 minutes, or until they are quite hot.

6 servings

ENCHILADAS

12 corn tortillas
vegetable oil, for shallow
   frying
1½ cups shredded
   muenster or Monterey
   Jack cheese

Chili Con Carne

Most commercially made chili powders are a spice blend that contains salt. This chili, a little on the fiery side, includes that spice blend without the salt.

In an 8-quart dutch oven heat oil and sauté onions, peppers, and garlic until onion is translucent. Add beef and stir, breaking into little pieces, until browned.

Add tomatoes, tomato sauce, cumin, oregano, and pepper. Simmer, covered, on low heat for 1 hour, stirring occasionally.

Stir in soybeans and simmer, uncovered, for 30 minutes. Serve hot.

6 to 8 servings

2 tablespoons vegetable oil
2 medium-size onions,
   finely chopped
2 red or green peppers,
   finely chopped
2 cloves garlic, minced
2 pounds ground beef
1 can (28 ounces) crushed,
   peeled tomatoes with
   juice
1 cup tomato sauce
2 teaspoons ground cumin
1 teaspoon dried oregano
1 teaspoon cayenne
   pepper, to taste
3 cups cooked soybeans

1 cup dry soybeans
½ cup large dry lima
  beans
1 tablespoon vegetable oil
1 fresh hot chili pepper,
  split and seeded
1 pound chicken wing
  drumlits*
1 clove garlic, minced
1 large onion, chopped
3 cups Chicken Stock
  (page 243)
1 can (16 ounces) whole,
  peeled tomatoes packed
  in juice (about 1½ cups)
½ teaspoon dried
  marjoram
1½ cups sliced carrot
  (¼-inch thick)
2 cups fresh or frozen
  green beans, cut into
  1½-inch pieces

*Drumlits are the meaty
portion of the wings that
resemble tiny drumsticks.
If your butcher doesn't carry
them, buy about 1½ pounds
of chicken legs.

Hot Bean and Chicken Drumlit Stew

This recipe can be attractively served as a skillet supper if the chicken "drumlits" are arranged around the edge of the pan and the beans and vegetables placed in the middle.

Soak soy and lima beans separately overnight (see Rehydrating and Cooking Soybeans, page 154).

Drain beans.

Heat oil in a large skillet. Add hot pepper and drumlits. Brown chicken well on all sides, remove from pan and reserve. Drain all but 1 tablespoon fat from skillet. Add garlic and onion and sauté until golden. Add soybeans and stock and bring to a boil. Reduce heat, cover and simmer for 1½ hours. Add limas and continue to simmer, covered, for 1 hour more.

Crush tomatoes slightly and add to the pan with their juice, chicken, and marjoram. Turn heat to high and heat until mixture comes to a boil. Reduce heat, cover, and simmer for 15 minutes. Taste to see if stew is spicy-hot enough, and if it is, remove pepper. If not, leave it in.

Stir carrots and green beans into mixture. Cook over high heat until mixture comes to a boil. Reduce heat, cover and simmer another 30 minutes or until beans and carrots are tender. If using frozen green beans, add during last 10 minutes.

6 servings

Macaroni, Beans, and Cheese

The slight crunch of soybeans adds the right textural contrast and the right complementary protein to a standard macaroni and cheese.

Cook the macaroni until just barely tender. Drain and place in a large bowl.

1 cup whole wheat elbow
  macaroni
1 cup cooked soybeans
1 onion, finely chopped

Sauté soybeans, onion, peppers, and chili in 1 tablespoon of the butter for 5 minutes. Add to macaroni.

Cook flour in remaining butter over medium-low heat for 2 minutes. Slowly add soymilk, stirring constantly, to prevent lumps. Bring to a boil. Remove from heat and stir in mustard, tomato, and parsley.

Combine sauce with macaroni and 1½ cups of the cheese. Pour into a buttered 1½-quart casserole. Top with remaining cheese.

Bake in 375°F oven until bubbly on the top, about 25 to 35 minutes.

This dish reheats well if covered loosely with aluminum foil.

4 servings

¼ cup chopped sweet red peppers
2 teaspoons finely chopped fresh red chili or dash of hot pepper sauce
3 tablespoons butter
2 tablespoons whole wheat pastry flour
1 cup soymilk
1 teaspoon dry mustard
1 tomato, chopped
1 tablespoon minced fresh parsley
2 cups shredded cheddar cheese

Peppers Stuffed with Corn, Beans, and Cheese

Cut tops from peppers. Chop tops, discarding stems. Reserve. Pull out soft white membranes. Steam peppers until they just begin to soften, about 4 minutes. Remove peppers from heat and drain thoroughly.

In a 2-quart saucepan sauté onion and chopped pepper in butter for 3 minutes. Remove from heat and stir in bread cubes, corn, soybeans, basil, and oregano. Let cool slightly, then stir in eggs, cayenne, cheddar and Parmesan cheeses.

Pack stuffing into peppers, dividing it evenly. Place peppers in a baking dish just large enough to hold them. Pour 1 inch of tomato juice around them.

Bake at 375°F until hot in the center, about 45 minutes.

4 to 6 servings

6 red or green peppers
1 onion, chopped
2 tablespoons butter
1 cup small slightly stale bread cubes
1 cup cooked corn
2 cups cooked soybeans
2 teaspoons finely chopped fresh basil or 1 teaspoon dried basil
½ teaspoon dried oregano
2 eggs, lightly beaten
dash of cayenne pepper
1 cup shredded cheddar cheese
¼ cup grated Parmesan cheese
tomato juice or Beef Stock (page 243)

¾ pound sausage, cut into
1-inch lengths

2 medium-size onions, cut
into thick wedges

2 tablespoons vegetable
oil, for shallow frying

4 carrots, cut into ¼-inch
rounds

1 stalk celery, chopped

2 to 3 cloves garlic, minced

3 tablespoons tomato paste

1 tablespoon soy sauce

1 cup bean cooking liquid
or stock

3 cups cooked soybeans

1 large unpeeled potato,
diced

1 tomato, chopped

½ teaspoon dried
marjoram

1 teaspoon dried sage

Ragoût of Sausage and Beans

A ragout is a French peasant-style stew of morsels of meat or fish and beans.

In a 3-quart saucepan over medium heat, cook sausage and onion in oil until onion becomes slightly limp, about 5 minutes.

Reduce heat and add carrots, celery, and garlic. Stir once and cook for 2 minutes.

Stir tomato paste and soy sauce into bean liquid. Add to sausage mixture along with soybeans, potato, tomato, marjoram, and sage. At this point, the ragoût can be cooked on top of the range or in the oven.

To cook on top of range, cover pan and simmer until carrots and potatoes are tender, 30 to 40 minutes.

To bake, pour ragoût into a 2-quart casserole, cover tightly, and bake at 350°F until potatoes and carrots are tender, about 1¼ hours. Check occasionally while baking, adding liquid if necessary.

Serve hot, perhaps with bread and a salad.

6 servings

Side Dishes

Calico Vegetable Salad

6 tablespoons vegetable oil

2 stalks celery, chopped

1 medium-size onion,
chopped

1 red pepper, chopped

1 large carrot, chopped

2 cups cooked soybeans

4 teaspoons vinegar or
lemon juice

1 teaspoon French-style
mustard

In a large saucepan or skillet heat 2 tablespoons of the oil over medium heat. Add celery, onion, pepper, and carrot, and sauté for about 5 minutes. Add soybeans and remove from heat.

Combine remaining oil, vinegar, mustard, soy sauce, chives, and dill. Beat well with a whisk.

Pour dressing over vegetable-soybean mixture and toss to combine thoroughly. Refrigerate for several hours to allow flavors to mingle. Stir occasionally.

When ready to serve, transfer to serving plate or bowl and garnish with tomatoes and parsley.

6 to 8 servings

2 teaspoons soy sauce
2 teaspoons chopped fresh chives
1 teaspoon chopped fresh dill
Garnish
10 cherry tomatoes
½ cup chopped fresh parsley

Rosemary, Bean, and Pasta Soup

This soup is easy to make. It is based on a standard Italian soup which is a relative of minestrone.

In a 3-quart saucepan over medium heat, sauté onion, rosemary and garlic in oil. When onion wilts, add soybeans, tomato juice, and stock. Simmer, covered, for 20 minutes.

Add pasta and cook until tender, about 7 minutes. Pass cheese to sprinkle on the soup.

4 to 6 servings

1 large onion, diced
2 teaspoons fresh rosemary, coarsely chopped, or ¾ teaspoon dried rosemary, crumbled
2 cloves garlic, minced
3 tablespoons olive oil
1½ cups cooked soybeans
2 cups tomato juice or chopped fresh or canned tomatoes
3 cups Beef Stock (page 243) or water
1 cup uncooked small pasta, such as shells or elbows
grated Parmesan cheese

½ cup peanut oil

½ cup sorghum syrup or
Barbados molasses

2 eggs

¾ cup finely chopped
cooked soybeans

1½ cups whole wheat
flour

1 teaspoon baking soda

1 teaspoon baking powder

1¼ teaspoons ground
cinnamon

¼ teaspoon ground
nutmeg

¼ teaspoon ground ginger

¼ cup buttermilk or
yogurt

½ cup coarsely chopped
raisins

½ cup finely chopped
peanuts

½ cup Toasted Soynuts
(page 173)

Soy-Nut Bread

Beat together oil and sorghum. Beat in eggs alternately with soybeans.

Sift flour with baking soda, baking powder, cinnamon, nutmeg, and ginger. Beat flour mixture into egg mixture alternately with buttermilk. Stir in raisins, peanuts, and soynuts.

Place in a buttered and floured 9 × 5 × 3-inch loaf pan and bake at 325°F for 50 minutes, or until bread tests done.

Cool on wire rack.

Makes 1 loaf

Soy-Raisin Pastry Filling

Use this filling in cookies, sweet breads, or tiny pastries. This versatile filling can also be seasoned with curry powder and stirred into hot rice for a spicy accompaniment to chicken.

Bring soybeans, oil, honey, molasses, and water to a boil. Cover, and reduce to a simmer. Cook, stirring occasionally, for 30 to 45 minutes, or until beans have softened to a nutlike texture. Add raisins. Uncover and cook to reduce liquid to a thick shiny glaze. Cool.

Stir in vanilla and peanut butter.

Yields 1¼ cups

WHOLE DRY
SOYBEANS

1 cup soaked soybeans,
  coarsely chopped*
2 tablespoons vegetable oil
3 tablespoons honey
2 tablespoons molasses
1½ cups water
⅓ cup raisins
1 teaspoon vanilla extract
¼ cup peanut butter

*Soak soybeans in enough water to cover 8 hours or overnight. You can chop the drained soybeans by hand, using a long sharp knife and a cutting board or chop them quickly in a food processor.

Soy-Sesame Relish

Chop the beans coarsely. Stir in onion, tomato paste, sesame seeds, and parsley. Refrigerate for at least 2 hours to let flavors mingle before serving. Serve with crackers.

Yields 1½ cups

1 cup cold cooked
  soybeans
1½ tablespoons chopped
  onion
2 tablespoons tomato paste
¼ cup toasted sesame
  seeds
2 tablespoons chopped
  fresh parsley

2 cups uncooked macaroni,
  such as small shells,
  bowties, or spirals
1 tablespoon vegetable oil
2 teaspoons soy sauce
1 cup cooked soybeans
2 tomatoes, cut into bite-
  size pieces
1 stalk celery, finely
  chopped
1 carrot, very thinly sliced
1 scallion, finely chopped
¾ cup cubed semi-soft
  cheese (mozzarella,
  gouda, port salut, or
  muenster)
1 can (6½ ounces) water-
  packed tuna, drained

Tuna Pasta Salad

This basic salad can be varied easily with different dressings. We recommend Creamy Dill Dressing (page 130) or the Basil Walnut Dressing that follows.

Cook macaroni in boiling water until just tender. Drain in a colander and cool quickly by rinsing with cold water. Shake off extra water.

In a large bowl toss macaroni with oil and soy sauce. Gently stir in soybeans, tomatoes, celery, carrot, scallions, cheese, and tuna. (Be careful not to break up the tuna too much.) Toss with desired dressing. Chill and toss again before serving.

8 servings

Basil Walnut Dressing

6 tablespoons olive oil
2 tablespoons white wine
  vinegar
3 tablespoons finely
  chopped fresh basil
1 clove garlic
black pepper, to taste
3 tablespoons Parmesan or
  Romano cheese
¼ cup finely chopped
  walnuts

Combine oil, vinegar, and basil in a jar. Put garlic through a garlic press, then add to jar. Cover jar and shake well. Pour over salad ingredients and toss to coat evenly with dressing. Sprinkle with pepper, cheese, and walnuts. Toss again.

Yields about ⅓ cup

Snacks

Nutty Maple Popcorn

This treat is a cross between nut brittle and popcorn balls. You will have best results if prepared on a clear day.

Combine honey, maple syrup, and butter in a skillet. Cook over medium heat, stirring constantly, until syrup becomes thick and sticky, about 10 to 15 minutes.

Test syrup for doneness by dipping a cold metal spoon in it. When syrup cools on spoon, it should be hard. If syrup is still soft, cook further.

Pour syrup over popcorn and soynuts, and stir until popcorn is coated. Spread on aluminum foil-covered cookie sheet. Bake at 300°F for about 10 minutes. Cool before removing from aluminum foil.
Yields 6 cups

¼ cup honey
¼ cup maple syrup
¼ cup butter
6 cups popped corn
1 cup Soynuts (page 173)

Pizza Nuts

Toss soynuts in a pan with olive oil. Add remaining ingredients and toss. Bake at 375°F for about 10 minutes until sizzling hot. Cool completely before storing in a sealed jar or container.
Yields 3 cups

3 cups Soynuts (page 173)
1 tablespoon olive oil
1 teaspoon dried oregano
1 teaspoon dried basil
pinch of garlic powder
pinch of crushed red pepper
3 tablespoons grated Parmesan cheese

1 cup Soynuts (page 173)
1 cup lightly toasted
    almonds
½ cup lightly toasted
    hazelnuts
¼ cup toasted sunflower
    seeds
2 tablespoons vegetable oil
2 teaspoons soy sauce
½ teaspoon ground cumin
¼ teaspoon cayenne
    pepper
½ teaspoon ground
    turmeric
½ cup raisins

Spicy Nut Mix

Soynuts are very compatible mixed with other nuts, so feel free to adjust this recipe to suit what is on hand, except for peanuts which are too similar to soynuts.

Preheat oven to 375°F.

Combine soynuts, almonds, hazelnuts, and sunflower seeds in a medium-size bowl. Toss with oil and soy sauce to coat completely. Stir in cumin, cayenne, and turmeric. Spread mixture in a jelly roll pan.

Bake, stirring occasionally, until crisp and almost dry, about 15 minutes. Remove from oven, add raisins and cool before storing in a sealed jar or container.

Yields 3 cups

The Soy Shop, Atlanta, Georgia

When Sara and Steve Yurman started making tofu in their Soy Shop in 1979, they had no idea whether their new business would succeed. Like many other beginning soyfoods entrepreneurs, all they knew was that they were doing something they believed in. They hoped it would be profitable.

"We had almost no money at all," Sara remembers. They managed to buy some basic equipment and get started in a church kitchen. Steve made tofu with the improvised equipment at an agonizingly slow rate. Sara stayed home, taking care of the business end and their son Matthew.

As the popularity of tofu and soyfoods spread throughout the country, many changes occurred, and the Soy Shop grew. Steve and Sara moved the business into more suitable quarters, increased the volume of tofu they made, invented new soy products, and hired nine employees. Today the Soy Shop makes tofu as well as tempeh in several flavors, tofu dips, and a sausagelike product from okara. "We develop new products constantly and have come a long way since our rudimentary beginning, but there's still a long way to go," Sara feels.

Sara tells people, who ask if she is getting rich, a simple no. She describes her business as "terrible, draining, fulfilling, and intense."

The Soy Shop, Atlanta, Georgia. Steve and Sara Yurman proudly display a tub of warm tofu cakes fresh off the line.

But she loves it. After 4 years, she is still thrilled by the craft that turns dull-colored soybeans into appetizing cakes of tofu.

Since their uncertain beginning, the Yurmans have covered a great deal of uncharted territory in the business of soy. Future strides in the realm of soyfoods will no doubt be backed by their sense of commitment, satisfaction, and high standards.

"First, we put out quality products. We can be proud of what we do. We make good, firm protein-packed tofu from organically grown soybeans using traditional methods. All our products must meet high standards, or they don't leave the shop," says Steve. "Second, we are usually able to buy the soybeans from a local farmer. That way, we are able to play a small part in keeping a small farmer on his land taking care of the soil. Third, and most importantly, we are providing good protein at a price people can afford."

Fresh Green Soybeans

I had never tasted or seen fresh green soybeans before my work on this cookbook. Then during 1980 and 1981, the Rodale Press Research Center conducted tests on many different varieties of fresh green soybeans. Rodale employees were invited to participate in the sensory analysis—evaluating the beans' aroma, taste, and texture. Sometimes the test monitors slipped in a cupful of fresh peas or fresh limas, easily confusing some of us. To the unfamiliar, fresh green soybeans are very similar to those two vegetables. Despite the sleight of hand I found the little afternoon snacks very enjoyable—even without the desserts, we were rewarded for our hard work.

William Shurtleff and Akiko Aoyagi, who are writing a definitive book on the history of soyfoods, provided my first perspective on fresh green soybeans. For although fresh green soybeans are a rare treat in our Western countries, throughout East Asia they are a common sight growing near rice paddies or wheat fields. The tender young beans are bundled off to the market to be sold still attached to the vine.

Fresh green soybeans are picked as soon as the pod has grown to full size, but before it begins to toughen and dry (becoming whole dry soybeans). Most soybeans in the world today are allowed to dry in order to be eaten as such or processed into various soyfoods. But the Eastern world has long given the fresh green soybean its due attention in the kitchen.

Treatment of this delicate, tasty fresh vegetable is, more often than not, quite basic. In Japan fresh green soybeans, a favorite summertime vegetable, are cooked in the pod, then served chilled as an hors d'oeuvre. Restaurants may serve them piled on small bamboo colanders, lightly seasoned, if at all. Fancier preparations consist of briefly simmering the beans in the pod in a little shoyu and sweetener. In Korea and Thailand fresh soybeans may be savored as an ingredient in rice dishes or boiled in the pod, tied into bundles, and sold as snacks.

Fresh green soybeans are almost always cooked in their pods to facilitate the otherwise difficult task of shelling them. After several minutes of boiling in seasoned or unseasoned water, they are more easily shelled, either by the cook for use in other recipes or by each individual diner who wishes to eat them out-of-hand. Fresh green soybeans may be used in much the same way as fresh lima beans, or other green vegetables. They are prepared just as easily, requiring no soaking or long cooking period as do whole dry soybeans. Their flavor is delicate and sweet, reminiscent of carrots or pistachio nuts, their texture smooth and buttery—unlike the somewhat drier texture of fresh limas. With a flavor and texture that stand on their own merits it is no wonder fresh green soybeans are often enjoyed alone. However, for variety's sake, or to boost the nutritional value of other dishes, they readily combine with many other ingredients. We offer you some very easy, but interesting, uses for the beans here. The Chicken Curry and Salad Niçoise are some favorites. For a real quick but elegant and tasty entrée, try the Fettuccine and Fresh Green Soybeans.

Like whole dry soybeans, fresh ones add a hefty dose of protein —somewhat lower than the dry bean—but remarkably high for a fresh green vegetable. Like dry soybeans, fresh soybeans have about half the carbohydrates of other beans. Unlike the dry soybeans, fresh beans are an outstanding source of vitamin A.

The only problem in using fresh soybeans is that they are not readily available commercially in this country. Several decades ago supermarkets did stock their shelves with canned fresh green soybeans. However, canners labelled them immature soybeans, an unfortunate word choice that probably put off consumers who did not wish to pay for anything immature.

If you grow your own soybeans (as many home gardeners find easy enough to do), harvest the fresh green soybeans when the pods are plump and green and before the leaves turn yellow. If you cannot grow your own, you can easily mail order fresh green soybeans from any of several mail order sources (see Mail Order, page 247).

Although fresh green soybeans offer a basic eating pleasure with easy cooking and preparation, you will no doubt find scores of ways to be as creative with them as you are with the dried beans.

Soups, stews, salads, casseroles, pasta and grain dishes are all welcome hosts for them. Substitute fresh green soybeans for any green vegetable or bean in your favorite recipes and you not only have a pleasant taste variation, but a good dose of extra nutrition.

Preparing Fresh Green Soybeans

To shell fresh green soybeans: Cover the pods with boiling water and allow them to soak for about 5 minutes. Drain and rinse them with cold water. The pods can be snapped open easily lengthwise with your fingers.

To eat fresh green soybeans alone: Boil or steam the shelled beans for 15 to 20 minutes, or until tender but not mushy. You needn't pre-cook them if you intend to mix them into a recipe where they will be cooked.

You can completely eliminate the shelling step if you wish to serve fresh green soybeans in the pod. Drop the pods gently into enough boiling water to cover them. Cover the pot and cook them for 30 minutes, then drain and rinse under cold water. Allow the pods to cool to room temperature, or chill them in the refrigerator and serve as an appetizer or snack.

Storing Fresh Green Soybeans

Before storing fresh green soybeans, it is wise to first blanch them in the pods as described above. The 5-minute soaking in the boiled water will greatly improve their keeping quality. Shell them and refrigerate in tightly sealed containers for up to a week. You may freeze fresh soybeans for up to one year. Seal them tightly in freezer containers and label.

Drying Fresh Green Soybeans

Drying fresh green soybeans turns them into a delicious crunchy, nutty snack—similar in taste and appearance to shelled pistachio nuts. You can dry them in a food dryer following the manufacturer's directions or in a slow oven at 175°F for 8 to 10 hours. When completely dried the beans will be hard and crunchy, no longer soft or pliable. Store them in a jar or plastic bag in the kitchen cupboard.

Main and Side Dishes

Bread and Butter Bean Medley

We give two methods for making this pickle. If you wish to keep this pickle for a long time use the canning method.

REFRIGERATED PICKLE

Steam soybeans for 15 to 20 minutes, or until tender. Toss together soybeans, carrots, cauliflower, pepper, and onion. Slightly crush each clove of garlic. Put 1 clove garlic and 1 bay leaf in each of 5 pint jars. Fill jars with the vegetable mixture to within 1 inch from top. Sprinkle each with ½ teaspoon of the celery seeds.

Bring vinegar, water, honey, mustard, and turmeric to a boil. Pour over vegetables to ½ inch from top. Seal tightly, cool, and store in refrigerator. Allow flavors to develop at least one week before opening. This pickle must be refrigerated.
Yields 5 pints

PROCESSED PICKLE

Sterilize 5 pint jars. Steam beans for 5 minutes. Combine beans, carrots, cauliflower, pepper, and onion. Slightly crush each clove of garlic. Put 1 clove garlic, 1 bay leaf, and ½ teaspoon of celery seed in each of 5 jars. Bring vinegar, water, honey, mustard, and turmeric to a boil in a 4-quart pot. Add vegetables, return to a boil, and boil about 5 minutes. Cover pot to prevent evaporation. Spoon vegetables into jars leaving 1 inch of headspace. Fill with liquid to ½ inch from the top. Seal and process in a boiling water bath for 5 minutes. Store jars in a cool dark place. No need to refrigerate until after opening. Chill to serve.
Yields 4 to 5 pints *

4 cups fresh green
    soybeans
1 carrot, cut into ¼-inch
    slices
2 cups cauliflower
    flowerets
1 red pepper, cut into
    1-inch strips
1 large onion, coarsely
    chopped
5 cloves garlic
5 bay leaves
2½ teaspoons celery seeds
3 cups white vinegar
1½ cups water
¾ cup honey
1½ teaspoons dry mustard
½ teaspoon ground
    turmeric

*Processed variety may yield less because vegetables shrink slightly in cooking.

Cornbread and Bean Stuffing

Especially good for stuffing chicken breasts or pork chops (see suggestion below).

Soak bread in milk.

Lightly toast seeds in a dry skillet for a few seconds. Add butter, onion, and celery. Sauté until celery softens. Stir in parsley, soybeans, basil, marjoram, sage, and pepper. Sauté for another minute. Add this mixture to soaked bread along with eggs and stir well. Especially good for stuffing chicken breasts or pork chops.

Yields 6 cups

Stuffing suggestion: Halve and debone 3 large chicken breasts, leaving skin on. Flatten them by pounding with a mallet. Put some stuffing in the middle of each and roll up, wrapping the skin around tightly. Place seam-side down in a large baking pan, surround with any extra filling and some sliced onions. Sprinkle with about ¼ cup water. Bake, covered, at 375°F for 40 minutes. Uncover and bake about 30 minutes more until golden brown.

4 to 6 servings

FRESH GREEN SOYBEANS

5 cups crumbled cornbread
⅓ to ½ cup milk
2 tablespoons sesame seeds
¼ cup butter, melted
2 medium-size onions, finely chopped
1 stalk celery, finely chopped
1 tablespoon finely chopped fresh parsley
1 cup fresh green soybeans
1 teaspoon dried basil
¼ teaspoon dried marjoram
½ teaspoon dried sage
¼ teaspoon black pepper
2 eggs, slightly beaten

Fettuccine with Green Soybeans

This sauce is especially good if you make your own fresh pasta, but try it on any long noodle.

Steam soybeans until tender, 15 to 20 minutes. Keep beans warm.

Mix cream, butter, cheese, parsley, pepper, and nutmeg together in an ovenproof serving bowl. Place in a warm oven (250°F) about 10 minutes before serving time, just until the butter melts.

Cook fettuccine in plenty of boiling water. (Thin homemade pasta will only take about 4 minutes to cook.) Drain cooked pasta quickly (do not rinse it) and toss it with the sauce. Mix in cooked soybeans and serve.

4 servings

½ to ¾ cup fresh green soybeans
½ cup heavy cream
2 tablespoons butter
¼ cup grated Parmesan cheese
1 tablespoon chopped fresh parsley
¼ teaspoon freshly ground black pepper
freshly grated nutmeg, to taste
¾ pound whole wheat or spinach fettuccine

Fresh Green Soybean and Chicken Curry

3 whole chicken breasts
(about 1½ pounds)
boned and skinned
2 tablespoons vegetable
oil, for shallow frying
1 tablespoon soy sauce
2 tablespoons cornstarch
3 tablespoons water
2 cups yogurt
2 tablespoons butter
1 medium-size onion,
chopped
1 tablespoon minced fresh
ginger root
¼ teaspoon ground
turmeric
½ teaspoon cayenne
pepper
1½ teaspoons ground
cumin
½ teaspoon ground
coriander
2 teaspoons paprika
3 cups fresh green
soybeans
1 cup cashew pieces

This dish has a mild curry flavor, yet it is spicy hot. For a quick and easy dinner prepare the chicken and fresh green soybeans ahead. Then you only have to make the curry sauce and heat the other ingredients.

Cut chicken into bite-size pieces. In a large skillet warm oil and sauté chicken until tender. Transfer chicken to a bowl. Sprinkle with soy sauce and set aside.

In a medium-size bowl stir together cornstarch and water. Stir in yogurt, and set aside.

In the same skillet melt butter and sauté onion and ginger until onion is golden and tender, about 10 minutes. Stir in turmeric, cayenne, cumin, coriander, and paprika. Cook over low heat for 2 minutes.

Slowly add yogurt mixture. Stir until thoroughly mixed. When yogurt mixture is hot, add cooked chicken pieces, soybeans, and cashews. Cover, but stir occasionally, until all ingredients are hot. Serve immediately.

6 servings

Green Soybean and Cabbage Soup

Combine soybeans, cabbage, onion, garlic, water, celery seeds, pepper, and dillweed in a 2-quart saucepan. Bring to a boil. Reduce heat, cover, and simmer for 45 minutes. Set aside to cool slightly.

Purée until smooth in a blender. Transfer to a 4-quart pot and keep warm over low heat. In a small saucepan melt butter and add flour. Cook and stir over low heat for about 2 minutes. Slowly stir in milk and continue to cook on medium-low heat until mixture thickens and begins to bubble. Slowly stir sauce into soybean mixture and then add soy sauce. Bring to a boil and serve.

4 to 6 servings

FRESH GREEN
SOYBEANS

2 cups fresh green
soybeans
2 cups coarsely chopped
cabbage
1 medium-size onion,
coarsely chopped
1 clove garlic, crushed
4 cups water
¼ teaspoon celery seeds
¼ teaspoon black pepper
1 teaspoon fresh dill weed
or ½ teaspoon dried
dillweed
2 tablespoons butter
2 tablespoons whole wheat
flour
1 cup milk
1 tablespoon soy sauce

Green Soybeans with an Herb Butter

A simple herb butter complements the subtle sweet flavor of fresh green soybeans very well. Since the bean's own flavor is so pleasing, go lightly when adding herbs, and use no more than two herbs in combination. Ideally, the herb butter should be made a few hours in advance so that the flavor of the herbs can permeate the butter. Suggested herbs are chervil, dill, thyme, fennel, summer savory, tarragon, or parsley in combination with chives.

With a fork mash herbs and butter together well in a small bowl. Cover and refrigerate for several hours before using.

Steam beans until tender, about 15 to 20 minutes. Toss hot beans with herb butter before serving or pass butter at the table.

4 to 6 servings

1 teaspoon minced fresh
herbs
3 tablespoons butter,
softened
3 cups fresh green
soybeans

TOFU, TEMPEH, & OTHER SOY DELIGHTS

2 large cloves garlic, minced

2 cups sliced mushrooms

2 tablespoons olive oil, for shallow frying

2 cups fresh green soybeans

1 tablespoon dried basil

½ teaspoon dried oregano

pinch of dried tarragon

2 tablespoons wine vinegar

2 cups stewed Italian tomatoes, crushed

½ cup grated Romano cheese

cooked spaghetti or favorite pasta

Italian-Style Green Soybeans

Sauté garlic and mushrooms in oil for 2 minutes. Add soybeans, basil, oregano, tarragon, vinegar, and tomatoes. Cover and simmer for 10 minutes. Remove lid and simmer for 10 minutes more. Stir in half the cheese. Spoon sauce over pasta and sprinkle with remaining cheese.

4 servings

Monastery Bean Soup

2 onions, coarsely chopped

3 small carrots, diced

2 tablespoons butter

2 yellow or red frying peppers or ½ green pepper, chopped

5 cloves garlic, finely chopped

½ teaspoon caraway seeds

6 cups Beef Stock (page 243), pork broth, or water

This garlicky soup is prepared by Bulgarian monks, formerly to feed faithful pilgrims, and now to feed the tourists who come to visit their isolated mountain retreats. The monks are outstandingly vigorous; many are over 100 years old. Thinner than most bean soups, this is served with a splash of a mild rose wine vinegar, although any mild-flavored vinegar can be used. Our Bulgarian friends also add a pat of butter. This soup improves with reheating and can be frozen.

In a 3-quart saucepan sauté onion and carrots in butter. When onion is lightly browned, stir in peppers, garlic, and caraway seeds. Cook 1 minute more.

Add stock to onion mixture. Stir well to deglaze pan. Add soybeans and simmer covered, until beans are tender, about 20 minutes more. Thicken soup a little by crushing some of the beans with a wooden spoon or potato masher. Add tomatoes and soy sauce and cook 5 minutes more.

Sprinkle each serving with parsley and croutons. Pass vinegar at the table.

6 servings

1½ cups fresh green
  soybeans
½ cup canned or fresh
  chopped tomatoes
1 tablespoon soy sauce
2 tablespoons finely
  chopped fresh parsley
½ cup croutons
wine vinegar

Pennsylvania Dutch-Style Bean and Corn Custard

Although similar to a souffle, this custard is much less fragile.

Preheat oven to 400°F.

Steam soybeans until they begin to soften, about 15 minutes. Add corn and steam just until tender, about 5 minutes. Cool slightly.

Put butter in a 9-inch round baking dish. Place baking dish in preheating oven while you mix remaining ingredients.

Put egg yolks in a medium-size bowl. Beat yolks thoroughly. Stir in cream, soy sauce, black pepper, onion, green pepper, and parsley. Stir in soybeans and corn.

Beat egg whites in a bowl until they form soft peaks. Fold these into vegetable mixture. Pour mixture into hot baking dish. Bake for 10 minutes. Reduce heat to 350°F and bake 15 minutes more, or until top is browned and center of custard is just set.

4 servings

NOTE: The eggs need not be separated; the result is different but good. If the eggs are not separated, bake at 375°F for 20 minutes.

1 cup fresh green soybeans
½ cup corn
1 tablespoon butter
4 eggs, separated
½ cup heavy cream
½ teaspoon soy sauce
⅛ teaspoon fresh ground
  black pepper or a dash
  of cayenne
¼ cup finely chopped
  onion
3 tablespoons finely
  chopped green pepper
1 tablespoon minced fresh
  parsley or 2 teaspoons
  minced fresh parsley
  and 1 teaspoon minced
  fresh dill

Salad Niçoise

This is a variation of the classic French salad. Feel free to change the proportions to accommodate your garden's supply. Salad Niçoise is excellent for serving as a composed salad. Arrange the ingredients in a low-sided salad bowl in artful groups.

SALAD

¾ cup fresh green
    soybeans
1 can (6-ounces) water-
    packed tuna
1 cucumber, thinly sliced
4 handfuls of bite-size
    lettuce pieces (romaine,
    butter, or loose leaf
    lettuce)
5 very thin slices red
    onion
¼ cup feta cheese chunks
¼ cup croutons
2 hard-cooked eggs, sliced

DRESSING

1 large clove garlic
1 teaspoon minced fresh
    parsley
¼ teaspoon dried oregano
½ teaspoon dried basil
¼ teaspoon dried thyme
½ cup olive oil
¼ teaspoon dry mustard
3 tablespoons lemon juice
1 teaspoon vinegar
½ teaspoon soy sauce
freshly ground pepper

To make the salad: Steam soybeans until tender, about 20 minutes. Place them in the refrigerator to chill. Arrange beans, tuna, cucumber, and lettuce in a large salad bowl. Top with sliced onion, cheese, croutons, and egg.

To make the dressing: Chop garlic and herbs together until they are pasty. Transfer to a small bowl. Pour in a bit of the olive oil and the dry mustard and mix well. Add the rest of the olive oil, lemon juice, vinegar, and soy sauce. Whisk together well.

Just before serving, pour dressing over salad and toss gently until all ingredients are coated. Grind black pepper over salad and serve.
4 to 6 servings

Sweet-Pungent Stir-Fried Beans

A quick spicy side dish.

Drain pineapple and reserve juice. Dissolve cornstarch in juice and set aside.

Heat oil in a wok. Add onion and garlic and fry for 30 seconds. Add soybeans, ginger, and pepper. Fry for 3 minutes. Stir in pineapple, vinegar, and soy sauce. Then add cornstarch and stir for about 2 minutes more. Serve over cooked rice.

4 servings

FRESH GREEN
SOYBEANS

1 can (16 ounces) unsweetened pineapple chunks
1 tablespoon cornstarch
1 tablespoon sesame oil
1 large onion, halved and sliced lengthwise from top to bottom
1 clove garlic, minced
3 cups fresh green soybeans
¼ teaspoon grated peeled ginger root
⅛ teaspoon black pepper
3 tablespoons rice vinegar
2 teaspoons soy sauce
cooked brown rice

Tortas de Soyas

These patties can be served plain or with a hot chili, tomato, and onion sauce. Leftover cooked vegetables can be used in place of some of the beans.

Steam soybeans until soft, about 25 to 30 minutes.

Purée soybeans, green pepper, onion, garlic, chili powder, tomato paste, cheese, and egg to a smooth paste. A food grinder or processor works best though it can be done in a blender or by hand with a potato masher.

Stir in ¼ cup of the bread crumbs and set mixture, uncovered, in refrigerator for about 10 minutes to firm. Form into 12 2-inch patties. Dredge patties with remaining bread crumbs.

Lightly coat bottom of a heavy skillet with oil. Fry patties over medium heat, turning once, until browned on each side. If the patties won't be served immediately, transfer them to an ovenproof serving dish and reheat them later in the oven.

4 to 6 servings

1¼ cups fresh green soybeans
¼ cup finely chopped pepper
1 tablespoon chopped onion
2 cloves garlic, finely chopped
½ teaspoon chili powder
1 tablespoon tomato paste
¼ cup shredded cheddar cheese
1 egg
1¼ cups fine whole grain bread crumbs
vegetable oil, for shallow frying

Soy Sprouts

You have probably eaten soy sprouts many times if you ever eat in Chinese restaurants. Mung and soy sprouts, crisp and juicy, are the chopped spaghetti look-alikes that are prominent additions to Chinese stir-fry dishes and in the ever-popular eggroll appetizer. What amazes me most about soy sprouts is that though mild-tasting they seem to be essential to the overall goodness of the dishes where they appear. They are a very edible garnish, but you will see they also work well in more demanding roles.

You can grow soy sprouts right in your own kitchen. Unlike the fresh green soybean with its 2- to 3-month growing season, soy sprouts can be harvested in 3 to 4 days. Soy sprouts are fresh produce that can be grown and harvested at any time of year, and added to your diet in many novel ways. The growing sprouts are nearly maintenance-free and are a quick economical way to turn whole dry soybeans into fresh crispy vegetables.

Sprouted soybeans require no soaking or special preparation and just a few minutes cooking—a fraction of the cooking time of dry soybeans. Stir-frying soy sprouts with other ingredients is one popular easy way to enjoy them.

Fresh sprouts lend themselves to a wide variety of uses on your menu. Add them directly to soups, casseroles, or main dishes for a tasty nutritious texture variation. Salads and sprouts have a natural affinity for each other. Combined with a handful of soy sprouts, fresh vegetable salads become more flavorful and visually appealing. Add sprouts to Mexican tacos along with the other salad ingredients, or add a handful of fresh sprouts to meat mixtures for meat loaves, meatballs, and the like. Sautéing sprouts briefly develops their nutty attributes, making them an excellent ingredient in sauces, breads, cakes, cookies, and other sweet baked goods. Substitute coarsely chopped sprouts for the nuts in any cookie (as we have in the Giant Old-Fashioned Cookies) or bread recipes for a nice crunchy product. The complementary protein that soy has to wheat (and other grains) makes soy sprouts a delicious and nutritious element in sauces for pasta. Pasta with Nut Sauce is a delicious variation on a classic. Because soy sprouts are so easy to cook with, you will discover scores of imaginative ways to enrich your meals with sprouts.

Soy sprouts are an excellent resource during times of the year when availability of fresh produce is limited. Sprouts can be even more nutritious than many other fresh vegetables, offering a noteworthy amount of protein, vitamins, and minerals. When you sprout soybeans you unlock a store of nutrients lying dormant. The sprouts are seeds that have begun to germinate. Soaking the seed activates the life forces packed away for its growth. Feeding itself on the embryo-containing starch, the seed can grow for several days without acquiring nutrients from soil, thus increasing its own store of certain nutrients. Sprouting soybeans generates significant increases in vitamin C, thiamine, and iron. The vitamin C in sprouts continues to increase even while the sprouts are in storage.

The calorie-conscious will find a special appeal in sprouts. Because the growing sprout uses up the starch in the seed, sprouts are very low in carbohydrates. One cup of soy sprouts has only 65 calories.

You can find soy sprouts in some supermarkets and more often in natural foods stores. They should look crisp and firm, not bruised or broken, and they should smell sweet. Sprouting is so easy you may find it more rewarding to grow your own.

How Much to Sprout

The first thing to know about sprouting soybeans is that their original volume will expand by about five times when fully sprouted. Therefore, one cup of soybeans, which will grow into about five cups of sprouts, is a sensible amount to sprout at one time. This way you can use the sprouts at their peak freshness, rather than storing them too long.

Sprouting Equipment

Sprouting equipment is quite basic and usually available commercially in supermarkets or natural foods stores. However, you will very likely have suitable sprouting equipment right in your home, and not need to purchase anything except the soybeans. The whole dry soybeans that you purchase from the supermarket for cooking are fine for sprouting. Do not attempt to sprout soybeans from farm seed dealers intended for use in gardening—they may be treated with insecticides.

To sprout you can use a jar, a plastic colander, or similar container. The most important thing the container should provide is a means of drainage, as you will need to rinse the beans during sprouting. Another consideration for the sprouting receptacle is depth. The experts say that deep containers are better than shallow ones for sprouting. The sprouts grown in deeper containers seem to be the most tender. I have found the sprouting jars available in natural foods stores to be very effective for the amount of sprouts I need. Whatever container you choose to use, avoid those made of wood or metal. Wood absorbs moisture and may grow mold or mildew, and metal may give sprouts a bad taste.

If you use a jar to sprout, you can cover it with a piece of cheesecloth fastened with a rubber band. If you use a colander for sprouting, you will need to soak the beans in a bowl first. You can cover the colander lightly with cheesecloth, a dish cloth, or a plate to protect the sprouting beans from dust and other airborne debris. It is best to set the colander with the growing sprouts on a dish lined with paper towel to absorb any excess moisture.

How to Sprout

Measure out about 1 cup whole dry soybeans. After measuring the beans, wash them thoroughly, removing any chaff or broken or cracked beans. To begin the sprouting process soak the beans in the sprouting jar (quart-size), or in a bowl if using a colander, with enough water to cover them over by at least three inches. Refrigerate the soaking beans overnight or for about eight hours.

Drain the soaked beans well. Rinse and transfer them to their sprouting container if not using a jar or sprouter. Rinse the soaked beans in a strainer or colander or in the jar, straining the water through a cheesecloth. If using a jar stretch the cheesecloth over the

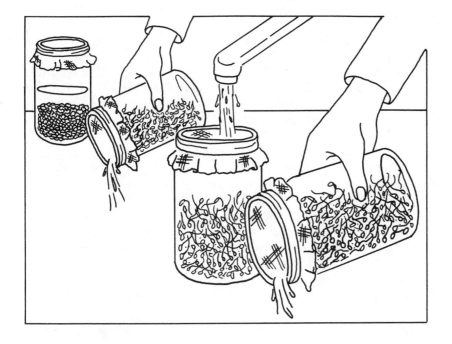

top and secure with a rubber band. Place the container of sprouting beans in an upright position in a dark warm place—under the sink, in the oven, or in a deep drawer.

The sprouting beans should be rinsed at least twice a day, but they will thrive well on more rinsings. The rinsing provides them with water and washes away any by-products of growth that encourage spoilage.

When rinsing the sprouts agitate them as little as possible to avoid having tough sprouts. Too much agitation—like too much exposure to light—tends to toughen the sprouts.

To rinse sprouts in a jar simply run the water through the cheesecloth filling the jar with water. Turn the jar over, cheesecloth-side down and allow the water to drain out thoroughly. Do not shake the water out. If sprouting in a colander, simply uncover it, run the water gently over the sprouts, and allow them to drain well.

The sprouts can be harvested in 3 to 5 days, depending on the air temperature where they are sprouted. The colder the air, the longer they will take to sprout. Full-grown soy sprouts should be about 2½ to 3 inches long. Allowing sprouts to grow too long will make them tough.

TIPS ON USING AND STORING SPROUTS

- If soy sprouts are to be served in dishes where no cooking is involved such as in cold salads, they should be blanched first. Place the sprouts in a steamer, and steam them over boiling water for 30 seconds. Chill them by running cold water over them.
- If the sprouts' hulls (or skins) become loose or seem an unappetizing color, they may be removed. Place the sprouts in a large bowl, and run cold water over them while rubbing the sprouts gently with your hands. The hulls will float to the top, and can be poured off with the water. Refill the bowl with water and let the sprouts settle for a minute. Pour off the loose hulls again. Drain the sprouts well, using a salad spinner if necessary to dry them well.
- If you find you have sprouted more beans than you can use or store, dry them for longer and more convenient storage. Spread the sprouts thinly on a baking sheet and place them in a 250°F oven for about 45 to 60 minutes, or until they are almost thoroughly dried and the tails are very brown. Turn the oven to off, but leave the sprouts in until thoroughly dried. When dried the sprouts will have a pleasant baked potato-like flavor and can be eaten as a snack. Or you can store them in a jar in the cupboard. Make sure sprouts are thoroughly dry or they will give way to mold growth in a short time. Use dried sprouts to replace the nuts or enhance the nutrition in baked goods and in other recipes.

Storing Sprouts

Sprouts are most tasty and crisp when they are first harvested. Store those that are not used immediately after harvesting in the refrigerator. Place them loosely in a covered plastic or glass container with a folded paper towel on the bottom of the container to absorb any remaining moisture. Do not use plastic bags for soy sprouts as tender shoots are easily crushed or broken in non-rigid containers, and bruised sprouts will quickly spoil. Store sprouts for up to ten days in the coldest part of the refrigerator. Never freeze sprouts—the shoots become soggy and limp when defrosted. For longer storage, blanch the sprouts for 30 to 60 seconds in boiling water. Dry well before refrigerating.

Main and Side Dishes

Chinese Chicken and Sprouts in Hot Pepper Oil

Serve this over hot rice. Preparing hot pepper oil may briefly irritate the cook's throat so turn the exhaust fan on high or open windows.

Cut chicken into ¾-inch cubes. Place chicken in bowl; sprinkle with 1 tablespoon of the soy sauce, ½ teaspoon of the cornstarch and ¼ teaspoon of the ginger. Stir. Cover and refrigerate for 1 hour.

Remove as many hulls as possible from sprouts (see page 186) and spread sprouts on a towel to dry.

Make a seasoning sauce by mixing remaining cornstarch with remaining soy sauce, vinegar, stock, and honey.

In a wok heat oil to about 360°F, or until a scallion slice spins about on oil. Fry chicken, a few pieces at a time, for 30 seconds. Drain on paper towels. Fry sprouts in 2 batches until lightly browned. Remove from oil, and drain on paper towels. Drain all but 2 tablespoons oil from wok.

Heat oil over medium-high heat. Fry pepper pods until dark brown but not burnt. Remove pods.

Add garlic, onion, and remaining ginger; stir 1 minute. Add chicken, and stir 1 minute. Pour in seasoning sauce. Reduce heat, and stir until mixture thickens. Add sprouts, and heat through. Drizzle with sesame oil and serve.

4 servings

1½ pounds chicken breasts, skinned and boned
2 tablespoons soy sauce
1½ teaspoons cornstarch
1½ teaspoons finely chopped fresh ginger root
1 cup soy sprouts
1 tablespoon red wine vinegar
¼ cup Chicken Stock (page 243) or Vegetable Stock (page 244)
1 teaspoon honey
peanut or other vegetable oil, for deep frying
2 or 3 small dried hot pepper pods, stem and seeds removed
2 cloves garlic, minced
1 small onion, diced
1 teaspoon Chinese sesame oil*

*Available in Oriental food shops.

Indonesian Sprout Fritters

Serve these as an appetizer or as a side dish.

1 clove garlic, coarsely
chopped
⅔ cup brown rice flour
¼ teaspoon ground
coriander
1 teaspoon curry powder
dash of cayenne pepper
¼ teaspoon baking soda
⅓ cup water
1 egg, beaten
1 cup soy sprouts
peanut or other vegetable
oil, for shallow frying
Dipping Sauce (recipe
below)

Using a pestle or a wooden spoon, crush garlic in the bottom of a medium-size bowl. Add flour, coriander, curry powder, cayenne, and baking soda. Blend thoroughly with a wire whisk. Stir in water and egg, making sure to scrape garlic from bottom. Fold in the sprouts.

Heat oil in a wok or skillet to 365°F, or until a scallion slice spins about on the oil.

Fry 3 or 4 fritters at a time, using about 1 heaping tablespoonful of batter for each. Regulate oil temperature so that fritter browns in 2 to 3 minutes. Turn fritters with tongs to brown other side. Drain on paper towels. Keep warm in oven while frying remaining fritters.

Serve with Dipping Sauce.

4 servings

DIPPING SAUCE

2 tablespoons soy sauce
3 tablespoons Chicken
Stock (page 243) or
water
2 teaspoons honey
⅛ teaspoon ground ginger
1 teaspoon chopped fresh
chives

Combine soy sauce, stock, honey, and ginger. Stir to dissolve honey. Serve in a shallow bowl topped with chives.

Yields ⅓ cup

Pasta with "Nut" Sauce

Sauces made with walnuts, butter or oil, and herbs are favored highly by Italians. This sauce is adapted to use soy sprouts.

Cook fettuccine in boiling water until tender.

Meanwhile, in a covered saucepan simmer rosemary, garlic, onion, and sprouts in olive oil. When onion is tender, but not brown, remove and discard garlic. Add tomatoes, but cook only enough to heat them.

Drain pasta. Toss pasta with butter in serving bowl. Top with sauce and pepper. Pass cheese at the table.

4 servings

¾ pound long flat egg noodles, such as fettuccine
1 tablespoon chopped fresh rosemary, or 1 teaspoon dried rosemary
2 cloves garlic, split in half lengthwise
1 onion, finely chopped
1¼ cups soy sprouts, coarsely chopped
2 tablespoons olive oil
2 firm ripe tomatoes, cut into ½-inch pieces
2 tablespoons butter
freshly ground black pepper, to taste
½ cup grated Parmesan cheese

Pineapple, Sprout, and Rice Salad

Toss together rice, sprouts, scallions, celery, carrots, pineapple, apple, and lemon juice. Stir in mayonnaise and sour cream until all ingredients are well blended. Chill and serve on a bed of greens. Garnish with carrot curls or shredded carrot, if desired.

4 to 6 servings

2 cups cooked brown rice
1 cup blanched soy sprouts
2 tablespoons finely chopped scallions
½ cup thinly sliced celery
½ cup shredded carrots
1 cup crushed pineapple, drained
½ cup chopped apple
2 tablespoons lemon juice
½ cup mayonnaise
¼ cup sour cream

Sautéed Apples, Cabbage, and Sprouts With Noodles

1 large onion, thinly sliced
4 cups shredded sweet or
  pungent cabbage
1½ cups mung or soy
  sprouts, or walnuts
¼ cup butter
2 medium-size apples,
  sliced into ½-inch ×
  2-inch pieces
½ cup raisins
1 cup cooked noodles
ground cinnamon, to taste

The combination of apples and cabbage appears in regional cuisines wherever the two are grown, in varying degrees of sweet and sour. This is a flavorful accompaniment to chicken or pork.

Sauté onion, cabbage, and sprouts in butter in a skillet for 5 minutes over medium-high heat. Add apples and raisins, and continue to sauté until apples are tender, about 10 minutes.

Stir in noodles and a sprinkle of cinnamon. Cook until heated through, about 2 minutes. Serve hot.

4 servings

Shrimp Egg Roll

3 dried shiitake
  mushrooms*
½ cup lukewarm water
1 pound celery cabbage or
  pungent cabbage
2 tablespoons vegetable oil
½ pound uncooked
  shrimp, shelled and
  deveined
8 fresh mushrooms, thinly
  sliced
1 cup mung or soy sprouts
½ cup chopped scallions,
  including tender green
  tops
2 cloves garlic, minced

*Available in Oriental food stores.

Varying the fillings for egg rolls is easy. The only rule is that the filling must be very dry and cooled to room temperature. Have three cups of filling for 12 fat egg rolls. For a poor man's egg roll substitute partially cooked carrots and/or tofu for the shrimp.

Soak shiitake mushrooms in the lukewarm water for 30 minutes. Remove mushrooms, reserve the flavorful water for soup, discard hard stems, and cut mushrooms into ½-inch pieces. Reserve.

Remove the tough cabbage stalks from the leaves. Cut the stalks across the fibers at a slight angle, into thin slices. Chop the leaves into ½-inch squares (keep separate from stalks).

Place wok over high heat, add 1 tablespoon oil. When hot, stir-fry shrimp for about 2 minutes, or until opaque. Remove from wok. Cool slightly. Chop shrimp into small pieces.

Add remaining tablespoon of oil to wok. When hot, add cabbage stalks and fresh mushrooms. Stir-fry 1 minute, then, stirring constantly, add shiitake mushrooms, sprouts, scallions, garlic, and ginger.

Add cabbage leaves; stir until completely wilted. Cook until liquid is absorbed without overcooking. Drain mixture in colander if necessary. Add shrimp and soy sauce. Cool completely.

Make a paste to seal the loose ends of the egg rolls by mixing flour with 2 tablespoons water.

Place 6 egg roll skins on a counter. Fill according to diagram, using ¼ cup filling for each. Fold egg roll, sealing edge with flour paste. Repeat with remaining skins.

Preheat oven to 300°F. Place an 8 × 13 × 2-inch baking dish in oven. Put enough oil in a clean wok so that 2 egg rolls can be shallow-fried at one time. Heat oil until a scallion slice spins about on oil. Fry egg rolls, 2 at a time, turning with tongs to brown both sides. Drain on paper towels, and transfer fried egg rolls to dish in oven.

Bake egg rolls at least 10 minutes before serving. Serve hot with soy sauce for dipping, if desired.

Makes 12 egg rolls

1 teaspoon minced fresh ginger root
2 teaspoons soy sauce
1 tablespoon whole wheat flour
2 tablespoons water
12 large egg roll skins
vegetable oil, for shallow frying

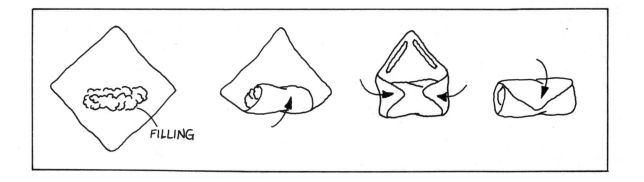

FILLING

Sprouted Meatballs with Mushroom Sauce

These can be served with toothpicks as an appetizer, or with the mushroom sauce. With the sauce the meatballs can also be served over rice or noodles.

MEATBALLS

1 cup soy sprouts, finely chopped
1 medium-size onion, finely chopped
1 stalk celery, finely chopped
2 cloves garlic, minced
2 tablespoons vegetable oil
2 cups crumbled whole grain bread
2 tablespoons water
1 pound ground pork
¼ teaspoon black pepper
2 eggs

To make the meatballs: Sauté sprouts, onion, celery, and garlic in 1 tablespoon of the oil until celery is tender. Moisten bread with water, and combine in a bowl with sauteed vegetables, pork, pepper, and eggs. Mix well and form into 1-inch balls. Brown meatballs in remaining oil. Drain off excess fat. Reserve.

SAUCE

1 large onion, chopped
2 cups chopped mushrooms
2 tablespoons butter
1 tablespoon wine vinegar
3 cups Beef Stock, page 243 or Chicken Stock, page 243
¼ cup cornstarch
2 teaspoons soy sauce
¼ teaspoon black pepper

To make the sauce: Sauté onion and mushrooms in butter for 5 minutes. Add vinegar and 2½ cups of the stock. Bring mixture to a boil. Dissolve cornstarch in remaining stock and stir into boiling liquid. Reduce heat and cook, stirring constantly, until mixture thickens and begins to bubble. Add soy sauce, black pepper, and meatballs. Cover and simmer for 10 minutes.
Makes about 30 1-inch meatballs

Herb or Curry Sprout Sauce for Vegetables

Use this easy sauce to add crunchy texture and a nutty flavor to soft vegetables, such as zucchini, cauliflower, or green beans.

Five minutes before serving time, sauté sprouts in butter until butter browns slightly. Add herbs; cook 1 minute more, and serve over hot cooked vegetables.

Yields 1 cup

½ cup coarsely chopped soy sprouts
½ cup butter
2 teaspoons chopped fresh herbs, such as chives, basil, and parsley, or ½ teaspoon curry powder

Mustard Bean Sprouts

This relish tastes best refrigerated overnight before serving.

Dissolve mustard and turmeric in 2 tablespoons of the water in a saucepan. Add onion, vinegar, and honey and bring mixture to a boil.

Dissolve cornstarch in remaining water and combine with egg. Stir about 3 tablespoons of the hot liquid into the egg. Reduce heat, and slowly stir egg mixture back into liquid. Cook, stirring constantly, until mixture thickens and begins to bubble. Cook 2 minutes more, remove from heat, and add sprouts and beans. Chill overnight before serving. This will keep for 1 month in the refrigerator; however, the sauce becomes thinner.

You can preserve this relish for future use by pouring it into sterile canning jars and sealing as for other relishes. Allow to cool, check seals, and store in the refrigerator.

Yields 3 cups

2 teaspoons dry mustard
¼ teaspoon ground turmeric
¼ cup water
1 small onion, chopped
¾ cup cider vinegar
2 tablespoons honey
2 teaspoons cornstarch
1 egg, well beaten
1½ cups soy sprouts
1½ cups 1-inch green bean pieces, steamed just until tender

1 slice day-old whole grain
  bread
½ cup Fish Stock (page
  244) or water
⅓ cup coarsely chopped
  soy sprouts
1 or 2 cloves garlic,
  minced
1 tablespoon olive oil
⅓ cup tahini (sesame
  butter)
2 tablespoons lemon juice
3 tablespoons chopped
  fresh parsley

Tahini Sauce for Baked Fish

*Traditionally this sauce is made with pine nuts. Here soy sprouts replace those
expensive nuts, giving the sauce the same nutty flavor.*

Remove crust from bread and discard. Crumble bread and sprinkle with 2 tablespoons of the fish stock.

Sauté sprouts and garlic in oil until tails begin to turn brown. Reduce heat to low.

Stir in tahini, lemon juice, parsley, and bread. Add enough remaining stock to make sauce with consistency of thick cream. Keep warm but not hot.

Yields about 1 cup

Baked Goods

Giant Old-Fashioned Cookies

1 cup soy sprouts
1 tablespoon corn oil
1¾ cups whole wheat
  pastry flour
½ teaspoon ground
  cinnamon
1 teaspoon baking soda
¼ cup butter, at room
  temperature
¾ cup mild honey
1 egg yolk
1 teaspoon vanilla extract
⅛ teaspoon almond
  extract
½ cup raisins
½ cup unsweetened carob
  chips

Rinse sprouts, remove loose hulls, drain well, and chop coarsely. Sauté sprouts in medium-hot oil until tails brown. Cool.

Butter 2 to 3 heavy steel cookie sheets.

Sift flour, cinnamon, and baking soda into a bowl.

In a second bowl, cream butter. While beating, add honey to butter in a stream. Stir in egg yolk, vanilla and almond extracts. The mixture may curdle slightly.

Stirring only enough to blend, add flour mixture to butter mixture. Fold in sprouts, raisins, and carob chips.

Preheat oven to 350°F.

Drop batter by heaping tablespoonfuls onto cookie sheets, leaving about 4 inches between cookies.

Bake for 14 to 16 minutes, or until center of cookie springs back when touched. If cookies brown unevenly, reverse the cookie sheets. Remove cookies from sheets carefully with a metal spatula since the cookies tend to stick. Cool completely before storing.

Yields 16 large cookies

Tomsun Foods, Greenfield, Massachusetts

The Tomsun Foods soy dairy is a large plant, humid and rife with the sweet pleasant aroma of cooking soybeans. The stainless steel equipment bought from an old dairy farm and a very efficient crew of nine produce 40,000 pounds of fresh tofu weekly. The plant workers divide up the chores of soaking the beans, turning them into soymilk in the 250-gallon cauldrons, making and pressing the curds, cutting up the finished tofu into various-sized blocks and pasteurizing and packaging the tofu.

"Tomsun Foods is a company with its roots deep in the soyfoods movement," explains Tom Timmins, one of its owners. Tom has had the joy of watching a struggling young company grow from its early beginnings as a craft shop employing devoted, muscular, vegetarian laborers, to its next stage as a high-quality, high-volume tofu production facility.

Like many other soyfoods businesses, Tomsun Foods began very modestly in the late seventies when "three young entrepreneurial couples joined forces to start the first tofu shop in New England." Half the group developed the production end of business and the others began developing Americanized tofu recipes. Eventually the business became established as the New England Soy Dairy in Greenfield, Massachusetts, its present location. The New England Soy Dairy experimented with products, such as, sweetened tofu puddings, salads, deep-fried products, a soymilk called Nu Mu, and a salad dressing called Soy Mayo.

Tomsun Foods, Greenfield, Massachusetts. A soy craftsman deftly divides freshly pressed tofu into uniformly sized cakes.

The owners realized educating the consumer was important for the success of their business. So part of the soy dairy's growth strategy included a large scale educational program designed to teach people how to incorporate tofu into their diets. The highly productive New England Soy Dairy became Tomsun Foods in the fall of 1983, a long way from its first days as a small business called Laughing Grasshopper Tofu Shop in Millers Falls. A quality assurance laboratory with trained microbiologists, pull-dating of products, and the pasteurization of tofu help to produce a very high-quality tofu.

Soy Flour and Soy Grits

As a home baker do you like to make quick breads, cupcakes, muffins, and other such goodies with nature's most wholesome ingredients: honey, nutty whole grain flours, sweet creamery butter, nuts, and dried fruit? If you are like me, you prefer the fuller flavors of these slightly richer and heavier baked goods. But if you'd like to lighten your baked goods, yet keep the full flavor, make soy flour your secret ingredient.

Commercial bakers have long recognized the merits of soy flour, adding small amounts of it to their baking mixes for lighter textures, and also to prevent the absorption of fat in deep-fried foods such as doughnuts. As a home baker, I was delighted to discover these qualities of soy flour, too. Just a little soy flour makes my baked goods lighter and fluffier. (Pancakes made with soy flour are so airy they almost float away!) This is especially handy when baking with the various whole grain flours, which tend to make baked goods slightly heavier. Used in small amounts soy flour will hardly affect the overall taste of baked goods. In larger amounts it imparts a sweet mellow flavor.

Flour is in reality a misnomer. This creamy yellow powder—ground from whole dry soybeans—is quite different from the flour ground from wheat and other grains. Soy flour is actually a high-pro-

Nutrients in Soy and Wheat Flours
100 g.

	Calories	Protein (g)	Fat (g)	Carbohydrates (g)	Fiber (g)	Calcium (mg)	Phosphorus (mg)	Iron (mg)	Potassium (mg)	Vitamin A (IU)	Thiamine (B_1) (mg)	Riboflavin (B_2) (mg)	Niacin (mg)	Vitamin C (mg)
Soy Flour (full-fat)	421	36.7	20.3	30.4	2.4	199	558	8.4	1,660	110	.85	.31	2.1	0
Soy Flour (defatted)	326	47.0	.9	38.1	2.3	265	655	11.1	1,820	40	1.09	.34	2.6	0
Whole Wheat Flour	333	13.3	2.0	71.0	2.3	41	372	3.3	370	0	.55	.12	4.3	0

tein concentrate that is almost starch-free. Though its baking qualities differ somewhat from those of wheat flour, soy flour has many benefits when used in the right proportions with wheat flour.

Soy flour lacks gluten, the protein substance in wheat flour responsible for a successful rising; therefore, it cannot totally replace wheat in baking. However, soy flour can replace up to 15 percent of the wheat flour in your favorite yeasted baked goods, for a nutritionally superior product. (Recipes in this book use soy flour in a higher proportion to wheat flour because they have been specially developed to use soy flour.) Soy flour can replace slightly more of the wheat flour in chemically-leavened products, such as quick breads, muffins, biscuits, pancakes, cakes, and cookies, resulting in large, tender-crumbed products.

MAKING SOY FLOUR AT HOME

You can grind your own soybeans into flour if you have a steel-plate grinding mill. A stone-plate mill will not work as well. The high-oil content of the beans can gum up the stone plate. It is possible to grind a small amount of soybeans in a stone mill, if you first mix the beans with an equal amount of wheat.

For richer flavor toast the whole dry soybeans before grinding them. Spread them on a baking sheet, and place in a preheated 375°F oven for 20 minutes, or until the beans are lightly golden. Cool before grinding.

Because it is gluten-free and very low in starch, soy flour is an ideal element in a wheat-free regimen (see Nutrients in Soy and Wheat Flours, page 198). A combination of soy flour and several whole grain flours yields a delicious wheat-free cake. Soy flour is also an excellent ingredient in flat breads such as tortillas and crepes.

The high-fat content in soy flour promotes faster browning in baked goods. Therefore, when substituting soy flour for wheat flour in a recipe, lower the oven temperature by 25°F. In most cases, it is best to use metal instead of glass bakeware (unless a dry, crispy outer crust is desired, as for pies and pastries) since glass contributes to faster browning of the outer crust.

Because it is not starchy, soy flour does not replace wheat flour as a thickening agent for sauces, puddings, and soups, but it can be added to these foods as a nutritional enhancement. We have developed a zesty soy mayonnaise with soy flour, using no eggs or dairy products. You will be happy to know that, since it is simply ground soybeans, soy flour contributes all the protein, vitamins, minerals, and fiber of the whole beans and in a form more readily assimilated by our bodies.

Buying and Storing Soy Flour

Soy flour may be full-fat or whole soy flour, or it may be low-fat or defatted—the oil removed with chemical solvents (which are then steam-removed). The soybeans may also be lightly toasted before they are ground to give the flour a nuttier flavor.

Some confusion may arise when buying soy flour. There is no standard labeling for soy flour (as is required by law for many foods), so it may be difficult to know if you are buying whole or defatted soy flour—they both look alike. The storekeeper may be able to tell you, if he is familiar with the manufacturers he buys from. Fortunately, the differences resulting from using one soy flour instead of the other are insignificant. Whole soy flour (with a fat content of about 22 percent) is preferred over defatted soy flour (with a fat content as low as 6 percent) whenever possible, because it contains more of the overall goodness of the soybeans and because its higher oil content lends more moisture to baked goods so they stay fresh longer.

Though soy flour will keep well at room temperature for several weeks, it is best to store it in the refrigerator or freezer—especially for long-term storage. This will protect the flour from bug infestation and keep it from turning rancid due to its oil content. (Even defatted soy flour at 6 percent fat is significantly higher in oil than whole wheat flour.) Be sure to first wrap the flour securely in several plastic bags, or in an airtight container, so it does not absorb moisture in storage. Stored this way soy flour will keep well for about a year.

LECITHIN IN SOYBEANS

Lecithin, commonly used as a nutritional supplement, occurs naturally in soybeans. It is composed of two B vitamins and oil, and is readily available in natural foods stores in oil and granular form. Liquid lecithin is useful in baking. Mixed half-and-half with vegetable oil, it is perfect for lightly oiling muffin tins, baking pans, and casserole dishes. A thin layer prevents sticking and adds no taste to baked goods. Mix and keep on hand on the pantry shelf.

Soy Grits

Soy grits are very similar to soy flour in origin—both are ground from whole dry soybeans. However, flour refers to a finely ground powder and grits refers to a larger particle size of the mechanically chopped soybeans. Soy grits, like soy flour, may be ground from full-fat whole soybeans. But most often they are ground from defatted soybeans. The smaller particle size of soy grits reduces the cooking time to about half of the cooking time for whole dry soybeans.

Soy grits resemble cracked wheat in appearance and may be used in much the same way as grains—simply boiled as a side dish, in pilaf, puddings, hot or cold salads, casseroles, soups, stews, and meat mixtures. Soy grits are also a nice addition to baked goods, grain dishes, and granola mixtures. Soy grits lend a nutty taste, and a pleasant chewy texture to many dishes.

Unlike other starchier beans and grains, soy grits do not thicken their cooking water. The water, which turns a milky white, may be cooked down or drained off and saved for soup or baking uses. Soy grits foam while cooking and may stick to the pot, so it is best to use a large pot and add a little oil to the cooking water.

Soy granules, another soyfood you may encounter in food stores, are made from hulled precooked soybeans. Although soy granules resemble soy grits in appearance, they cook even more quickly—about 5 minutes. Soy granules may be used in the same way as soy grits.

NOTE: At the risk of confusing you further, I mention a product called soy flakes, resembling rolled wheat or oats in appearance. However, our Test Kitchen sees no special value in soy flakes. Little time is saved using this product in place of the whole soybean.

Soy Flour Recipes

Cranapple Quick Bread

1¼ cup whole wheat flour
¼ cup soy flour
½ teaspoon ground
  allspice
½ teaspoon ground
  cinnamon
2 teaspoons baking
  powder
¼ cup vegetable oil
½ cup honey
2 eggs
½ cup apple juice
½ cup chopped
  cranberries
¼ cup chopped dried
  apples
½ cup chopped nuts

In a large bowl sift together the flours, allspice, cinnamon, and baking powder. Add oil, honey, eggs, and apple juice. Stir together just until mixed. Fold in cranberries, apples, and nuts.

Preheat oven to 350°F.

Put batter into an oiled 8½ × 4½ × 2½-inch or 9 × 5 × 3-inch loaf pan, and bake for 55 to 60 minutes, or until bread tests done. Cover with foil after 40 minutes so that bread will not overbrown. Cool in pan on wire rack 5 minutes. Remove from pan, and cool completely.

Yields 1 loaf

Flour Tortilla

½ cup soy flour, sifted
½ cup water
1¼ to 1½ cups whole
  wheat pastry flour

This traditional Mexican bread is very easy to make and an excellent wrap for many fillings.

Mix soy flour and water together with a wire whisk. Blend in enough of the wheat flour to make a soft dough. Knead dough on a floured surface until smooth. Divide into 8 small balls.

Roll out each ball to a 7-inch circle on a heavily floured surface. Shake off excess flour from tortilla.

Heat a cast-iron skillet over medium-low heat. Lay the tortilla in the pan and bake until very lightly browned, then turn to brown other side. Wipe out any excess flour that collects in skillet, or it will burn and give tortillas an off-flavor. The tortilla should remain soft and flexible for use in burritos, or it can be cooked until crisp for use as a chip.

Makes 8 7-inch tortillas

Golden Almond Shortcake

SOY FLOUR
AND SOY GRITS

Plan to serve this while it is still warm. Unused shortcake can be wrapped in foil and reheated.

In a large bowl combine fruit and honey. Add lemon juice to taste, if using peaches. Set aside.

Butter and flour an 8-inch square baking pan. In a medium-size bowl mix together soy flour, wheat flour, and baking powder.

In a separate bowl mix together egg and honey with a wire whisk. Gradually whisk in milk and vanilla.

Preheat oven to 425°F.

Using a pastry blender, 2 knives, or a food processor, cut butter into flour mixture until small crumbs are formed. Add almonds. Stir liquid ingredients into flour mixture. Work quickly; do not mix more than necessary. Spread batter evenly into prepared baking dish.

Bake 15 minutes, or until lightly browned. Cool slightly.

Cut into serving-size pieces. Split each piece as it is removed from the pan. Spoon a layer of fruit onto bottom half of each piece, and replace top half. Top with more fruit and whipped cream. Serve immediately.

Serves 6 to 8

- 1 quart sliced strawberries or other berries, or 6 cups sliced peaches
- 1 tablespoon lemon juice (if using peaches)
- ½ cup soy flour, sifted
- 1 cup whole wheat pastry flour
- 1½ teaspoons baking powder
- 1 egg
- ¼ cup plus 2 tablespoons honey
- 3 tablespoons milk
- 1 teaspoon vanilla extract
- ½ cup cold butter
- ½ cup coarsely chopped toasted almonds
- 2 cups sweetened whipped cream

½ cup cold butter
¼ cup Barbados molasses
¼ cup honey
1 egg yolk
1 teaspoon vanilla extract
1½ cups whole wheat
    pastry flour
¾ cup soy flour, sifted
1 teaspoon baking powder
¾ cup finely chopped
    pecans
⅓ cup raspberry preserves

Linzer Cookies

Cream butter. Slowly beat in molasses and honey. Beat in egg yolk and vanilla. Continue beating until mixture is light and fluffy; it should look like buttercream frosting.

Mix together the flours and baking powder. Add flour mixture to butter mixture, ½ cup at a time, stirring no more than is necessary to blend mixtures. Fold in pecans.

Divide dough in half. Pat each half into a circle 1 inch thick. Wrap in wax paper and place in freezer or refrigerator until completely chilled, about 1 to 2 hours. It is important to keep the dough chilled or it becomes sticky and hard to manage. While working, keep unused portions of dough and dough scraps refrigerated.

Preheat oven to 350°F.

The cookies will not stick to black steel cookie sheets. Lightly grease other types. Gently roll out the first dough circle on a lightly floured surface to ⅛ inch thickness. Cut with round cookie cutters. Cut a small round hole in the center of half the cookies. Transfer cookies to baking sheets.

Bake for 6 to 10 minutes, or until cookies brown lightly around edges. Cool on wire racks. Repeat with remaining dough.

Knead dough scraps into a ball, flatten and roll out. Cut into diamonds or rectangles and bake. The rerolled cookies have a less delicate texture.

Spread the preserves in a thin layer on the whole cookies and top with the cookies with holes.

Makes 18 to 22 filled cookies

Russian Caraway Bread

SOY FLOUR
AND SOY GRITS

Sift soy flour into a large bowl. Gradually whisk in boiling water. Whisk to combine thoroughly and remove lumps. Stir in caraway seeds, grain beverage, butter, malt syrup, molasses, soy sauce, and vinegar. While this cools, dissolve yeast in warm water.

When the soy mixture has cooled to about 100°F, stir in dissolved yeast and then gradually add 2 cups of the whole wheat flour. Stir until dough is very smooth. Scrape dough down from sides of bowl.

Cover with a damp towel. Let dough rise in a warm place (about 80°F) until doubled in bulk, about 1 hour.

When doubled, sprinkle dough with 1 cup of flour. Scrape underneath dough with a rubber spatula to allow the new flour to fall under it. Knead briefly while still in the bowl; then turn out onto floured surface and knead until dough is smooth and elastic, 8 to 10 minutes. Use remaining flour if needed.

Place dough in an oiled bowl, and flip over to coat surface with oil. Again, cover bowl with a damp towel. Allow dough to rise in a warm place until doubled in bulk, about 1 hour.

Punch down dough, and knead gently into a ball. Let dough rest for 5 minutes. If dough is sticky, flour rolling area lightly. Roll out dough into a 12 × 17-inch rectangle.

Roll up dough, beginning with shorter edge, and crimp to seal the final edge. Place, crimped edge down, on a buttered baking sheet. Set aside to rise until doubled in bulk, about 30 minutes.

Preheat oven to 375°F. When loaf has almost doubled (about 20 minutes), cut 3 ¼-inch deep diagonal slashes across the top with a razor blade or very sharp knife.

Bake until crust begins to brown, about 25 minutes. Then brush with egg white glaze.

Return loaf to oven and bake for 10 to 15 minutes more. When done, bottom of loaf will sound hollow when tapped. Cool on rack before slicing. This bread keeps well.

Makes 1 large loaf

Ingredients

- ¾ cup soy flour
- 1¼ cups boiling water
- 2 teaspoons caraway seeds
- 2 tablespoons grain beverage coffee substitute
- ¼ cup melted butter
- 1 tablespoon malt syrup or honey
- 2 tablespoons Barbados molasses
- 1½ teaspoons soy sauce
- 2 teaspoons vinegar
- 2 teaspoons dry yeast
- ¼ cup warm water
- 3 to 3¼ cups whole wheat flour
- 1 egg white mixed with 1 tablespoon water

Shoo Fly Pie

Soy flour adds a new twist to an old Pennsylvania Dutch favorite.

1 cup Barbados molasses
1 teaspoon vanilla extract
1 teaspoon baking soda
1 cup hot water
2 cups oat flour
1 cup soy flour
1 cup date sugar
2/3 cup butter
2 unbaked Whole Wheat
   Piecrusts (page 242)

In a medium-size bowl, stir together molasses, vanilla, baking soda, and water. Set aside.

In a large bowl sift together the flours. Add date sugar and butter. Use a fork or a pastry blender to cut in butter until crumbs form.

Preheat oven to 375°F.

Pour molasses mixture into prepared pie shells. Top each with the crumbs.

Bake for 45 minutes.

Makes 2 9-inch pies

Soft Cheese Pretzels

1 teaspoon dry yeast
¾ cup warm water
1 teaspoon honey
2 tablespoons vegetable oil
2 teaspoons soy sauce
1 cup soy flour, sifted
1 cup shredded sharp
   cheddar cheese
1½ to 1¾ cups whole
   wheat flour

Dissolve yeast in 2 tablespoons of the water. Add honey, and let stand until bubbly.

Meanwhile, stir together remaining water, oil, and soy sauce. Stir in yeast mixture and soy flour, using a whisk. Stir in cheese.

Work in enough wheat flour to form a soft dough. Knead on a floured board for several minutes until dough is smooth and elastic.

Divide dough into 12 balls. Roll each into 14-inch rope and form into pretzel shape. If you use a floured board, put a little water on places where dough overlaps to make it stick. If you use an unfloured board, the water is not necessary.

Place pretzels on well-greased baking sheets.

Bake in a 350°F oven on the lower-middle rack for 10 minutes. Shift to top middle rack and bake 5 to 10 minutes more until golden brown. These burn very easily because of the cheese so watch them closely. Cool pretzels on a wire rack. Serve warm or cooled.

Makes 12 pretzels

Soy-Banana Nut Bread

Combine the flours, baking powder, and baking soda in a large bowl. Beat together eggs, butter, honey, vanilla, and banana and add all at once to the flour mixture. Mix just until dry ingredients are moistened. Stir in walnuts.

Preheat oven to 350°F.

Pour batter into a buttered and floured 8½ × 4½ × 2½-inch loaf pan.

Bake for 1 hour, or until toothpick comes out clean. Cover with foil if loaf is browning too fast.

Remove from pan and cool on wire rack.

Makes 1 loaf

1½ cups whole wheat flour
½ cup soy flour, sifted
1 teaspoon baking powder
½ teaspoon baking soda
2 eggs, beaten
½ cup butter, melted
½ cup honey
1 teaspoon vanilla extract
1 cup mashed ripe banana
1 cup chopped walnuts

Soy Crepes

These easy-to-make crepes are delicate-flavored and excellent with savory or sweet fillings.

Combine eggs, milk, honey, and butter. Whisk to combine well. Whisk in the flours until smooth. Cover and let stand for at least 1 hour.

Heat a 7- or 8-inch cast-iron skillet over medium-low heat. Lightly oil pan. Bake crepes in skillet, turning once, until browned on both sides. Keep finished crepes warm in a 200°F oven until ready to serve.

Makes 12 to 14 crepes

2 eggs, beaten
1 cup milk
1 teaspoon honey*
2 tablespoons melted butter
¼ cup plus 2 tablespoons whole wheat flour
¼ cup soy flour

*If making a dessert crepe, increase honey to 1 tablespoon.

207

Soy Flour Pie Crust

1 cup soy flour, sifted
¼ cup cold butter
2 to 3 teaspoons cold
 water

Double the ingredients for a double-crust pie. This mild-tasting crust is best with a flavorful filling.

Cut butter into flour with a pastry blender until crumbs are the size of small peas. Sprinkle with water, and toss with a fork until just slightly moistened and crumbs cling together.

Form into a ball and knead briefly. Roll out carefully on a piece of wax paper using more soy flour if necessary. Do not roll too thinly. Crust is delicate and breaks apart easily.

Set greased 8-inch pie plate upside down on top of dough, and holding the wax paper, invert. Remove wax paper, and fit dough into plate.

Crimp crust, and fill and bake as directed. Or bake at 425°F for 8 minutes, or until golden brown. Cover edges with aluminum foil to prevent overbrowning, if necessary.

Makes 1 8-inch piecrust

Soy Mayonnaise

¼ cup soy flour
½ cup water
½ teaspoon paprika
1 teaspoon dry mustard
⅛ teaspoon cayenne
 pepper
1 teaspoon grated onion
1½ to 1¾ cups vegetable
 oil
¼ cup lemon juice or 3
 tablespoons vinegar

This tangy eggless, dairy-free dressing is easiest to make in a food processor, but a blender can be used, scraping the sides frequently with a rubber spatula.

In a food processor or blender combine flour, water, paprika, mustard, cayenne, and onion. Process while slowly adding oil, drop by drop at first, then faster as the mixture begins to thicken. When mixture has reached desired thickness, add lemon juice, 1 tablespoon at a time, and blend well. Chill before serving.

Yields 2½ cups

Walnut Sticky Buns

To make the dough: Soften yeast in warm water. Add a teaspoon of the honey and let stand until bubbly.

Scald soymilk. Stir in butter and remaining honey. Let cool to lukewarm.

Beat eggs in a large bowl, then beat in milk and yeast mixtures, lemon juice, and rind. Sift soy flour with 3 cups of the wheat flour. Whisk flour into liquid ingredients, one cup at a time. Add enough remaining flour to make a soft dough.

Knead dough on a floured surface until smooth and elastic, about 8 to 10 minutes. Put into an oiled bowl and turn once to coat top of dough. Cover and place in a warm place until doubled in bulk, about 1 hour.

To make the filling: Mix together ½ cup of the butter, ½ cup honey, molasses, cinnamon, and nuts. Generously butter a 9 × 13 × 2-inch pan. Spread one-third of the filling over the bottom of the pan. If a stickier bun is desired, combine remaining butter and honey, and drizzle over filling in pan.

When dough is ready, divide into 2 balls. Roll each to a 10 × 15-inch rectangle and spread one-third of the filling evenly over the dough. With long side facing you, roll as for a jelly roll, then cut into 12 slices. Place rolls, cut-side down, in pan. If extra butter was not added to pan, brush sides of dough with some melted butter to make them easier to pull apart. Cover and let rise in a warm place until doubled in bulk, about 30 to 45 minutes.

Preheat oven to 350°F.

Bake for 30 to 35 minutes, or until just browned. Turn out immediately. Spoon any filling left in pan on top of rolls. Best served warm.

Makes 2 dozen buns

DOUGH

1 tablespoon dry yeast
½ cup warm water
⅓ cup honey
¾ cup soymilk
½ cup butter
2 eggs
juice and grated rind of ½ lemon
2 cups soy flour
3½ to 4 cups whole wheat flour

FILLING

½ to ¾ cup melted butter
½ to 1 cup honey
¼ cup molasses
1 tablespoon ground cinnamon
2½ cups chopped walnuts

2⅔ cups brown rice flour
⅔ cup millet flour*
⅔ cup soy flour
1 cup carob powder
2 teaspoons baking soda
1 cup instant nonfat dry
  milk
1 cup vegetable oil
1½ cups honey
4 eggs
4 teaspoons vanilla extract
1½ cups water

*Can be made by grinding whole millet in a blender.

Wheat-Free Carob Cake

Sift all the flours, carob, baking soda, and milk powder together 3 times.

Combine oil and honey and beat thoroughly. Add eggs, vanilla, and water, and beat again.

Preheat oven to 350°F.

Make a well in flour mixture and stir in egg mixture. Beat until smooth. Pour into 2 oiled 9-inch round cake pans.

Bake for 35 to 40 minutes, or until cakes test done.

Makes 2 9-inch layers

1 cup whole wheat pastry
  flour
½ cup soy flour
6 tablespoons cold butter
3 to 4 tablespoons yogurt
  or sour cream

Wheat-Soy Piecrust

Adding soy flour to a basic whole wheat pastry results in a more delicate crust. Because soy flour is richer in oil, the butter or shortening can be reduced.

Combine the flours in a bowl. Cut in butter with a pastry blender or two knives. When mixture is the size of small peas, work in yogurt, 1 tablespoon at a time, until a soft dough is formed.

Knead lightly into a ball. On a sheet of floured wax paper, roll out dough, a little larger than a 9-inch round, flouring as needed. Flip dough into pan. Peel off wax paper and gently ease in dough to fit pan. Trim and crimp edges. Prick bottom with a fork in several places. Refrigerate until ready to fill.

To bake crust, preheat oven to 400°F. Bake for 10 to 14 minutes until lightly browned.

Makes 1 9-inch piecrust

Soy Grits Recipes

Basic Cooked Soy Grits

Bring water to a boil in a 2½- to 3-quart saucepan. Sprinkle grits into the water slowly, so that boiling does not stop. Stirring occasionally, cook at a slow boil, about 10 minutes. Cover and remove from heat.

Let stand 20 minutes. Stir in oil. Return to heat and simmer, covered, until tender, about 50 minutes. Stir occasionally. Uncover, increase heat and, stirring frequently, reduce liquid until grits are thick.

Yields 4 cups

5 cups water
2 cups uncooked soy grits
1 tablespoon vegetable oil

Barley, Beef, and Grits Pilaf

In a large pan sauté garlic, onion, and celery in butter until they begin to turn translucent. Add mushrooms, and continue to sauté until vegetables are just lightly browned.

Stir in grits, 3 cups of the stock, pepper, savory, and soy sauce. Bring mixture to a boil. Reduce heat, cover, and simmer for 45 minutes.

Stir in barley and remaining stock, and bring to a boil. Reduce heat, cover, and simmer about 50 minutes more, or until grain and grits are tender and most of the liquid is absorbed. Check mixture during cooking, and add extra broth, if necessary. Add tomatoes, cook 10 minutes more and serve hot.

4 to 6 servings

3 cloves garlic, minced
3 small onions, chopped
3 stalks celery, chopped
6 tablespoons butter
½ pound mushrooms,
  sliced
¾ cup uncooked soy grits
4½ cups Beef Stock (page
  243)
¼ teaspoon black pepper
1½ teaspoons dried savory
2 tablespoons soy sauce
  (optional)
¾ cup barley
2 large tomatoes, chopped

211

¼ cup butter
½ cup uncooked soy grits
½ cup rolled oats
1 cup ground almonds
¼ cup maple syrup

Crumb Piecrust

Great for ice cream or frozen pudding pies.

Melt butter in a medium-size saucepan. Stir in grits and saute lightly for 1 or 2 minutes. Add oats, almonds, and maple syrup, and cook over very low heat, mixing well. Mixture will be sticky. Press mixture into a greased 9-inch pie plate. Bake at 350°F until lightly browned, about 15 minutes.
Makes 1 9-inch crust

NOTE: To make a 10-inch pie crust, add 1 more tablespoon each of soy grits, rolled oats, and ground almonds.

Granola Bars

3 tablespoons butter
3 tablespoons honey
1 tablespoon molasses
1 tablespoon sorghum
   syrup, or 1 more
   tablespoon molasses
¼ cup frozen pineapple
   juice concentrate
3 cups Soy Granola Cereal
   (page 215)

Place butter, honey, molasses, sorghum, and juice in a medium-size skillet. Cook over medium heat, stirring constantly, until mixture becomes golden brown and caramel-like. It takes several minutes to get to this point, but once it is reached you must work quickly or mixture will burn.

Immediately turn off heat, and stir in granola, making sure to coat all pieces well. Pat evenly into a well-greased 8-inch square baking pan. Cool. Cut into 1 × 2-inch bars with a sharp knife.
Makes 32 bars

Italian Meat Loaf with Tomato Sauce

To make the meat loaf: Combine beef, eggs, grits, pepper, tomato, soy sauce, onion, garlic, marjoram, and tarragon. Mix thoroughly. Pat firmly into an oiled 9 × 5 × 3-inch loaf pan.

Bake for 60 to 75 minutes at 375°F, depending on how well done you like it.

To make the sauce: Meanwhile, sauté marjoram, tarragon, and garlic in butter for 2 minutes. Add tomato sauce, and simmer for about 20 minutes, or until heated through, stirring occasionally. Pour over hot meat loaf on a serving platter. Sprinkle with Parmesan cheese.

6 to 8 servings

MEAT LOAF

1½ pounds lean ground
  beef
2 eggs
¾ cup uncooked soy grits
1 red or green pepper,
  finely chopped
1 small tomato, finely
  chopped and drained
2 teaspoons soy sauce
1 small onion, chopped
1 clove garlic, minced
1½ teaspoons dried
  marjoram
1½ teaspoons dried
  tarragon

SAUCE

½ teaspoon dried
  marjoram
½ teaspoon dried tarragon
1 clove garlic, minced
1 tablespoon butter
4 cups mildly seasoned
  tomato sauce
2 tablespoons grated
  Parmesan cheese

213

Lamb and Apricots with Soy Grits

1 tablespoon olive or
vegetable oil
1 pound lean boneless
lamb stewing meat, cut
into 1-inch cubes
2 large onions, coarsely
chopped
3 cloves garlic, finely
chopped
7 cups water
2 cups uncooked soy grits
¾ cup dried apricots,
coarsely chopped
½ cup raisins
1 tablespoon soy sauce
½ cup slivered almonds

Grits cooked this way can make a delicious stuffing—use lamb bones in place of the meat and remove bones before serving.

Heat oil over medium heat in a large Dutch oven or soup pot. Add lamb and onion. Cook, stirring constantly, for 3 minutes. Add garlic and cook a few minutes more, allowing the bottom of the pan to brown. Remove meat, cover, and reserve meat.

Add water to Dutch oven and stir well to loosen the browned particles from the bottom. Add grits, cover and simmer, stirring occasionally, for 1 hour until almost tender.

Add lamb, cover, and simmer until lamb is very tender, about 45 minutes, adding extra liquid if necessary. Add apricots, raisins, and soy sauce.

Uncover grits and boil, stirring constantly, to evaporate extra liquid. Transfer grits to center of a warm serving dish, arranging lamb mixture around grits. Top with almonds and serve. (This reheats easily in a 300°F oven.)

4 to 6 servings

Orange-Apricot Muffins

½ cup uncooked soy grits
1 cup milk
2 cups whole wheat pastry
flour
1 teaspoon baking powder
1 teaspoon baking soda
½ teaspoon ground
cinnamon
1 egg
¼ cup corn oil
¼ cup honey
½ cup orange juice
1 teaspoon grated orange
rind
½ cup diced dried apricots

Preheat oven to 400°F.

Combine soy grits and milk in a medium-size saucepan. Bring almost to a boil over medium heat, stirring occasionally. Remove from heat.

Sift together flour, baking powder, baking soda, and cinnamon. Set aside.

Beat egg into grits mixture when it is lukewarm. Stir in oil, honey, orange juice, and orange rind.

Stir egg mixture into dry ingredients just until blended. Fold in apricots. Fill lightly buttered muffin tins ¾ full with batter. Bake until muffins are lightly browned at edges, about 12 minutes.

Makes 12 to 15 muffins

Soy Granola Cereal

In a large mixing bowl combine grits, flaked grains, coconut, sunflower seeds, wheat germ, and sesame seeds. Stir together juice, oil, honey, and vanilla, and add to dry ingredients. Mix well.

Spread mixture in a large shallow oiled jelly roll pan (15½ × 10½ × 1-inch). Place on the middle rack of a 250°F oven and bake for 1 hour, stirring every 15 minutes. Add almonds and bake for another 15 minutes more, or until mixture is dry and lightly toasted.

Remove from oven and stir in dried fruit. Cool and store in an airtight container.

Yields 10 cups

1½ cups uncooked soy grits
3 cups flaked grains (rolled oats, rolled wheat, or rolled rye)
1½ cups unsweetened dry coconut
1 cup sunflower seeds
½ cup wheat germ
¼ cup sesame seeds
¾ cup apple juice
¼ cup vegetable oil
¼ cup honey
1 tablespoon vanilla extract
1 cup slivered almonds
1½ to 2 cups chopped dried fruit

½ pound ground beef
2 cups cooked soy grits
1 small onion, finely
  chopped
1 teaspoon finely chopped
  fresh sage, or ½
  teaspoon dried sage
2 tablespoons finely
  chopped fresh parsley
1 egg
1 large head of cabbage
1 tablespoon vegetable oil
2 cups Beef Stock (page
  243)
2 cups tomato juice
1 tablespoon soy sauce
2 teaspoons red wine
  vinegar
sour cream or yogurt

Stuffed Cabbage

Soy grits replace rice in this satisfying winter meal. Serve a crusty slice of dense rye bread to sop up the sauce.

In a bowl mix together beef, soy grits, onion, sage, parsley, and egg. Set aside.

Remove all damaged or loose leaves from the cabbage. To free the leaves, cut around the core with a paring knife. Steam the whole head for 8 minutes. Cool slightly and gently remove 15 or more whole leaves. If leaves aren't flexible toward the center of the cabbage, steam for a few minutes more. Slightly ripped leaves may be patched with pieces torn from another leaf. Trim the thick rib from each leaf.

Place ¼ cup of filling in a flattened ball near the base of the cupped side of each leaf. Roll the leaves up firmly, tucking the loose ends of the leaves into the rolls. This keeps the leaves from unrolling.

Cover the bottom of a very large skillet or Dutch oven with the oil. Place cabbage rolls in skillet in a single layer, seam-side down. Cover with stock, tomato juice, soy sauce, and vinegar. Cover pan. Bring to a boil over medium heat. Reduce heat, and simmer for 1½ hours. Shake pan gently occasionally.

Serve in shallow bowls with sauce and sour cream or yogurt.

5 to 8 servings

Stuffed Grape Leaves

These Greek dolmas *are commonly served as appetizers or to accompany meat, especially lamb. The stuffing may also be used for chicken or pork.*

If using fresh grape leaves, soak them in boiling water for 2 minutes to soften, then rinse under cold water. Rinse preserved grapevine leaves in hot water to remove brine. Spread washed leaves on paper towels to drain.

Bring water to a boil in a 2-quart saucepan and stir in grits. Reduce heat to low, cover, and cook for about 2 to 3 minutes, or until the water is absorbed.

Add 2 tablespoons of the oil and onion to grits. Stirring frequently, cook over medium-low heat until onions are limp.

Stir in mushrooms, currants, garlic, mint, parsley, oregano, soy sauce, and ¼ cup of the tomatoes. Simmer, uncovered, about 20 minutes, or until almost dry. Stir in pine nuts and cayenne. Remove from heat.

Place individual leaves face down on counter with stem-end facing edge. With a small sharp knife, trim stems from leaves.

Choose a leaf that is ripped. Use it to patch any holes in remaining leaves.

Place 1 level tablespoon of filling 1 inch from bottom of each leaf in a short strip. Fold stem-end over filling, then fold leaf sides in over this, and roll tightly toward tip.

Heat remaining olive oil and tomato puree in a 10- or 12-inch skillet. Add *dolmas,* seam-side down, in a single layer. Simmer, covered, for 30 minutes, shaking pan occasionally.

Place lemon slices over *dolmas* and simmer 15 minutes more. Check during this time and add water if necessary to keep *dolmas* from sticking. They should be shiny when finished but not in a wet sauce.

Serve hot or at room temperature garnished with mint and lemon wedges.

4 to 6 servings

25 grape leaves (oak leaf size or larger)
⅓ cup water
¼ cup uncooked soy grits
¼ cup olive oil
1 large onion, finely chopped
1½ cups thinly sliced mushrooms
½ cup dried currants
2 cloves garlic, minced
1½ teaspoons finely chopped fresh mint, or ½ teaspoon dried mint
2 tablespoons finely chopped fresh parsley
1 teaspoon dried oregano
2 teaspoons soy sauce
1¼ cups pureed tomatoes
¼ cup pine nuts or sunflower seeds
cayenne pepper, to taste
½ lemon, cut into thin slices
Garnish
2 tablespoons chopped fresh mint or parsley
12 thin lemon wedges

2 cups ½-inch cubes of
  raw scrubbed sweet
  potato
1½ cups water
⅔ cup soy grits
2 tablespoons butter, at
  room temperature
¼ cup honey
3 eggs, lightly beaten
¼ cup milk
1 tablespoon orange juice
2 teaspoons grated orange
  rind
¼ teaspoon ground
  nutmeg
1 teaspoon ground
  cinnamon
1 unbaked Whole Wheat
  Piecrust (page 242)
whipped cream (optional)

Sweet Potato Pie

In a medium-size saucepan bring sweet potatoes and water to a boil. Add soy grits, cover, and simmer until potatoes are tender, about 20 minutes. Stir occasionally to prevent soy grits from boiling over. Uncover, and cook until mixture is reduced to consistency of thick soup.

Cool slightly and purée mixture in a food processor or blender. The rest of the mixing can be done in a food processor, or transfer mixture to a bowl.

Preheat oven to 400°F.

Add butter, honey, eggs, milk, orange juice, orange rind, nutmeg, and cinnamon, beating after each addition. When well mixed, pour into piecrust.

Bake until pie filling is set in the middle, about 30 minutes. Serve warm or cold with whipped cream, if desired.

Makes 1 9-inch pie

1 cup cooked brown rice,
  at room temperature
1 cup cooked soy grits, at
  room temperature
1 cup crumbled feta cheese
¼ teaspoon black pepper
2 eggs, beaten
2 scallions, finely chopped
10 ounces fresh spinach,
  finely chopped
¼ cup butter

Vegetable Terrine

Serve this terrine cold with yogurt seasoned with minced garlic and crackers, or French bread as a first course or at a buffet table. Although time-consuming to make, the terrine looks and tastes impressive.

Mix rice and soy grits with ½ cup of the cheese, ⅛ teaspoon of the pepper, 2 tablespoons of the egg, and scallions. Press half of the rice mixture into the bottom of a thickly buttered 10 × 3 × 3-inch collapsible paté pan or an 8½ × 4½ × 2½-inch loaf pan. Reserve remaining rice mixture.

Sauté spinach in 2 tablespoons of the butter with onion, garlic, and thyme until quite dry. Transfer spinach to a bowl, and set bowl in cold water. Stir occasionally to cool quickly.

When cool, stir in 2 tablespoons of the egg, 2 tablespoons of the bread crumbs, and ¼ cup cheese. Press evenly over rice layer in pan.

Mash carrots with remaining egg, bread crumbs, pepper, and ¼ cup cheese. Spread over spinach layer.

Press remaining rice firmly on carrot layer. Dot with remaining butter. Cover pan loosely with foil.

Bake in a preheated 350°F oven for 1 to 1¼ hours, or until terrine is firm and begins to brown at edges. To check doneness, insert a small thin knife into center of terrine for 20 seconds. When terrine is done the knife will come out very hot to the touch. Chill terrine completely before serving.

To serve, run knife between terrine and pan. Place pan in hot water for 30 seconds, then turn bottom-side up onto a cutting board. Cut into ¾-inch thick slices with a very sharp knife. Serve slices with garlic-seasoned yogurt, if desired.

8 to 10 servings

1 large onion, finely chopped
2 cloves garlic, minced
1 teaspoon chopped fresh thyme, or ½ teaspoon dried thyme
¼ cup fine whole grain bread crumbs
3 carrots, cooked

Walnut Torte

This torte can be made into an elegant dessert, layered with fresh peaches, strawberries, or other berries and whipped cream.

Combine ground walnuts, butter, honey, maple syrup, eggs, and vanilla, and beat well.

Sift flour and baking powder together twice. Beat egg mixture into flour mixture, while gradually adding milk. Fold in chopped walnuts and soy grits.

Preheat oven to 350°F.

Divide batter into 3 8-inch buttered and floured cake pans.

Bake for 30 minutes or until cake tests done. Remove from pans immediately and cool on wire racks.

Serve torte layers filled with a fruit glaze or whipped cream, if desired.

Serves 8

1 cup finely ground walnuts
4 tablespoons butter
¼ cup honey
¼ cup maple syrup
3 eggs
2 teaspoons vanilla extract
1¼ cups whole wheat pastry flour
2 teaspoons baking powder
1 cup soymilk
1 cup coarsely chopped walnuts
¾ cup uncooked soy grits

Blair Island Natural Foods Restaurant, Eugene, Oregon

Toby Alves, who is a vegetarian, always thought of tofu as that bland watery health food floating in soups in Chinese restaurants. Then her youngest son developed allergies to dairy products, wheat, peanut butter, and other foods. Toby searched for non-meat protein sources that would appeal to the tastes of her young children. "I knew that if I wanted to keep my family vegetarian, I would have to come up with some pretty imaginative and delicious dishes," says Toby.

Toby began experimenting with tofu and other soyfoods. She discovered that freshly made tofu with the moisture pressed from it could be incredibly versatile. The Tofu Tia is one of her proudest creations, and she serves it at Blair Island, a restaurant serving natural foods with a flair.

To make her Tofu Tia, she cubes the pressed tofu, sautés it lightly in oil until crispy and golden, and spices it in a variety of ways. "We prefer the Mexican spiced ones for tacos," she explains, "chili, garlic, onion, cumin, plus a little curry for zip. We add soy sauce which gives it color and a wonderful taste." Toby's tofu invention is a popular dish at the Eugene, Oregon, restaurant as well as at the famous Northwest Oregon County Fair.

Blair Island Natural Foods Restaurant, Eugene, Oregon. Toby Alves displays some of the mouth-watering treats that keep customers more than satisfied.

The menu at Blair Island is diverse and has a wide appeal. People from all over the country try our uniquely prepared tofu, and say they have never tasted tofu like this before, according to Toby. A tofu meatball hero sandwich, burritos with tofu, tempeh, or Mexican blackbeans, sweet and light fruit-flavored tofu cheesecakes, a delicious dairy-free sour cream, and waffles and hot cakes are just some of the simple but good-tasting fare.

Toby is happy she discovered tofu, tempeh, soymilk, and other soyfoods. They came to her first as a healthful, delicious solution to her son's dietary restrictions, only to take on a more significant role in her life. "Our food is our politics at Blair Island. We see tofu and tempeh as wholesome high-protein foods and a more efficient way to feed people," Toby says.

SOY FLOUR
AND SOY GRITS

Soy Sauces

Soy sauce like soy sprouts and tofu is one of those soyfoods you have tasted scores of times in Chinese restaurants. Unfortunately, you may very likely have tasted a product very different from the one I will tell you about here. Soy sauce is one of those foods that fell prey to our Yankee ingenuity of taking short-cuts and producing more for less. Read on and learn about real and not-so-real soy sauce.

Soy sauces, like many other soyfoods, had their beginnings in ancient times when the Chinese discovered that the soybean could be preserved and aged in salt to improve its flavor. They also discovered that these various soy sauces added robust meatlike flavors to a bland rice diet. What's more, the Chinese unwittingly added missing amino acids and B-vitamins to their foods with these rich flavor concentrates.

Most Westerners have known and used the American version of soy sauce for years. So the very savory miso, tamari, and shoyu I will introduce you to may not be totally exotic spices. But the quality and taste difference between these authentic varieties and a quickly manufactured ersatz soy sauce is startling to most. Check the ingredients list when buying soy sauce. Water, soybeans, salt, and sometimes a grain are the only necessary ingredients. The rapidly produced Western copy of soy sauce, using acid-hydrolyzed protein, corn syrup, caramel coloring, monosodium glutamate (responsible for MSG headaches in many people), and preservatives, is a weak rival for the naturally aged and fermented soy condiments that Asians have produced for centuries.

SOY SAUCES

Shoyu and Tamari

In Japan and China many variations of these tasty sauces are made from soy. In this country we are becoming more familiar with at least three of these natural soy sauces—shoyu, tamari, and the very rich and versatile paste-like sauce, miso. All three can be found in natural foods stores.

Shoyu is simply the Japanese name for soy sauce. Natural shoyu, brewed using a natural, rather than temperature controlled, fermentation process, is made from an equal proportion of wheat to soybeans. Shoyu mistakenly came to be called tamari in the West years ago because Western distributors believed the word tamari easier to pronounce. However, genuine tamari unlike shoyu is made without wheat. The word tamari means that which accumulates, and it refers to the salty-sweet tasty liquid that accumulates during the ripening process of miso. Some soy sauce producers distinguish tamari-shoyu containing a small amount of wheat, about 10 to 20 percent.

Shoyu and tamari are both quality sauces with differing appeal. Much of the flavor and aroma of shoyu results from wheat fermentation, which creates volatile alcohols and esters. These attributes are heat-sensitive and so they diminish somewhat during cooking. Tamari, with its slightly deeper flavor, richer brown color and consistency keeps its native flavor and aroma even with extended cooking. It is the amino acids created by the fermentation of soy protein and the glutamic acid (naturally occurring monosodium glutamate) that are largely responsible for the flavor of tamari. Tamari is more intensely flavored so you need less for seasoning.

These natural soy sauces have many uses that go beyond their obvious role as salt replacements. In marinades they help tenderize and flavor meats, poultry, or vegetables. They are an excellent flavoring agent in sauces for fish. They fill out the flavor of dips, salad dressings, soups, casseroles, and many other types of dishes.

SODIUM CONTENT OF SOY SAUCES

Despite their salty taste, soy sauces are not nearly as high in sodium, the nutrient associated with high blood pressure and other health disorders, as is salt. A teaspoon of tamari has about 268 mg so-

223

dium and a teaspoon of soy sauce (or shoyu) has 343 mg. By comparison, a teaspoon of salt has about 2,000 mg sodium. With soy sauces, however, you further reduce your sodium intake because the seasoning power is about three times as great as that of salt so you use less. Low-sodium soy sauces, containing about half as much sodium as regular soy sauces, are also available in some areas of the country. Their taste is just as rich.

Miso

Miso is a unique soy condiment with no counterpart in Western food culture. Unlike other soy sauces, it is not pourable, but has a peanut butter consistency that is spreadable and easily dissolved. Miso is a high-protein, thick salty paste that is most often served as a highly concentrated soup base. But it has scores of other uses as a seasoning. It comes in a rainbow of earthy colors and varying textures, depending on the type of miso: tans, russets, ambers, and rich browns. Each miso has its own distinctive flavor and aroma ranging from savory and beefy to mild and subtly sweet.

Traditional types of miso are prepared essentially the same way today as they were thousands of years ago: Rice or barley is soaked overnight, steamed until tender, and mixed with spores of a special mold. The molded grain, called koji, supplies essential enzymes needed for fermentation and is combined with an equal amount of soybean cooking liquid. The ingredients are mashed together, packed into deep cedar vats, and allowed to ferment for 1 to 2 years. The result is a rich-flavored, very robust seasoning.

Miso has a slightly higher nutritional value than shoyu and tamari. Miso has been called a living food, containing millions of very beneficial living organisms—yeast, molds, and bacteria—suspended in a mixture of oils, sugars, minerals, and amino acids. Miso is one of the few vegetarian sources of the essential vitamin B-12, and is also rich in enzymes and lactic acid bacteria beneficial to digestion. Miso is about 12 percent salt. It has a high ratio of protein to calories. One tablespoon has 27 calories and 2.5 grams of protein.

Storing Soy Condiments

The salt content in miso and the other soy condiments protects them from bacterial growth. Miso, shoyu, and tamari can be stored indefinitely at room temperature.

SOY OIL

Soybeans are rich in a cooking oil that is cholesterol-free and very high in polyunsaturates. Much of the oil labeled vegetable and sold in supermarkets contains some proportion of soy oil, though this oil is generally refined, bleached, and deodorized. Cold-pressed, unrefined soy oil (generally available in natural foods stores) is a deep amber color with a distinct flavor, somewhat nutty and fruity. Its taste is probably too marked for use in sweet or delicate-flavored baked goods and desserts. But it can be used successfully for sautéeing vegetables, meat, poultry, or fish or in piecrusts for quiche or other savory fillings.

When using soy oil in salad dressings, add it slowly to other ingredients, tasting until the desired strength of flavor pleases you. If you desire, you may also lessen the strength of taste of soy oil in salad dressings by combining the soy oil with a mild-flavored vegetable oil, such as corn, sunflower, or safflower.

USING MISO

Although miso replaces the need for salt in food, it should not be used to salt food, but rather to enhance flavor.

Use miso as a stock base, or to flavor sauces, dips, dressings, and marinades. To add miso to soup, stock, or liquid dishes, first dissolve the miso in some of the liquid from the dish, then combine it with the rest of the dish. It is important to avoid boiling miso as this will destroy some of its friendly organisms. The sharp cheesy flavor of miso can also enhance casseroles and spreads. You will also find that miso makes a delectable sandwich spread that can be used instead of mayonnaise or mustard.

DIFFERENT TYPES OF MISO

Miso is generally classified according to the length of time it has been allowed to ferment. The longer the fermentation period, the deeper and richer flavor, aroma, and color. The highly prized Hatcho miso is subject to the longest fermentation period—2 to 3 years. Its name reflects the city of its origin. Deep chocolate-colored Hatcho miso has a very ripe zestful flavor and an aroma that is immediately apparent.

225

SOME QUICK AND EASY USES FOR SOY CONDIMENTS

- Baste skinned chicken pieces or fish fillets with shoyu or tamari before broiling.
- Brush slices of eggplant with shoyu or tamari and broil until tender.
- Use tamari, shoyu, or miso as a topping for baked potatoes instead of sour cream or other dairy products.
- Mix steamed green beans, carrots, or sliced squash, or cucumber slices with a few drops of shoyu or tamari for a simple tasty low-calorie vegetable snack.
- Spread a thin layer of miso on a slice of whole wheat bread, top with a tomato slice and serve as a light snack.
- Thin miso with a little melted butter and mix into hot cooked rice or other grains when serving as a side dish.
- Mix three parts peanut butter with one part miso and fill long crisp celery stalks with the mixture.

Some moderately fermented types of miso include brown rice miso, *mugi* miso, and *genmai*—all fermented a little over a year. These are milder tasting. Some American manufacturers also produce short-term miso—miso made in 6 to 12 weeks. Mellow-barley, white, yellow, and red miso are all short-term. Their flavors are very light and mild, and generally they tend to taste saltier (though the salt content is the same) than longer-fermented miso.

Shoyu and Tamari Recipes

Onion Dip

This dip tastes just like the dry onion soup dip that many people love, but this one is much less salty.

In a medium-size skillet melt butter and sauté onions over medium heat until dark caramel is brown but not burnt. Add soy sauce, while scraping bottom of skillet to deglaze. Remove from heat and cool mixture. When cool, stir onion mixture into sour cream. Place in a small bowl, cover, and refrigerate for at least 2 hours. Serve with vegetable crudites, potato chips, or crackers.
Yields 1½ cups

2 tablespoons butter
2 medium-size onions, finely chopped
2 tablespoons shoyu soy sauce
1½ cups sour cream

Sesame Seed Salad Dressing

This dressing with a Mid-Eastern flavor keeps well in the refrigerator. It is especially suited for simple salads of tender greens with tomatoes or cucumbers.

Combine oil, tamari, seeds, and garlic and mix well. Refrigerate overnight to blend flavors. Toss dressing with salad. Add lemon juice or vinegar just before serving, if desired.
Yields about 1¼ cups

1 cup vegetable oil
2 tablespoons tamari soy sauce
½ cup toasted sesame seeds
2 cloves garlic, minced
lemon juice or wine vinegar, to taste (optional)

227

Soy-Herb Marinade for Artichoke-Mushroom Antipasto

This recipe will give you those wonderful marinated vegetable salads that are so expensive in Italian delicatessens. Serve as an appetizer or as a salad on a crisp lettuce leaf. The marinade can be used for any lightly cooked vegetable, but we offer a combination artichoke-mushroom salad. You can use this basic recipe to improvise others; for instance, cooked green soybeans or soy sprouts would be an excellent addition.

To prepare the marinade: Combine all ingredients in a glass jar. Set aside.

To prepare the salad: Bring water and vinegar to a boil in a 2-quart saucepan. Add artichokes, cover, and cook for 3 minutes after water comes to a boil. Then add mushrooms, pepper, and celery. Cover and simmer about 4 minutes more, stirring occasionally, or until the mushrooms are barely cooked. Stir in the marinade immediately. Cover and let cool to room temperature.

Transfer to a glass jar and refrigerate at least 1 day before serving. Remove jar from the refrigerator 30 minutes before serving to allow the oil to become liquid again. Shake before serving.

6 servings

MARINADE

½ cup olive oil

¼ cup wine vinegar

2 tablespoons shoyu soy sauce

2 cloves garlic, peeled and quartered lengthwise

1 tiny dried chili pepper, seeded and finely chopped, or ½ teaspoon hot pepper flakes

1 teaspoon dried marjoram

2 teaspoons chopped fresh rosemary, or 1 teaspoon dried rosemary, crumbled

1 teaspoon fresh thyme leaves, or ½ teaspoon dried thyme

SALAD

½ cup water

¼ cup wine vinegar

1 package (9 ounces) frozen artichoke hearts

½ pound mushrooms, sliced

1 red pepper, cut into 2-inch strips

2 stalks celery, cut into ¼-inch slices

Sweet and Spicy Dressing

This salad dressing is an emulsion sauce made like mayonnaise, but it will not be as thick. It tastes delicious on both fruit and mixed green salads.

In a food processor or blender, combine egg yolks, mustard, cayenne, and 2 tablespoons of the vinegar. On high speed, add 1 cup of the oil, a few drops at a time, until mixture thickens. Then add oil by teaspoonfuls. When thick, blend in paprika, allspice, tomato paste, honey, and soy sauce. Taste and thin with remaining oil or vinegar, if necessary. This dressing stores well in the refrigerator for about two weeks.

Yields 2 cups

2 egg yolks, at room temperature
2 teaspoons dry mustard
⅛ teaspoon cayenne pepper
2 to 4 tablespoons cider vinegar
1 to 1¼ cups sunflower oil
2 teaspoons Hungarian paprika
½ teaspoon ground allspice
2 tablespoons tomato paste
3 tablespoons honey
2 tablespoons shoyu soy sauce

Tahini Dressing

This is the traditional dressing poured over shredded raw vegetables or falafel in pita sandwiches, but it is also good as a dressing for a standard mixed green salad.

Stir lemon juice and soy sauce into tahini, 1 tablespoon at a time. Add garlic, and thin with water, adding 1 tablespoon at a time until mixture is smooth and thin enough to pour.

Yields 1 cup

¼ cup lemon juice
1 tablespoon shoyu or tamari soy sauce
½ cup tahini
1 clove garlic, pressed
¼ to ⅓ cup water

Tamari-Marinated Mushrooms

1 pound button
  mushrooms
½ cup tamari soy sauce
¼ cup honey
1 tablespoon lemon juice
1 cup water
1 tablespoon vinegar
2 tablespoons butter

Clean and dry mushrooms. In a medium-size bowl mix together tamari, honey, lemon juice, water, and vinegar. Add mushrooms. Marinate for about 30 minutes at room temperature.

Drain and reserve marinade. In a large skillet melt butter. Add mushrooms and ¼ cup reserved marinade, and simmer uncovered for 5 minutes. Serve hot. Use remaining marinade as a dipping sauce.

4 servings

Teriyaki Beef

½ cup tamari soy sauce
2 tablespoons Barbados
  molasses
2 tablespoons rice vinegar
1 tablespoon vegetable oil
2 tablespoons honey
1 teaspoon dry mustard
2 cloves garlic, minced
1 teaspoon minced peeled
  ginger root
¼ teaspoon black pepper
1 pound round steak, cut
  into thin strips
1 tablespoon vegetable oil
1 tablespoon butter
½ cup water
2 tablespoons cornstarch
2 tablespoons water

This sauce is delicious for marinating beef strips. Use it to make a gravy, too. Larger cuts of beef, such as roasts, should be marinated overnight in the refrigerator.

In a medium-size bowl mix together tamari, molasses, vinegar, oil, honey, mustard, garlic, ginger, and pepper. Immerse beef in marinade for about 30 minutes at room temperature.

Heat oil and butter in a large skillet. Remove beef strips from marinade with a slotted spoon. Reserve marinade. Add beef to skillet and brown over medium-high heat. Add ½ cup reserved marinade and ½ cup water.

In a small bowl whisk together cornstarch and 2 tablespoons water. Add to beef and simmer 2 minutes to thicken sauce. Serve hot over rice.

4 servings

Miso Recipes

Chinese Cooking Sauce

Similar to bottled hoisin sauce, this cooking sauce is thick and shiny, spicy, fruity and sweet and sour. In short, it is a sauce with a delightfully complex flavor that is very easy to put together. It will keep in the refrigerator up to two months. An unusual use for the sauce is to spread one side of a Chinese pancake with the sauce, then mound a dry stir-fried chicken or pork mixture on one quarter of the pancake. Next fold the pancake around the filling to form a tidy package for eating by hand.

This type of sauce is also used to flavor and thicken seafood and chicken dishes that are cooked with a little stock. Add the sauce toward the end of the cooking time to preserve its delicate flavors.

2 tablespoons water
1 tablespoon cornstarch
¼ cup Barbados molasses
2 tablespoons cider vinegar
¼ cup frozen orange juice concentrate
½ teaspoon ground ginger
1 to 2 teaspoons minced fresh chili pepper, or ½ teaspoon cayenne pepper
¼ cup gen mai or mugi miso
2 cloves garlic

In a small saucepan combine water and cornstarch to form a smooth paste. Stir in molasses, vinegar, orange juice, ginger, and chili. Cook while stirring, over medium heat, until mixture thickens and begins to bubble. Stir in miso with a wire whisk. Press garlic, and add to mixture. Cook over lowest heat for 4 minutes more. Store in a glass jar.

Yields 1 cup

Eggplant with Miso and Sesame Seeds

Serve this as a vegetable side dish or as a sauce over Japanese noodles.

2 small eggplants
2 to 4 tablespoons peanut oil
2 cloves garlic, minced
3 tablespoons sesame seeds
3 tablespoons miso
1 scallion, thinly sliced

Cut eggplants into small cubes. Sauté eggplant in 2 tablespoons of the oil in a loosely covered large saucepan. Stir occasionally until lightly browned, about 8 minutes. Add garlic and remaining oil if necessary; stir, then reduce heat to lowest setting. Cover and cook until tender, about 10 minutes more.

Meanwhile toast sesame seeds in a dry skillet until lightly browned, about 5 minutes. Reserve.

When eggplant is tender, stir in miso and cook 3 minutes. Add sesame seeds, garnish with scallions and serve. Leftovers are also good served cold.

4 servings

2 tablespoons miso
¼ cup Vegetable Stock
   (page 244) or water
4 eggs
3 cups hot cooked rice or
   noodles
2 scallions, thinly sliced

Miso and Egg Omelets with Rice

This very savory Japanese-style egg dish needs to be balanced by a bland food such as rice or noodles. Served hot or cold, this is a protein-packed, quickly prepared meal. This is a good recipe for trying different misos in order to become familiar with their different flavors and aroma. A light-colored miso makes this dish most eye-appealing.

Place miso in a small saucepan. Stir in stock, 1 tablespoon at a time, until smooth and spreadable, but not runny. Cook over low heat, stirring, for 4 minutes. Remove from heat and reserve.

Place lightly oiled 9- to 10-inch skillet over medium heat. When sizzling hot, add 1 beaten egg and swirl it around the pan to spread as thinly as possible. When set but not brown on the bottom, flip egg. Remove to a plate when done. Spread top thinly with miso mixture. Roll up omelet as tightly as possible. Repeat with remaining eggs.

With a sharp knife, cut eggs into 1-inch pieces. Place eggs on top of rice or noodles, top with scallions, and serve.

4 servings

1 tablespoon butter
1 tablespoon vegetable oil
1 onion, finely chopped
2 cloves garlic, minced
½ cup 1-inch pieces of
   uncooked vermicelli
1 tablespoon miso
3¾ to 4 cups hot water
1 cup brown rice
1 tablespoon minced fresh
   parsley
1 tablespoon grated carrot
1 tablespoon minced red
   peppers
1 cup cashew pieces

Miso, Rice, and Noodles

An all-natural version of the flavored rices you can buy. It tastes better and is better for you.

In a large skillet melt butter and oil. Sauté onion, garlic, and vermicelli until browned.

In a 4-cup measure dissolve miso in hot water. Pour into skillet. Add rice, parsley, carrot, and pepper. Stir until mixed. Cover and simmer over medium-low heat until rice is done, about 45 minutes.

Remove cover, stir in cashews, and simmer until excess liquid evaporates, if necessary. Serve immediately.

6 servings

Miso Soup

Adding miso to soups is as simple as using a bouillon cube. This recipe proves it. In Japan this soup is eaten at any time of the day. The kelp, which is available in Oriental food stores, can be omitted. A simple soup such as this is another good way to familiarize yourself with the characteristics of different types of miso.

Wipe kelp lightly with a damp cloth. Do not wash it. With scissors, cut kelp into 4-inch lengths. Cut these into thin strips. Place kelp and water in a saucepan over medium heat. As soon as water begins to boil, remove kelp. Reserve kelp for another use.

Simmer carrot, mushrooms, garlic, and tofu in cooking water for 1 minute. Stir miso and warm water together in a small bowl. When miso is dissolved, add mixture to soup. Keep hot for 8 minutes more without letting soup simmer. Sprinkle with scallions and serve.

4 to 5 servings

2 pieces giant kelp
(kombu), 2 × 8 inches
1 quart cold water
1 carrot, sliced into paper-thin ovals
6 mushrooms, thinly sliced
1 clove garlic, pressed or minced
½ cup diced or slivered tofu
2 to 3 tablespoons miso
1 cup warm water
2 scallions, thinly sliced

Rice Salad with Miso

A chunky style miso is best for this.

Bring water to a boil in a 6- or 8-quart saucepan. Add rice slowly, so water continues boiling. Cook uncovered at a slow boil, stirring occasionally, until rice is tender, 40 to 45 minutes. Drain rice in a colander, saving ¼ cup of the water. Rinse rice with cold water. Thin miso with reserved water.

Return rice to pot and stir in miso mixture, oil, vinegar, and black pepper. Then fold in onion, red pepper, peas, and basil. Chill thoroughly before serving. If storing salad for more than one day, taste at time of serving and adjust seasonings if necessary.

4 to 6 servings

8 cups water
2 cups long grain brown rice
3 tablespoons miso
⅓ cup vegetable oil
3 to 4 tablespoons white wine vinegar
freshly ground black pepper, to taste
¼ cup finely chopped red onion
1 red pepper, diced
1 cup blanched peas or sugar peas
1 tablespoon finely chopped fresh basil

233

1 teaspoon finely chopped
    fresh hot pepper
¼ cup finely chopped
    onion
2 teaspoons curry powder
2 tablespoons butter
¼ cup red miso
1 cup peanut butter
¾ cup apple juice,
    approximately
hot pepper sauce
    (optional)

Spicy Peanut Butter Spread

Try this spread as a filling for celery sticks or as a sandwich ingredient, perhaps with bananas. Add extra apple juice to make a dip or sauce.

Over low heat cook hot pepper, onion, and curry powder in butter in a covered saucepan for 2 minutes, stirring occasionally. Stir in miso and cook 2 minutes longer. Remove from heat and stir in peanut butter. Add apple juice, 1 tablespoon at a time, or until mixture is thin enough to spread. Add a few drops of hot sauce, if desired.
Yields 2 cups

1 tablespoon miso
¼ cup hot water
3 tablespoons corn oil
2 medium-size zucchini,
    sliced into ¼-inch
    circles
1 teaspoon minced peeled
    ginger root
1 clove garlic, minced
1 pound snow peas
2 medium-size tomatoes,
    cubed

Three-Color Vegetables

Green peppers, red tomatoes, and white zucchini make an easy festive dish.

Dissolve miso in hot water. Set aside.
In a wok heat corn oil. Add zucchini, ginger root, and garlic. Stir-fry for 5 minutes. Add pea pods and stir-fry for 4 minutes more. Add tomatoes and fry for about 30 seconds more.
Pour miso mixture down the side of wok, reduce heat, and simmer over medium heat for 2 minutes. Serve immediately.
4 servings

Wildwood Natural Foods, Fairfax, California

On a bay-laurel and oak-lined street, nestled at the foot of Mount Tamalpais is Wildwood Natural Foods. Not far from the craggy northern California coastline, this idyllic locale sets the tone for the bustling healthy business of Wildwood. The company's three owners, Bill Bramblett, Paul Orbuch, and Frank Rosenmayer, are all vegetarians and macrobiotic eaters. They insist on preparing their many soyfoods recipes from their own homemade tofu without frying or using animal products.

When they first bought Wildwood, the brown rice and tofu sandwich (BRT) seasoned with a miso-tahini sauce was a favorite. Bill, Paul, and Frank introduced it to many people throughout the San Francisco and surrounding Bay areas. Its popularity grew quickly, and soon they varied the flavors of the sandwich with curry, mustard, and hot peanut sauce.

At Wildwood they make small batches of tofu daily, adding up to 2200 pounds weekly, and deliver it as soon as it is made to stores in the surrounding area. "It's very important that Americans learn to adopt the Japanese concept of fresh tofu. It should be eaten the day it is made," Paul says.

Wildwood Natural Foods, Fairfax, California. The famous "BRT" (brown rice and tofu) sandwich assembly line helps meet the growing demand.

235

Wildwood has a varied menu that keeps changing. Some of the popular creations are Tofu Steak Sandwich, Marinated Tempeh Burger, Avocado-Tofu Salad, Tofu-Vegetable Salad, Tofu-Dill Salad, Tempeh Salad with Vinaigrette, Potato Salad with Tofu Mayonnaise, Vegetarian Sushi, and Sea Vegetable-Rice Pie. Desserts and beverages include *Kanten*, a traditional Japanese gelatin flavored with fresh fruit, a carob brownie called Seventh Heaven Bread, and soymilk drinks sweetened with honey and flavored with fruit.

Wildwood's owners find their customers are active, health-conscious people who like good-tasting food. The owners distribute their soyfoods to stores in many corners of Marin County and San Francisco, including the city's financial district where many business people like the original BRT.

Paul, Bill, and Frank are very busy keeping up with demands of their many customers, but are always looking for new ones, too. They have distributed some of their soyfoods sandwiches and salads to the large food chain, Safeway Supermarket. Soon Paul, Bill, and Frank will probably have to increase the volume of tofu they make to meet new demands.

The Soyfoods Pantry

Some of the following recipes are for foods that I use often in small amounts as ingredients in many other recipes. I like to keep them on hand when possible. You'll find the following homemade ingredients much more satisfying than their commercially bought counterparts. You can make many of these recipes ahead of time and store them for quick easy use as directed.

Directions for cooking whole grains, tomato sauce, and gravy are also given as these may appear in serving suggestions throughout the book.

Basics

Baking Powder

This easily made baking powder does not contain aluminum as some commercial brands do.

Mix ingredients together in a small bowl with a wooden spoon. Crush any lumps. Store in a tightly covered jar in a cool dry place.
Yields: ¼ cup

1 tablespoon baking soda
2 tablespoons cream of tartar
2 tablespoons arrowroot

2 tablespoons cumin seeds,
  or 2 tablespoons ground
  cumin
2 teaspoons ground chili
  pepper, or 4 dried hot
  peppers
2 teaspoons dried oregano
2 teaspoons garlic powder
2 teaspoons onion powder
1 teaspoon ground allspice
⅛ teaspoon ground cloves

Chili Powder

Combine all ingredients in an electric grinder or blender, and grind until mixture is a coarse powder. If using dried hot peppers, remove seeds before grinding, or mixture will be too hot. Store in an airtight container.

Yields ¼ cup

Curry Powder

2 teaspoons ground
  cinnamon (1- to 3-inch
  stick)
½ teaspoon ground
  cardamom (10 seeds)
½ teaspoon ground cloves
  (8 cloves)
3 teaspoons ground cumin
  (3 teaspoons seeds)
2 teaspoons ground black
  pepper (1 teaspoon
  peppercorns)
½ teaspoon ground
  coriander (2 teaspoons
  seeds, ground and
  sifted)
1 teaspoon ground
  turmeric
3 teaspoons ground
  fenugreek (2 teaspoons
  seeds)

Commercially mixed curries do not give you as varied a blend.

Combine all ingredients, except coriander seeds, if using. They should be ground and sifted separately and then added to mixture. Blend. Store in an airtight container.

Use an electric grinder or blender if ingredients are whole.

Yields ¼ cup

Variation

Hot Curry Powder: Add 1 teaspoon ground cayenne pepper to recipe.

Italian-Seasoned Whole Grain Bread Crumbs

Use these bread crumbs to coat meat, poultry, fish, or vegetables, or add them to stuffings.

Combine all ingredients except bread in an 8-ounce plastic container. Break bread into pieces and place in a blender. Grind finely, then add to herb mixture, and mix evenly. Store in an airtight container in the refrigerator for up to 3 months.
Yields about 2 cups

½ teaspoon dried sage
1 teaspoon dried basil
1 teaspoon dried parsley
1 teaspoon black pepper
1 teaspoon garlic powder
½ teaspoon dried marjoram
½ teaspoon dried oregano
½ teaspoon onion powder
4 thick slices stale whole grain bread

Meat, Poultry, or Vegetable Gravy

In a saucepan melt fat. Remove pan from heat; stir in flour to make a smooth paste. While pan is still off the heat, add stock slowly, stirring with a whisk to avoid lumps and scorching. Cook over high heat, stirring constantly, until gravy boils. Reduce heat, and simmer gravy for a few minutes until it is thickened. Season to taste with pepper. Serve immediately or freeze in a tightly sealed container for up to 6 months. Thaw in refrigerator before reheating.
Yields 2 cups

¼ cup meat or poultry drippings or butter
¼ cup whole wheat flour
2 cups rich Beef Stock (page 243), Poultry Stock (page 243), or Vegetable Stock (page 244)
black pepper, to taste

Variation
Herbed Gravy: Add 1 tablespoon any chopped fresh herb or 1 teaspoon dried herbs. Simmer 10 minutes longer.

Tarragon Vinegar

2 cups white vinegar
3-inch fresh tarragon sprig
1 clove garlic, halved
  (optional)

A sweet fragrant infusion, use this in place of regular vinegar, if you like.

Place ingredients in a small saucepan and heat, but do not boil. Remove garlic clove, if using. Place sprig of tarragon and vinegar in a sterile jar or the bottle in which vinegar was purchased. Store on pantry shelf.

Yields 2 cups

Tomato Paste

24 large, very ripe
  tomatoes

Place tomatoes in a large, heavy pot and cook, uncovered, over low heat for 1 hour.

Purée in a food mill, food processor, or electric blender and then strain through a fine sieve. Return mixture to pot, and continue to cook slowly, uncovered, until thick enough to mound on a spoon. Stir often while cooking to prevent tomatoes from sticking to bottom of pan. Spoon into containers and freeze, or freeze in ice-cube trays for small amounts. Defrost before using.

Yields about 4½ quarts

Tomato Sauce

You can easily double or triple this recipe to store in larger quantities.

Heat oil in a large skillet and sauté onion, carrot, and garlic until soft, about 5 minutes. Add pepper, tomatoes, and thyme. Cook, uncovered, over low heat for 30 minutes, stirring occasionally.

Purée in a food mill, electric blender, or food processor. Strain mixture to remove seeds. Return to pot and add soy sauce and parsley. Cook for 10 minutes longer. Serve sauce immediately or store in a container in the refrigerator for 3 to 5 days or in the freezer for up to 1 year.

Yields 3 cups

3 tablespoons olive oil
1 small onion, chopped
1 small carrot, finely minced (about ¼ cup)
2 cloves garlic, finely minced
¼ teaspoon black pepper
2½ pounds very ripe plum tomatoes, peeled and chopped, or 1 can (28 ounces) Italian plum tomatoes
½ teaspoon dried thyme
2 tablespoons soy sauce
2 tablespoons minced fresh parsley

Vanilla Extract

This natural flavoring does not contain the alcohol of commercial varieties.

Cut vanilla bean into small pieces, and place in a small bowl. Pour boiling water over bean pieces, cover, and allow mixture to steep overnight.

Place mixture in a blender, and process on medium speed until bean pieces are pulverized. Strain mixture through cheesecloth, then return liquid to blender.

Add honey, oil, and lecithin, and blend on medium speed until thoroughly combined. Pour the extract into a small bottle, cap tightly, and store in the refrigerator. Shake well before using. Measure the same amount as for any commercial vanilla extract.

Yields ¼ cup

1 vanilla bean
¼ cup boiling water
1 tablespoon honey
1 tablespoon sunflower or soy oil
1 teaspoon liquid lecithin

1¼ cups whole wheat
    pastry flour
3 tablespoons butter
2 to 3 tablespoons
    vegetable oil
2 to 3 tablespoons ice
    water

Whole Wheat Piecrust

This piecrust is good for sweet dessert fillings, or for savory quiche, vegetable, or meat fillings. You can make it ahead and store it.

Measure flour into a medium-size bowl. Add butter and cut into flour with a fork or pastry blender. Add oil slowly and continue to cut or mix until dough looks crumbly. Slowly add ice water and mix until you can gather the dough into a ball.

Place dough on a piece of floured waxed paper, either on a flat counter top or wooden board. Flatten dough with your hand, sprinkle a little flour over it, cover with another piece of waxed paper and roll out to form a circle about 12 inches in diameter, ⅛ to ¼ inch thick.

Remove top piece of waxed paper; invert dough over buttered 9-inch pie plate with waxed paper side up. Remove waxed paper and fit dough into plate. Flute edges, or simply trim away excess dough with a knife. If not using immediately, cover with plastic wrap and freeze. Do not thaw before baking.

If recipe calls for a baked crust, prick dough with fork and bake for 12 to 15 minutes at 425°F until lightly browned.

Makes 1 9-inch piecrust

Stocks

Stocks are easy to make, but most of them require long cooking. So it is best to make a large quantity of stock and store it. Stocks can be stored for a long time in the freezer. Divide the stock up among several small containers, and defrost only as much as you need.

NOTE: To make any of the following stocks richer, increase the cooking time, or reduce the cooked stock before using it by boiling it until its volume is decreased by one-third to one-half.

Beef Stock

Combine all ingredients in a 6- to 8-quart soup pot. Bring to a boil, reduce heat to low, cover, and simmer 2 hours.

Let stand 30 minutes, and then strain. When cold, skim fat off top.

Yields 4 quarts

3 pounds shin beef, cut into chunks
5 large onions, halved
10 medium-size carrots
8 medium-size tomatoes, quartered
16 cups water
½ pound mushrooms
pepper, to taste

Chicken (or Poultry) Stock

Place carcass and veal bone pieces in an 8-quart soup pot with the water. Bring to a boil, reduce heat, and skim off scum that rises to surface.

Add remaining ingredients, and simmer very gently 6 hours.

Strain stock through a fine sieve. Cool stock quickly, and refrigerate. When cold, remove the surface fat.

Yields 5½ to 6 cups

cooked or uncooked carcass of chicken, duck, or turkey, broken apart
1 pound veal bones, sawed into 2-inch pieces
12 cups water
1 large, unpeeled onion, halved, each half stuck with 1 clove
1 carrot
1 celery stalk
1 bay leaf
6 sprigs parsley
½ teaspoon dried thyme

243

Vegetable Stock

5 large onions, halved
10 medium-size carrots
8 medium-size tomatoes,
  quartered
1 clove garlic, minced
5 celery stalks
1 bunch fresh parsley
16 cups water

Combine all ingredients in a 6- to 8-quart soup pot. Bring to a boil, reduce heat to low, cover, and simmer 1 hour.

Let stand 30 minutes and then strain. Skim any scum that may form.

Yields 4 quarts

Fish Stock

2 pounds fish heads,
  backs, and bones
6 cups water
juice of large lemon
2 large onions, quartered
3 celery stalks, quartered
3 carrots, quartered
1 bay leaf
10 peppercorns
3 sprigs fresh parsley
1 sprig fresh thyme

Place all ingredients in a 5-quart soup pot. Bring to a boil, reduce heat, and simmer, uncovered, 30 minutes. Skim surface if necessary.

Soak a 3-layer piece of cheesecloth in cold water and wring it out. Strain broth through the cheesecloth into another large pot.

Cool strained broth, and refrigerate or freeze until needed. If large fish heads are used, remove meat to use in fish soup or salad.

Yields about 6 cups

Cooking Whole Grains

Grains are very easy to cook. Just add them to boiling water, cover, and wait. Unlike the other foods in this section you shouldn't make them too far in advance for best results. Grains do not freeze well. You can make them a day in advance and refrigerate. Then reheat the cooked grain over low heat in a covered pot with a little water to keep them from sticking. Or place the cooked grain in a covered ovenproof casserole and bake at 325°F until heated through.

Basic Cooking Method for all Grains:

1. Bring required amount of water to a boil in a saucepan with a tight-fitting cover.
2. Slowly add grains. Stir once and cover pot tightly.
3. Reduce heat and cook grains specified time. If water is absorbed before grain is cooked thoroughly, add a little boiling water, cover, and cook until all water is absorbed.

Cooking Grains

Grain	Amount Uncooked	Amount of Water	Cooking Time	Amount of Cooked Grain
Barley	1 cup	4 cups	30 to 40 minutes	4 cups
Buckwheat groats	1 cup	2 cups	20 minutes	4 cups
Bulgur	1 cup	2 cups	15 minutes	2½ cups
Cornmeal	1 cup	4 cups	30 to 40 minutes	4 to 5 cups
Millet	1 cup	2 cups	25 to 30 minutes	4 cups
Oatmeal	1 cup	3 cups	10 minutes	4 cups
Rice, Brown	1 cup	2 cups	35 to 40 minutes	2½ cups
Whole Wheat Berries	1 cup	4 cups	1 hour	2½ cups

Substitutes for Less Common Soyfoods

For the best results, you should not substitute ingredients called for in the recipes in this cookbook. If less common soyfoods such as okara and green soybeans are not readily available, it is possible to use substitute ingredients, but you should expect a slightly altered recipe. When possible, we suggest using a more common soyfood as a substitute. The following chart provides some guidelines for substituting for less common soyfoods:

Substitutes for Less Common Soyfoods

Soyfood	Substitute Food	Ratio of Substitution	Adjustments to Make	Results to Expect
Dried-Frozen Tofu	Fresh firm tofu or frozen tofu	1 cup fresh or frozen tofu for every ½ cup dried-frozen tofu	Omit liquid used to rehydrate dried-frozen tofu.	If using fresh tofu texture will be less chewy and meaty and much smoother.
Dried Okara	Wheat, oat, or corn bran or germ, or crushed breakfast cereal	1 cup bran, germ, or crushed cereal for every cup dried okara	None	Depending on type of bran, germ, or cereal used, flavor may be sweeter or nuttier.
Fresh Green Soybeans	Cooked dry soybeans or fresh lima beans	1 cup cooked soybeans or fresh lima beans for every cup green soybeans	If using soybeans add another ingredient to give color to the dish.	The bean used will dominate the taste and texture of recipe.
Okara, fresh	Ground cooked dry soybeans or cooked soy grits	1 cup ground soybeans or soy grits for every cup okara	May be necessary to adjust liquid to obtain proper consistency recipe calls for.	Recipe will be slightly richer or heavier.
Soy Flour	Chick-pea flour	1 cup chick-pea flour for every cup soy flour	In baked goods it may be necessary to add about 2 tablespoons extra liquid for every cup chick-pea flour, since it absorbs more liquid than soy flour.	Baked goods will be slightly denser.

Soyfoods Mail Order Sources

The following places carry a variety of soyfoods including soybeans, dry and fresh, soy grits, soy flour, soy flakes, soy sauces, and other soyfood products that can be shipped by mail. Since inventory and price changes occur periodically it is best to call or write for the most current information.

Chico San Inc.
PO Box 810
Chico, CA 95926
(916) 891-6271

Erewhon Trading Company
236 Washington Street
Brookline, MA 02146
(617) 738-4516

Fearn Soya Foods
Division of Richard Foods
  Corporation
4520 James Place
Melrose Park, IL 60160
(312) 345-2335

Walnut Acres
Penns Creek, PA 17862
(717) 837-0601

TOFU-MAKING KITS

CIS
2813 Arizona NE
Albuquerque, NM 87110
(505) 881-9881

The Learning Tree
PO Box 76
Sebastopol, CA 94922
(707) 829-2952

Aikenwood Corporation
1261 Howard Street
San Francisco, CA 94103
(415) 861-3377

HOME SOYFOOD EQUIPMENT BOOK

Build-it-yourself manual includes blueprints, construction manual, and cooking instructions for tofu, tempeh, and soymilk.

Rodale Press
33 East Minor Street
Emmaus, PA 18049
(215) 967-5171

TEMPEH STARTER, OTHER CULTURES, AND COAGULANTS FOR TOFU-MAKING

Gem Cultures*
30301 Sherwood Road
Fort Bragg, CA 95437
(707) 964-2922

*Gem Cultures carries powdered tempeh starter (PTS), and living tempeh starter (LTS). They also carry koji starters for making various types of miso: sweet white, red, barley, soy, and shoyu. Nigari and calcium sulfate (terra alba or powdered gypsum) are coagulants available from Gem Cultures for making tofu. Prices and further information are available upon request.

Index

References to illustrations are in italics.
References to tables are indicated by the
letter t.

249

INDEX